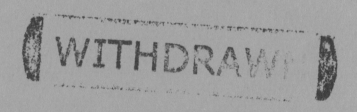

E. E. CUMMINGS

a reference guide

A
Reference
Publication
in
Literature

Ronald Gottesman
Editor

E. E. CUMMINGS

a reference guide

GUY L. ROTELLA

G.K.HALL &CO.

70 LINCOLN STREET, BOSTON, MASS.

Library of Congress Cataloging in Publication Data

Rotella, Guy L
  E. E. Cummings: a reference guide.

  (A Reference publication in literature)
  Includes index.
  1. Cummings, Edward Estlin, 1894-1962 — Bibliography.
I. Series.
Z8204.63.R67 [PS3505.U334]   016.811'5'2   79-9873
ISBN 0-8161-8079-2

This publication is printed on permanent/durable acid-free paper
MANUFACTURED IN THE UNITED STATES OF AMERICA

Contents

Introduction

A chronological survey of secondary materials on E. E. Cummings (1894-1962) reveals more or less continuous critical interest in his work since his first book in 1922. And, although the major outlines of the criticism were defined rather early on, such a survey also reveals a development of that interest which in many ways parallels the development of American literary scholarship in the last fifty or so years.

Cummings criticism in the twenties is dominated by reviews. Those of his World War I autobiographical novel, The Enormous Room (1922), run the gamut from extravagant praise to total condemnation, apparently depending on whether the reviewer looks upon the avant-garde with favor or scorn, but the critics' response is perhaps most typified by the "mixed" title of Robert Littell's review, "Garbage and Gold" (1922.7). Among the important reviews of The Enormous Room are John Peale Bishop's (1922.3), which anticipates later examinations of the pilgrimage-conversion motifs in the novel, George Carver's (1922.4), which notes Cummings' skill in realizing event, and John Dos Passos' (1922.6), which recognizes Cummings' use of American speech rhythms and his essential modernism. Other significant documents on The Enormous Room to appear in this decade are Edward Cummings' (the author's father's) introduction to the novel (1922.5), with its reprinting of some of the letters and telegrams involved in securing the release of Cummings from the French prison which is the work's setting, and Robert Graves' introduction to the British edition of the novel (1928.13), with its discussion of its style and of its historical accuracy (this countering the charges of exaggeration made by some reviewers).

Reviews of the four volumes of poetry Cummings published in the twenties, Tulips and Chimneys (1923), & (1925), XLI Poems (1925), and is 5 (1926), are also mixed. If some reviewers despair entirely of Cummings because of his "eccentric" typography and others are wholly enchanted by his originality, the majority expresses high praise for his themes and doubts about the effectiveness and/or necessity of his technical experiments. The extreme to which this latter attitude could go is characterized by Harriet Monroe's decision (1924.7) to "normalize" her quotations of Cummings' poems because his typography is no more than an irritating intrusion. The idea of most continuing importance to come out of the collective criticism of Cummings' poetry of the twenties, an idea that would become one of the major clichés of Cummings scholarship, is that he is a deeply traditional lyric poet despite the modernistic, experimental trappings of his poems.

Among significant reviews of Tulips and Chimneys are Slater Brown's (1924.2), which asserts the influence of painting on Cummings' technique and suggests the importance of tempo to his work, Thomas Seltzer's (1924.11), which notes Cummings' combining of pre-Elizabethan topics with a modern system of punctuation and insists that that system is essential to his treatment of those topics, and Edmund Wilson's (1924.13), with its charge--one that would be repeated frequently by later commentators--of immaturity.

As suggested above, the treatment of the other three volumes of verse Cummings published in the twenties more or less followed the lead set by reviewers of Tulips and Chimneys. Valuable comments are made by John W. Crawford (1926.1), who remarks on the improvisational element in the poems, Glenn Hughes (1926.4), who notes Cummings' use of the mannerisms of such seventeenth-century poets as Marvell, Herrick, and others, Maurice Lesemann (1926.5), who observes Cummings' use of line breaks for purposes of emphasis, and Marianne Moore (1926.7), who describes his shaping of the poems' graphics as "a kind of verbal topiary-work."

Cummings' first play, Him, appeared in 1927. It too, in book form and in production, received much attention from the critics. Again, there were extremely positive and negative reactions to the work (it revitalizes the theatre; it is boring and meaningless), some of which jousted in the letters-to-the-editor sections of newspapers and magazines. But the more typical responses (excepting the rather hysterical ones of some of the conventional theatre critics) registered delight at the play's verbal and other innovations and despair at its lack of concern for "produceability" and/or meaning. Few commentators on Him go beyond assertion, description, or summation, but relatively undeveloped remarks that indicate areas which would be explored by later critics are made by Genevieve Taggard (1927.6), who notes that its preoccupation with expressing inner realities makes the play continuous with Cummings' preceding work, S. Foster Damon (1928.11), who discusses Him in psychological terms, and John Dos Passos (1928.12), who emphasizes the play's replacement of statement and description with expression. Also of interest is Gilbert Seldes' "him" and the Critics (1928.19), a sixteen-page pamphlet which collects excerpts from twenty-seven contemporary newspaper reviews of the play's production at the Provincetown Playhouse.

In addition to the reviews of specific works which characterize Cummings criticism in the twenties, three more general studies are worthy of attention. Gorham B. Munson's "Syrinx" (1923.8) discusses Cummings' combining of traditional lyric themes with original techniques and insists that his work marries content and form, that his new methods of presentation are not eccentric but are the means of renewing antique themes. Munson examines those new methods, defining them as converting reorganized punctuation and typography into "active instruments for literary expression," and describing them and their effects. The sort of careful analytic attention to technique afforded Cummings by Munson would not, with minor exceptions, become characteristic of Cummings scholarship for many years. Paul Rosenfeld, in the essay on Cummings in Men Seen (1925.5), notes his connection to the "old Puritanic stem" of New England literature, a connection that would, in various guises, be picked up and expanded on by later scholars. Laura Riding's and Robert Graves' comments on Cummings in their A Survey of Modernist Poetry (1927.4), like Munson's, emphasize and demonstrate the expressive functions of his technical devices, with special attention to punctuation and spelling.

Cummings criticism in the thirties is again typified by reviews, but the number of important general studies increases slightly. Works of the thirties receiving significant attention from the reviewers are Viva (1931), Eimi (1933), no thanks (1935), and Collected Poems (1938). Reviews of Viva follow the pattern we have already seen. Positive responses emphasize Cummings' originality and his revitalizing of hackneyed themes, negative responses charge him with writing trivial nonsense. But again, most of the reviews are mixed and are perhaps most important for their recognition of the increased import of the satiric element in Cummings' verse, a recognition that will eventually lead to the common division of his poetry into lyric and satiric categories. The most significant reviews of Viva, a collection of poems, are two which make charges that, whether repeated or refuted, would become major subjects of subsequent Cummings criticism. They are Horace Gregory's (1931.6), which asserts that Cummings' poetry is static, without development, and Allen Tate's (1932.7), which charges that Cummings' work is so personal as to be private, to put the origins of the work above the work itself.

Responses to Cummings' record of his trip to the Soviet Union, Eimi, range from describing it as a "comic masterpiece" to charging it with exhibitionistic obscurantism. Other reactions include the following: the book is witty but affected, it is a radical defense of the individual and the artist against the threat of collectivism, it is a brilliant experiment in poetic prose, it willfully confuses the techniques of poetry with those of prose. Perhaps the most intriguing reviews of Eimi are those by pro-Soviet avant-gardists who view Cummings' critique of Communist Russia as a betrayal of the revolution by a man once thought an ally. Ben Hecht (1933.11), for instance, describes the Cummings of Eimi as an anti-revolutionary aesthete of "the ivory toilet set." Responses to the poems collected in no thanks generally fit the mold of earlier reviews and continue the attention to the satiric poems that began in the reviews of Viva.

Introduction

Reactions to <u>Collected Poems</u> are somewhat less frequently mixed
than those to the previous volumes, tending toward purer condemnation
or praise. For example, Yvor Winters (1939.3) describes Cummings'
work as "infantile exhibitionism, at once mildly unpleasant and in-
finitely tedious," while John Holmes (1938.11) describes Cummings as
"one of the funniest, frankest, tenderest, most passionately ribald
poets we have produced." In other significant reviews, Horace
Gregory (1938.8) comments on the legitimacy of Cummings' "typographical diversions" as "devices of poetic inversion and transposition,"
complains that he ignores the artist's responsibilities to his time
and place, and reiterates his earlier charge that Cummings' work is
marred by a lack of development from its youthful anti-intellectual
stance; S. I. Hayakawa (1938.9) discusses Cummings' combination of
lyric and satire as resulting from a capacity "for unaffected delight
and wonder" which, in a modern world, has "been compelled to tragic
adjustments"; Philip Horton (1938.12) finds Cummings' poetry repetitive, confused because of its anti-intellectualism, and without technical or thematic development; and Sherry Mangan (also 1938.12)
refutes, point by point, many of the charges typically made against
Cummings, although she agrees that his subject matter needs broadening.

Cummings' more minor works of the thirties, such as <u>The Red Front</u>,
a translation of Louis Aragon's revolutionary poem, and <u>Tom</u>, a ballet
based on <u>Uncle Tom's Cabin</u>, received some, although largely perfunctory, critical attention. His work also begins, in this decade, to
receive comment, usually brief and descriptive, in general studies of
American literature, the literature of the twenties, and so on. The
most important developments in Cummings criticism in the thirties,
however, occur in several essays on his work. The most important of
these is R. P. Blackmur's "Notes on E. E. Cummings' Language"
(1931.1). Blackmur's argument, one which for years Cummings' critics
would repeat or try to refute, charges that Cummings' anti-intellectual, romantic-egoistical poetry, with its special vocabulary, is
unintelligible. The argument is buttressed by a "philosophical"
framework (true meaning requires contact between the abstract and the
concrete; Cummings moves away from the concrete and, therefore, away
from meaning into imprecision) and by extensive demonstration. The
charge is so serious and so well made that it colored Cummings scholarship for years. Its influence is indicated by its frequent reprinting and by the number of critics who would, in direct or indirect,
major or minor ways, respond to it. But if Blackmur's essay is damn-
ing, it also contains the germ of its own refutation in its suggestion
that the continued practice of Cummings' more or less private system
of notation might eventually "produce a set of well-ordered conventions susceptible of general use." This hint would become precisely
the argument of many critics who would attempt to counter Blackmur's
strictures and is, in fact, the basis of Blackmur's own later partial
recanting (1941.2) of his almost wholly negative view. Another important, although far briefer and less influential, negative criticism
of Cummings is Yvor Winters' description of him (1937.4) as a "pseudo-
experimentalist...who confuses tradition with convention."

Other significant essays on Cummings to appear in the thirties
are John Peale Bishop's (1938.4), John Finch's (1939.2), and Paul
Rosenfeld's (1939-1940.1). Bishop's "The Poems and Prose of E. E.
Cummings" is a major effort to place Cummings as an artist. It describes the influence of the romantic tradition on his early work and
argues that, although technically he soon left this influence behind,
he maintained the "romantic attitude" in the later work dominated by
the technical attempt to achieve what Cummings called "that precision
which creates movement." Cummings' technique of immediacy is discussed in terms of his concepts of the discontinuity of experience
and of the mind and in terms of the influences of Ulysses and modern
painting on it. Finch's "New England Prodigal" is important for relating Cummings' work to the tradition of transcendentalism. He
argues that the nineteenth-century stance of rejecting external in
favor of internal authority is at the center of Cummings' poetry and
feels that, to the extent that such a stance is out of date, it is
the source of his obscurity, while, to the extent that it provides
him a "platform of moral isolation," it is what allows the lyric intensity which is his greatest achievement. Rosenfeld's "The Enormous
Cummings" discusses The Enormous Room and Eimi as "serio-comic" anti-
novels recapitulating themes of the Thoreau, Emerson, Whitman tradition.

One additional piece of thirties criticism deserves notice here,
the reading of "Buffalo Bill's" in Cleanth Brooks' and Robert Penn
Warren's Understanding Poetry (1938.5). This avatar of the New Critical technique of close analysis signals what will become a major
method of subsequent Cummings scholarship.

In the thirties, the lines of Cummings criticism were clarified.
On the one hand, he is praised for his transcendent individualism,
his social criticism, his technical innovations, and his revitalizing
of conventions. On the other, he is condemned for excessive personalism, for being out of touch with his times, for "false" experimentalism, obscurantism, and anti-intellectualism, for imprecision and
unintelligibility, and for a lack of both thematic and technical
growth. The weights of these opposing judgments (at times held by
the same critic) are generally in balance in terms of both the status
and number of the critics who hold them. They become, in various
guises, the poles of what would be a continuing controversy over
Cummings' artistic merit.

The amount of critical attention given Cummings in the forties
increased (to the extent that this is measurable by the number of
items devoted to him and his work) by approximately ten percent over
that of the previous decade, a rather impressive figure when it is
recalled that half the decade was dominated by World War II and that
Cummings published only two major volumes, thus lowering the percent-
age of reviews in the criticism as a whole. Part of this increased
attention is accounted for by more and more frequent mention of Cummings in general studies of literature and literary history, in books

and essays on modernism, and in biographical and other sorts of dic-
tionaries and encyclopedias; but the major development of Cummings
criticism in this decade is the increasing number and length of serious general critical essays on his work, an increase dominated by the
devoting of an entire issue of The Harvard Wake to Cummings.

The two major volumes published by Cummings in the forties are
50 Poems (1940) and 1 X 1 (1944). Both were reviewed by influential
critics in influential newspapers, magazines, and journals. Clearly
Cummings' claim to serious attention was established, but the nature
of that attention remained complex and qualified. Perhaps the most
important review of 50 Poems is R. P. Blackmur's (1941.2), which contains at least a partial recantation of some of the strictures in
"Notes on E. E. Cummings' Language." Blackmur expresses admiration
for Cummings' continuing immediacy and energy but insists that his
vocabulary is excessively general (although this view is held less
extremely than in the earlier essay) and that his scatology fails to
achieve levels of disgust or gesture. More significantly, however,
and implicitly developing his previous suggestion that Cummings' personal notation might eventually develop a usable precision, Blackmur
attends to Cummings' "use of prepositions, pronouns, and the auxiliary
verbs in the guise of substances, and of words ordinarily rhetorical--
mere connectives or means of transition in their ordinary usage--for
the things of actual experience." If Blackmur's assessment of 50
Poems is largely a balanced one, many critics of the work were harsh
in their judgments, especially on grounds of Cummings' failure to
develop as an artist, a charge that had become common in the reviews
of the thirties. Two examples will suffice to characterize this
criticism: in The New Yorker, Louise Bogan (1941.3) describes the
book as "irrevocably stuck in the past"; and Howard Nemerov, in the
New York Herald-Tribune (1941.11), finds Cummings to have "produced
something undeniably the same." Other reviews worth mention here are
Weldon Kees' (1941.10), which provides a kind of counter to the
charges of lack of growth in its suggestion that the absence of "progression" in Cummings' work is connected to his effort to preserve
the self in a world of constant and violent change, and Allen Tate's
(1941.15), which partially revokes his earlier criticisms of Cummings
by arguing that some of his poems "are among the best works of our
time."

As the reviews of 50 Poems were more often negative than those of
any previous Cummings work, those of his next volume, 1 X 1, were more
often positive. Peter De Vries (1944.4) finds that--as Blackmur had
in a sense predicted--Cummings' grammatical innovations have reached,
in this volume, the point at which they can be accepted not as tricks
but as "his natural kind of vocabulary," as speech. In support of
this argument, De Vries examines Cummings' tendency to make nouns of
other parts of speech and describes it as the key to his essential
desire "to express...the fact and experience of being." Ruth Lechlitner (1944.8) agrees with earlier critics that Cummings is repetitive
and lacks development (a charge made very infrequently by reviewers of

this volume), but finds that his work remains fresh nonetheless. If
Lechlitner finds Cummings' lack of development real but no liability,
other critics argue that his poetry does, in fact, show growth. For
example, Alan Swallow (1944.13) asserts that if 1 X 1 shows little
thematic change from earlier volumes it does demonstrate two significant changes in method: an "attempt to achieve greater complexity,
especially with the pun" and increased "use of interruption and
qualification to the argument." And, along similar lines, Robert
Penn Warren (1944.14) suggests that the pure polarities of the early
poems have in the later ones "been drawn into more elaborate combina-
tions and fused under greater pressure." These largely positive
responses (which, by the way, suggest an approach to Cummings that
has never been fully exploited) are typical of the reviews of 1 X 1,
but one important negative review must also be remarked. Interesting-
ly, its major complaint is that Cummings' work has failed to develop.
In it, F. O. Matthiessen (1944.9) argues that, in direct contradiction
to his constant concern with growth, Cummings' themes and techniques
remain unchanged. Even uniqueness, when it becomes expected, yields
monotony. Clearly the question of Cummings' development or lack of
it remains central to Cummings criticism in the forties. Clearly it
is yet to be definitively answered.

Among significant more general treatments of Cummings in the
forties, the earliest is by John Arthos (1943.1). Arthos presents an
overview of Cummings' poetry and maintains that his pagan, anti-
puritan celebration of the life of the senses is balanced by his
Puritan discipline, integrity, and humility and is one with the common American trait of "refusing to be affected by experience." Arthos
also discusses Cummings' technique, concentrating on his treatment of
abstract words as if they were material ones, his economy and con-
creteness, and his use of slang and jazz idioms. He concludes that,
if Cummings' is not a poetry of intellectual subtleties, it is informed by a coherent intellectual stance: he "is a Platonist, absorbed in the discipline of contemplation and devoted to the
perception of being."

1946 was a banner year for Cummings scholarship. Of minor interest is Donald H. Andrews' brief essay (1946.1) arguing that Cummings'
obscurity is the result not of Dadaist non-meaning but of extreme condensation of meaning, a condensation Andrews relates to the symbolic
ones of algebra. But the item of major significance to appear in
this year, a clear, largely positive indicator of Cummings' stature,
is the Cummings number of The Harvard Wake, containing fourteen essays
by important writers and critics, among them Jacques Barzun (1946.3),
John Dos Passos (1946.6), Harry Levin (1946.14), Marianne Moore
(1946.15), Karl Shapiro (1946.19), Allen Tate (1946.21), Lionel
Trilling (1946.22), and William Carlos Williams (1946.23). Perhaps
the most important pieces in the special issue, however, are those by
Lloyd Frankenberg (1946.8), Paul Rosenfeld (1946.18), and Theodore
Spencer (1946.20). Frankenberg concentrates on Cummings' thematic
praise of an aristocracy based not on government, hierarchy, or class,

but on the qualities of aliveness and individuality, and discusses his technical ability to capture what is perpetually in motion. Rosenfeld presents a lengthy examination of *Eimi*, discussing its experimentation with prose technique and its central symbol, "the absurd contradiction of an expectation by an event," comparing it to *The Divine Comedy* and the comedies of Aristophanes, and considering its "Idealist vision" and its relation to the political and economic developments of the thirties. Spencer explores Cummings' poetic technique, arguing that it results from his thematic preference for the individual over the mechanical and regimented. This preference requires the poet to recreate the living moment and the living object in permanent form. To do this, Spencer explains, Cummings develops means for destroying the time content of language and replacing it with simultaneity. Another article from the Cummings issue of *Wake* deserving notice in this survey is Fairfield Porter's on Cummings' paintings (1946.16), the first critical attention to this aspect of his work beyond brief mentions of shows.

Two more important treatments of Cummings appeared in the remaining years of the forties. Robert M. Adams (1947.1) rehearses some of the major parameters of Cummings criticism, exploring his apparent technical radicalism and his potentially limiting theme of individualism and finding that his devices are used largely to control tempo and to reflect the chaos of reality. Adams concludes his essay with the intriguing suggestion that, because the theme of self-reliance rejects man and the world and thereby severely limits available subject matter, Cummings' style is not, in fact, radical, but is rather a substitute for a subject. Lloyd Frankenberg (1948.6) demonstrates, through extensive examinations of poems, plays, and prose works, that all of Cummings' methods, techniques, and innovations are addressed to one central conception of his work: the celebration of the individual. (Part of this essay is reprinted in a longer essay by Frankenberg [1949.7] which makes further contributions to Cummings scholarship in its examination of his development of "the metaphor-poem, a technique for internal mimicry" and in its examination of Cummings' ideas.)

Mention of three further matters will complete our survey of Cummings criticism in the forties. First of all, the "new" emphasis on close reading signalled by Brooks' and Warren's Understanding Poetry resulted in several such analyses of Cummings poems (see especially 1944.3; 1947.10; 1948.6; 1949.11; 1949.12), although these are only a foreshadowing of the explosion of such criticism in the fifties and sixties and although, as we shall see, the doctrines of the New Criticism would in many ways retard critical attention to Cummings' particular virtues. Second, the two plays Cummings published in the forties, Anthropos: The Future of Art (1944) and Santa Claus: A Morality (1946), received relatively little attention from the reviewers and were, when discussed at all, discussed in terms of their allegorical simplifications of Cummings' usual themes. And third, in 1948 there appeared, under the pseudonym of Michael Lee, an essay submitted for Harvard University's Bowdoin Prize which contains the seeds of some of the ideas and approaches which would inform the later work of its author, Norman Friedman, who was to become the ablest and most influential interpreter of Cummings' work.

Paralleling the remarkable growth of American literary scholarship in the fifties is an explosion of Cummings criticism. The number of items considering him and his work more than doubled the number in the previous decade, and if Cummings scholarship had not quite become an industry it was clearly a solidly established small business. This growth is characterized by more frequent and more extensive considerations of Cummings in literary and period histories and other sorts of general studies, by continuing and still more extensive reviews of his major works, by a great increase in the number of essays presenting close analyses of individual Cummings poems, by the first extensive bibliographic and biographical attention to him, by the first dissertations to take him as their subject, and, most significantly, by several lengthy scholarly articles which, if they continue to examine the by-then typical areas of question in Cummings criticism (the relationship of his techniques to his themes, his growth or lack of it), tend to treat those questions more maturely, with more evidence and less assertion than much of the earlier commentary and frequently to push beyond those questions.

The major works by Cummings published and reviewed in the fifties are: Xaîpe (1950), i: Six Nonlectures (1953), Poems: 1923-1954 (1954), and 95 poems (1958). To the extent that such a term is meaningful, the reviews are in general "respectful" and indicate that Cummings has become an established if not establishment writer. The most significant development in the reviews of Xaîpe is the insistence of several of its critics that Cummings' technical innovations are not only not mere eccentricities but are in fact essential to his particular form of expression. For example, Donald H. Andrews (1950.1) argues that Cummings' oddities and obscurities are part of an integral idea, and Lloyd Frankenberg (1950.10) calls him a major lyric poet whose typography and other techniques are definitely functional. The major negative point of the reviews of Xaîpe suggests that the absence of the tragic in his work trivializes both their lyric joy and satiric anger. This view is expressed most tellingly by Louise Bogan (1950.5) and Randall Jarrell (1950.13). The question of Cummings' growth as an artist also receives attention in these reviews. For instance, Robert H. Glauber (1951.7) complains that Cummings fails to move on from his old themes and skills, while Henry W. Wells (1950.24) maintains that, if Cummings continues to concern himself with the same ideas and modes of expression, he has refined those themes and techniques and become a more philosophical poet.

Reviews of i: Six Nonlectures, the talks given by Cummings while Charles Eliot Norton Professor of Poetry at Harvard during the 1952-1953 academic year, are generally descriptive, discussing their occasions and/or summarizing their autobiographical content and characteristically peculiar style. The most common analytical comment stresses the concern of the "non-lectures" with the individual in a mass society, the struggle of the self against "mobism." The most important reviews are those by Alfred Kazin (1954.18) and John Logan (1955.20). Kazin relates Cummings to certain transcendentalists and other American originals and complains of his incurable sentimentality. Logan discusses i̲ as an act of self-transcendence and a celebration of the human spirit.

In 1954, Cummings' second retrospective collection, Poems: 1923–1954, was published. It occasioned a number of lengthy essay-reviews reconsidering Cummings' poetic career. Some of these were enthusiastic. For example, John Logan (1955.20) describes Cummings' accomplishment as "monumental" and "prodigious." Others repeat some of the central criticisms of earlier commentators. For instance, Michael Harrington (1954.15) charges Cummings with superficiality, Carl Bode (1955.1) agrees with Blackmur's criticism of Cummings' language and finds that the poems lack development, and Hayden Carruth (1955.3) charges that Cummings loses sight of the precision of language which is the ultimate goal of experimentalism. More typical reviews are more "mixed." Babette Deutsch (1955.6) finds that if Cummings has not matured he has kept his energy, his love of movement, and his skill in recording it and comments on his mastery of rhythm, his unevenness, and his lapses into sentimentality. G. S. Fraser (1955.9) lists the "marks of permanent adolescence" in Cummings' poems and praises their readability and documentary value. Randall Jarrell (1954.17) describes Poems: 1923–1954 as a "formidable collection," but complains of its monotony and, reflecting the New Critical bias for dualistic complexity that dominated the age and sometimes distorted Cummings criticism, of its excessively clear split between lyrics of affirmation and satires of negation. In other significant reviews, Edwin Honig (1955.13) describes Cummings as "the expressionist par excellence," discusses his stylistic mastery, compares and contrasts him with his contemporaries, and places him in the context of modernism; David Burns (1954.9) argues that Cummings has reinvigorated modern poetry through the shock of his techniques; and Louise Bogan (1954.6), who had often charged Cummings with technical irrelevance, also finds that he has reinvigorated modern verse, but insists that he has done so by a persistent attempt to reintroduce "vital material that Victorian taste had outlawed" rather than by his typographical experiments.

In contrast to the many thoughtful reviews of Poems: 1923–1954, those of 95 poems are often perfunctory, issuing conventional praise, repeating the old charges of non-development or excessively private language, or asserting that the volume is not up to Cummings' previous standard. Exceptions to this are reviews by Paul Lauter (1958.16), James Dickey (1959.12), and Robert Maurer (1959.18). Lauter argues that Cummings has shown no "poetic growth" because his integrity has caused him to "reject the changing world...asserting in its place the ultimate validity of his own perceptions." Dickey, discussing Cummings in general because his books are "all alike," lists the characteristics of the verse he most admires--sharpness of observation, devotion to spontaneity, daring diction and imagery, and so on--and describes Cummings' poetry as often seriously flawed but constantly restoring itself "to an eminence which seals the critic's mouth and changes him into a more perceptive being." Maurer comments on the anachronism of Cummings' intense personalism in an era when poets have struggled to extinguish personality.

In addition to continued attention to Cummings' work by reviewers, the criticism of the fifties is marked by a large increase in the number of essays devoted to close analysis of individual poems, the majority of them appearing in the journal The Explicator. The most significant contribution of these analyses is their typical insistence on and demonstration of the interrelationship of Cummings' techniques and themes, thus implicitly countering the varieties of the frequent critical charge that his techniques are irritating irrelevancies.

Other signs in this decade of Cummings' increasingly established position as an important writer are the appearance of a bibliography, a book length biography, and four doctoral dissertations with Cummings as subject. Paul Lauter's bibliographic work (see 1953.9, 1955.17, 18, and 1957.14) presents an index of first lines of Cummings poems (giving publication data), a partially descriptive bibliography of his books, and a checklist of news stories, miscellaneous articles, and critiques and reviews. Charles Norman's biography, The Magic-Maker: E. E. Cummings (1958.19 and 1964.21), the first book on Cummings, is more "appreciative" than critical, but it does make available much factual, anecdotal, and atmospheric information on his life, works, and "environments." Of the dissertations, Robert Beloof's (1954.4) explores Cummings' prosody, Robert Maurer's (1955.21) examines the identity of Cummings' life and work and discusses in detail the unifying theme of both, "the isolation of the individual artist-human being from society," Louis Rus's (1955.28) uses linguistic analysis to explore structural ambiguity in the poems, and Robert Wegner's (1959.33) presents a sympathetic discussion of Cummings' themes and techniques.

If so far the survey of Cummings criticism in the fifties demonstrates increased attention to him and his work, the most important development of the decade is the number of mature, scholarly essays devoted to him. One of these, George Haines IV's "::2:1 The World and E. E. Cummings" (1951.8) elaborates on what had become a cliché of Cummings criticism by the thirties, the ease with which his poetry can be divided into and contained by lyric and satiric categories. Cummings loathes and loves. He loathes abstraction and expresses that loathing concretely, but his love often finds only abstract expression. This paradox Haines resolves by differentiating two types of abstraction. That loathed is the application of the laws of mechanical science to human life; this occurs in a concrete world and so Cummings' expression of it is concrete. The second abstraction, the alternative to the first, is the transcendence of self through love;

since this can never be realized in a concrete world, Cummings' expression of it is abstract. In addition to this thematic and technical analysis, Haines also relates Cummings' craft and ideas to expressionistic aesthetics and nineteenth-century romanticism.

If Haines' examination concerns itself with both theme and technique, other essays have a narrower focus. Norman Friedman (1958.10), Ralph J. Mills, Jr. (1959.19), and Barbara Watson (1956.15) take a thematic approach. Friedman maintains that the informing idea of Cummings' persona is the elevation of "freshness of response and accuracy in its expression" over the chief obstacles to such response and expression, submission to mass life. Mills explores Cummings' opposition of "'civilized' scientific method" with the appraisal of being and becoming. Watson, writing in The Kenyon Review, one of the most important journals of the fifties, places Cummings' themes in historical context by emphasizing his rejection of "the intellectualizing, devitalizing, and neutering of emotion" which makes possible the development of mass societies. S. V. Baum (1954.3) concerns himself with technique. He sees Cummings' technical denial of authority as an expression of his theme of individualism and examines the techniques for simultaneous presentation (in spite of the sequential nature of syntax) which he was forced to develop in response to his reduction of moral categories to affirmation and negation.

The question of growth which had frequently dominated critical comment on Cummings is taken up at length by Rudolph Von Abele in the first essay on Cummings (1955.31) to appear in the influential journal PMLA. Von Abele rebuts the charge that Cummings' poetry lacks development by demonstrating its growth through three periods in three technical categories (typographical rhetoric, syntactic dislocation, and word formation) and two thematic categories (romantic love and the satire of science) and concludes that he has moved from impressionist presentation and evocation to a more abstract concern with asserting, remonstrating, and defining. Cummings' satire is the subject of Eleanor M. Sickels' essay (1954.26) in another major journal, American Literature. She traces the process by which the satires have degenerated over the course of Cummings' career from effective propaganda and art into a nihilism which is the reductio ad absurdam of his individualism. Two essays take Cummings' language as subject. Robert Maurer (1955.22) partially rebuts the charges of imprecision made by R. P. Blackmur (1931.1) by arguing that if the language of Cummings' early poems is occasionally vague and inexact, in the later poems his language has grown increasingly precise, especially in terms of his technique of using certain words as a "metaphorical shorthand for concepts." Norman Friedman, in another essay published in PMLA (1957.11), also rejects Blackmur's strictures and explores the "diction, voice, and tone" of Cummings' style. This style is "mixed," has a "neutral" center and can vary to the "formal" on one side and the "burlesque" on the other. The effects of the juxtapositions of these styles are discussed in terms of Cummings' thematic concerns.

Louis C. Rus's examination of Cummings' "structural ambiguity" (1955.27) is important because it is the first of what will in the sixties and seventies become frequent linguistic approaches to Cummings' work, approaches which, like Rus's, often concern themselves with the work itself and with the question (or assertion) of the role of linguistic analysis in literary criticism.

Other important essays of the fifties concern themselves with two of Cummings' long individual works, Him and The Enormous Room. Eric Bentley (1952.2) presents an interpretation of Him by Theodore Hoffman which discusses the play as seeking modern remnants of ancient fertility rites. Robert Maurer (1956.11) explores the play's experimentation for the creation of active rather than static art and its treatment of the artist in relation to his self, his loved one, and his society. In these essays, the controversy marking most earlier commentary on Him is replaced by more objective analysis. The Enormous Room receives similar objective analysis from Kingsley Widmer (1958.25), who examines its violation of traditional prose forms, "mixture of aesthetic functions," and "experimentation with logical, causal, and temporal relationships."

In the fifties, then, Cummings received more, more sustained, and more serious attention. Commentary on him grew in depth and breadth. The questions of growth and of the relation of his technique to his themes which had become conventional continued to be asked and answered, but were typically treated more objectively and analytically than before and were generally answered in Cummings' favor. Essays as well as reviews appeared in many of the most influential literary and critical journals. It is important, however, that these developments not give a misimpression. In neither quantity nor level of praise did Cummings criticism reach the levels accorded such of his major contemporaries as Frost, Hemingway, Eliot, Faulkner, and Stevens. (There was still, for instance, no critical book on Cummings.) In part this is, as previously suggested, due to the fact that the personal, lyrical, anti-analytical, "anti-intellectual," "simple," unallusive nature of Cummings' poetry was (or seemed to be) out of step with the artistic and critical demands of the times for impersonal, dramatic, analytical, intellectual, complex, and allusive art. In the sixties and seventies, these demands would begin to change and, in some ways, to come closer to those Cummings' verse might meet, and his reputation in the next two decades would benefit, if more or less indirectly, from these changes. (An early indication of these changes and of their possible relation to Cummings criticism is Charles Olson's mention of Cummings' influence on "field composition" in his essay on projective verse (1950.16).) Yet for all the serious and praiseful attention Cummings would receive, he would never be accorded quite the major status achieved by such contemporaries as those mentioned above.

The thoughtful attention which typified much Cummings criticism in the fifties was consolidated and expanded in the sixties. This is true in terms of the number of items devoted to Cummings: the approximately twenty percent increase over the number in the previous decade is at once rendered more impressive by the small proportion of the total accounted for by reviews--only the posthumous 73 poems (1963) received significant notice--and less impressive by the fairly large proportion accounted for by reprints of earlier pieces, although these too show continuing interest. More importantly, however, it is also true in terms of the sustained increase in the length and seriousness of both interpretive and research scholarship on Cummings. This increase is signalled by more than double the number of analyses of individual poems that appeared in the fifties, by many more major essays than in any previous period, by significant treatments in parts of books, and, most importantly, by several books with Cummings as their subject.

The reviews of 73 poems are, not surprisingly in responses to a posthumous volume, typically respectful in tone, and few of them make any real contribution to the criticism. Two minor exceptions are the reviews of Horace Gregory (1964.10) and Louis Martz (1964.18). Gregory describes Cummings' achievement as a unique "lyrical integration of satire, religious feeling and art," while Martz suggests that Cummings' continuing acuteness is the product of his "archaic but nevertheless viable belief in the existence of a platonic ideal." Other reviews, even when properly respectful, continue to charge Cummings with insufficient development and ineffective techniques.

The latter charge, which is made far less often and less vigorously than before, is again rebutted, as it was in the fifties, by a large number of close analyses of individual poems. These studies persist in demonstrating--and their weight increases as the number of poems given such analysis mounts--a unity between Cummings' themes and forms, and it seems fair to say that by the early sixties it was generally accepted that, as some had long argued, Cummings was a serious craftsman whose techniques, if eccentric, are integral to his thematic expression.

Cummings received many other sorts of critical attention in the sixties as well. For instance, he was the subject of two doctoral dissertations and was considered in parts of three others. Of the major studies, James Dougherty, Jr. (1962.12) discusses the relationship of The Enormous Room to Cummings' poetry, arguing that both are informed by the belief that true individualism can only maintain itself through unending pilgrimage and growth; and Charles Stetler (1966.44) concentrates on Cummings' poems of love and transcendence, addressing the charge of nondevelopment by demonstrating the deepening of Cummings' belief, the clarifying of his vision, and his increasing control of his materials over the course of his career.

But all these matters are relatively insignificant in comparison to the major articles, important parts of books, and entire books on Cummings which dominate the scholarship of the sixties. The essays,

continuing to parallel the "boom" in literary criticism, fall generally into the categories we have seen in the articles of the prior
decade. (And if there are, inevitably, some which, although lengthy,
make little contribution, there are far more which make major ones.)
The category showing most growth is that including the essays taking
a linguistics approach to the poems. Of course, Cummings' typical
violation of the principles of conventional grammar makes him a prime
subject for the then developing use of the tools of linguistics in
literary analysis, both as a locus for arguments for the validity of
such an application and as the subject of actual practical analyses.
And if most of these essays are not especially important themselves,
they are worthy of attention as early examples of what was to become
an increasingly significant critical discipline. Samuel R. Levin
(1964.13) analyzes a line from "anyone lived in a pretty how town" in
a discussion of generative grammar. James Peter Thorne (1965.28) examines the same poem in its entirety and concludes that its total effect is "controlled by the fact that the kind of irregularity it
exhibits is regular in the context of the poem." John B. Lord
(1966.32) discusses "para-grammatical" structures in the same poem.
Roger Fowler (1969.14) discusses reader retrieval of the syntax of
"anyone lived in a pretty how town." Archibald A. Hill (1967.14) suggests that Cummings' adaptation of the linguistically unpredictable in
the poem exemplifies that modernist technique which violates linguistic convention in the hope of achieving something stylistically meaningful and, in another essay (1967.15), uses "nonsun blob a" as an
example of the recoverability of the normal from underlying deviant
sentences. William S. Chisholm (1967.4) employs syntactic stylistics
to isolate points of grammatical innovation in "what if a much of a
which of a wind." It will be clear from this that most of these essays are more concerned with using Cummings' poetry as a tool for
linguistics study than the reverse, but they do prepare the way for
essays which will in fact invert that relationship. These would multiply in the seventies, but only one such appears in the sixties.
Written by Irene R. Fairley, the major linguistics critic of Cummings,
this essay (1968.9) discusses syntactic violation as a stylistic device in "Me up at does," "Chansons Innocentes, III," and "a like a."

Among essays taking a general approach to Cummings, the most important are John Logan's (1961.9) and George Wesolek's (1965.32).
Logan examines Cummings' poetry in terms of its paradigms of love
(theme) and language (technique). Wesolek considers Cummings a more
profound writer than is usually recognized and maintains that his
alienation from "most-people" forces him to look within to the depths
of the self and without to a transcendent other. Yet, finally, an
unfilled emptiness remains at the heart of the poems, an emptiness
symbolic of man's condition. Perhaps the best thematic essay of the
sixties is Patricia Buchanan Tal-Mason Cline's (1968.4). She asserts
that Cummings demanded "a holistic experience of life." He posits
two realms, the real world of "growth and decay in time" and the ideal
world of "timeless and immeasurable absolutes." Man and nature in-
habit the real but participate in the ideal through love. Accepting

this, but wishing to go beyond it, Cummings strives for growth, for death in time and rebirth in timelessness. The development of these ideas over the course of Cummings' career is also discussed. The most significant sixties essay concentrating on Cummings' technique is Haskell S. Springer's (1967.29). Springer emphasizes and explores Cummings' use (and attempts to conceal that use) of "traditional prosodic principles."

In other important contributions in essays, Bernard Benstock (1960.4) discusses the dramatic characterizations which provide "a strong basis of reality" in Cummings' poems and James P. Dougherty (1968.6) argues that Cummings, in a methodology opposite from that of his major contemporaries, avoids the pitfalls of abstraction not by grounding his work in the particulars of phenomenological reality but by reference to "the tangibility of language itself." Several other essays of the sixties are also marked by attempts to provide context for Cummings and his works. Sister Mary David Babcock, O.S.B. (1963.2) connects Cummings' effort at the simultaneous capture of "aliveness" through typography to characteristics of the Chinese ideogram. John Clendenning (1963.5) suggests that Cummings' technique stems from the American humor tradition and insists that he is not a modernist because he is unaffected by modernist principles and themes. Cummings' place in the modernist movement is taken up in more complex fashion by Norman Friedman (1962.14), who maintains that Cummings combines romantic and modernist elements. For the modernist, two-dimensional reality is complex and, therefore, poems must be complex. But Cummings takes a different view. For him, "to lose the two-dimensional everyday world is to gain the threedimensional world of understanding," a world which is without conflict and is the source of all our values. Thus Cummings' view of poetry is relatively simple. On the other hand, his concept of poetic form is as organic as the modernists'. Still, his problem is, in a sense, the reverse of theirs, for rather than reflect a complex reality in a complex mirror he treats "simple subjects and attitudes in a complicated way." Another Friedman essay (1964.8) continues this theme in an examination of criticism of Cummings, asserting that his combination of romantic and modernist elements has caused many excessively monistic critics, with their insistence on the "twentieth-century view of the tragic vision," to misunderstand and undervalue him.

As in the fifties, Cummings' major individual works also receive attention from essayists. There are three important treatments of The Enormous Room. David E. Smith (1965.25) discusses the influence of John Bunyan's The Pilgrim's Progress on the novel, emphasizing both works' requirement that the respective pilgrims accept the reality of human filth as preliminary to the achievement of vision. Marilyn Gaull's ambitious essay (1967.12) explores Cummings' treatment of language and identity in The Enormous Room. Cummings "assumed the multiple task of demonstrating not only the discrepancy between language and experience but also the corrosive effects of this discrepancy on the human psyche, and, perhaps his most significant achievement,

offered a means of overcoming it in the creation of new relationships
between language and experience." James P. Dougherty (1969.6) examines The Enormous Room in terms of the birth of the modern spirit,
the well-known literature of disillusionment that followed World War
I, and the radical tradition of Whitman, Emerson, and Thoreau. He
also suggests that the work anticipates the "post-modern world of the
1960's." Two essays treat Him. Katherine J. Worth (1967.32) explores
the play's anticipation of the preoccupations of the modern theatre,
and Manuel L. Grossman (1968.16) discusses Him in the context of absurdist drama, pointing out such similarities as the lack of clear
plot and linear development and the use of the conventions of the
popular theatre and one major difference, Cummings' lack of pessimism.
An exception to the usual course of Cummings criticism is Charles
Stetler's essay (1968.25) on a single volume of Cummings' poems.
Stetler holds that Cummings' 73 poems continues to evidence his capacity for growth and suggests that in these last poems his persistent
affirmations arise out of the negative rather than, as in the earlier
ones, transcending it. (This reference to growth--a subject not taken
up as explicitly in the essays of the sixties as in those of the fif-
ties--is typical of the tendency of much of the serious Cummings
scholarship of the decade to refute the by now conventional charge of
nondevelopment by providing extensive evidence demonstrating development.)

The essays surveyed so far fall at least roughly into the categories established in the previous decade. Others, however, break
relatively new ground. Sister Joan Marie Lechner, O.S.U. (1960.14)
discusses Cummings as a "nature poet" who practices a romantic identification with the natural world. Fred E. H. Schroeder (1965.23) examines Cummings' use of obscenity, concluding that he consistently
employs it in connection with irony and satire to make moral statements. Mick Gidley (1968.14) discusses Cummings' "poem-pictures."
His hieroglyphs create "a vehicle for personal conviction and insight"
rather than, as those of most earlier practitioners, "a vehicle for
spiritual visions."

Our survey so far indicates, and will continue to indicate, that
the major scholarship of the sixties generally took a very positive
attitude toward Cummings' achievement. And this is surely accurate.
There are, however, at least two significant essays which complicate
this impression. Carl Bode (1961.2), while admiring the energy of
Cummings' indignation and irreverence and the experimental success of
some of his love poems, finds that much of his work fails because of
a constant search for the new. Clive James (1969.22) suggests that
the simplistic ideas expressed in Cummings' poems would, if effected,
bring about the end of civilization.

In addition to the continuing importance of critical essays as a
component of Cummings criticism in the sixties, it was in these years
that parts of books treating Cummings first made significant contributions to the scholarship. M. L. Rosenthal, in a study of modern poets

(1960.19), describes Cummings as "absorbed in the problem of definition through the trapping of a state of awareness" and asserts that
most details of his technical unorthodoxy are functional. In his
study of modern American poetry (1966.10), L. S. Dembo discusses Cummings' ideas of becoming, of "'instantaneous growth,'" and his combining of objectivist and mystic responses to objects. David R.
Weimer, in his study of the city as a literary metaphor (1966.49),
examines Cummings as an urban poet. In his book on Americans in
Paris (1969.32), George Wickes rehearses the details surrounding
Cummings' incarceration in a French prison, The Enormous Room, and,
especially, French influence on his work. The most important treatments of Cummings in books are in Roy Harvey Pearce's The Continuity
of American Poetry (1961.10) and Hyatt H. Waggoner's American Poets
from the Puritans to the Present (1968.27). Both these major and very
influential studies, presenting overviews of American poetry from the
beginning to the 1960's, take that "mixed" view of Cummings which had
been typical but which seemed to have diminished in more recent scholarship. (The difference this indicates between the specialists and
the generalists is multiply instructive.) Pearce concentrates on
the personal element in Cummings' poems, finding them at times successful, at times sentimental. If he is capable of rescuing language
from deadening abstractness, his self-transcendence usually "turns out
to be only self-realization." Waggoner examines Cummings' transcendentalist metaphysic, places him in the Emersonian tradition, and defends
him against the charge that he has failed to grow, but concludes that
his techniques are too often repetitive and unimaginative to make him
the "true poet" for whom Emerson called.

The increased stature indicated by these treatments of Cummings
in sections of books is signalled even more strongly by the appearance
in the sixties of several books devoted entirely to him and his works.
In 1960, George J. Firmage published E. E. Cummings: A Bibliography
(1960.7). This descriptive bibliography of primary works catalogues
not only books and pamphlets by Cummings, but also his contributions
to books, periodicals, catalogues, and the like, translations and
musical settings of his works, recorded readings, and reproductions
of his art works. Firmage also provides an index of titles and first
lines. (Secondary bibliographies are provided in books by Baum and
Friedman; see below.) A book collecting a sizeable selection of Cummings' letters (1969.7), edited by F. W. Dupee and George Stade, was
published in 1969 (a small selection relating to attempted censorship
of a Cummings' reading and edited by Robert G. Tucker and David R.
Clark [1963.20] appeared in The Massachusetts Review earlier in the
decade.) Charles Norman's revision of his biography, retitled E. E.
Cummings: A Biography (1967.25), adds a chapter updating the work to
the time of Cummings' death in 1962. The only other significant biographical work to appear in the sixties is Richard S. Kennedy's study
of Cummings' father (1966.27), which suggests the influence of his
world view on his son.

In addition to the works mentioned above, five critical books
and one pamphlet appeared in the sixties. The first of these, and
still the best study of Cummings' poetry, is Norman Friedman's E. E.
Cummings: The Art of His Poetry (1960.8). Friedman analyzes Cummings' vision and technique in much detail. He defines the major
themes and explores Cummings' poetic persona; examines the responses
typically acted out by this speaker, which involve all the usual lyric
stances except the meditative; discusses Cummings' style, rejecting
the idea that his language is unintelligible and defining its neutral,
formal, and burlesque modes; demonstrates the growth of Cummings'
figurative language and discusses many of his other distinctive techniques; and evidences his careful craftsmanship through a lengthy
analysis of "rosetree, rosetree." Friedman concludes by making explicit a judgment implicit throughout the book, that there is real,
sustained growth evidenced in the course of Cummings' career. S. V.
Baum's ΕΣΤΙ: eec E. E. Cummings and the Critics (1962.9) reprints
twenty-six reviews of and essays on Cummings' work and includes an
introductory essay by Baum tracing the growth of Cummings' critical
reputation and both primary and secondary bibliographies.

In 1964, Norman Friedman published a second major book on Cummings, E. E. Cummings: The Growth of a Writer (1964.9). As its
title suggests, the book's main intention is the final refutation of
the charge that Cummings' work is static. Friedman lays the groundwork for this refutation by defining Cummings' mature vision and
technique, the "goals" of his life's work. His mature vision is
summarized "under four related headings: the nature of the true
world, knowing it, acting in it, and depicting it." Cummings' true
world is "a timeless world of the eternal present." It is known by
wisdom rather than knowledge, since ultimate values lie beyond logic.
Cummings' paradigms for action are love and individuality. His aesthetic for depicting that world is Romantic. Turning to the method
by which these ideas are expressed, Friedman defines Cummings' mature
technique as combining tradition and experiment and as centrally concerned with "stripping the film of familiarity from language in order
to strip the film of familiarity from the world." Having provided
this foundation, Friedman examines all Cummings' works preceding 73
poems, including the prose works and plays, in relation to the development of the mature vision and art he has described.

Barry A. Marks' E. E. Cummings (1964.16), in Twayne's United
States Authors Series, aims to illuminate Cummings' attitudes and
themes as they appear in specific poems. After extensive analyses of
four representative poems, Marks, who confines his attention almost
entirely to the poems, takes up several subjects, always evidencing
his assertions by reference to particular poems. Among these subjects
are Cummings' use of children's open and imaginative response to the
world, his use of sex as subject and symbol, his relation to some of
the characteristic aesthetic principles of his age, his formalism
(the sections dealing with these matters are very valuable), and his
relationship to American attitudes and myths. Marks also discusses

Cummings as a religious poet. Robert E. Wegner, in his <u>The Poetry</u>
<u>and Prose of E. E. Cummings</u> (1965.30), explores the importance of
self-discovery as a motive for Cummings' art, compares and contrasts
him to his contemporaries, lists his central subjects as love, birth,
growth, death, and their opposites, and describes his favored images
as manifestations of the life force informing the universe. Wegner
also examines Cummings' emphasis on freedom and individuality and his
elevation of feeling over thinking, and refutes charges of anarchism,
solipsism, nihilism, anticultural attitudes, and nondevelopment.
Cummings' satire of all that opposes the vital in life and his characteristic forms and techniques are also discussed. Wegner's points on
these matters are supported by references to particular works. Eve
Triem's <u>E. E. Cummings</u> (1969.28), one of the University of Minnesota
Pamphlets on American Writers, presents an overview of Cummings' work
and describes him as a transcendentalist, a troubadour, and an artist
who uses the absurd to shock his readers into attention and, later,
to "mean the truth of earthly living and a promise of eternity" and
whose major themes concern sensory awareness, the integrity of the
individual, and the true meaning of love.

Lengthy and serious interpretive and research scholarship continues to increase in the Cummings criticism of those years of the
seventies covered by this survey. The more or less accepted estimate
established in the fifties and sixties of Cummings as a kind of major-
minor or minor-major poet, modernist in style and traditional in
theme, persists in the seventies, as do nagging doubts about the functional value of his experiments and his growth as a poet (despite the
major and largely convincing demonstrations of Friedman and others).
The most significant development of the criticism of these years is
not, then, any serious shift or revision of reputation, but, as we
shall see, a tendency to focus on increasingly specific subjects,
critical questions, and so on.

The only significant volumes of Cummings' work to be reviewed in
the seventies so far are <u>Selected Letters of E. E. Cummings</u> (1969) and
the American edition of <u>Complete Poems: 1913–1962</u> (1972). Not surprisingly, given their generally retrospective quality, both received
relatively little and relatively brief attention from reviewers. The
most interesting response to the letters (a few reviews of which also
appeared in 1969) is Robert B. Shaw's suggestion (1970.16) that their
revelation that Cummings' character was formed early and remained
largely unchanged may explain his frequently noted lack of poetic development. Among the few important responses to the <u>Complete Poems</u>,
Reed Whittemore (1972.29) notes Cummings' extraordinary isolation and
finds his social opinions finally antisocial, and Helen Vendler
(1973.37) bemoans his "great aborted talent" and considers him "abys-
mally short on ideas" and his optimism exclusionary.

If reviews play quite a small role in the Cummings criticism of
this decade, other areas increase markedly. Among these is attention
to Cummings in doctoral dissertations, fourteen of which consider him

in larger contexts. The greater specificity of the criticism of the
seventies noted above is demonstrated in many of these studies which,
unlike the typically general approaches of earlier dissertations,
consider such subjects as syntactic deviance in the poems (1971.7),
the early long poems (1971.16), stylistics (1972.22), the plays
(1973.30), the sonnets (1975.13 and 1976.23), and so on. Another
area of criticism showing an increase is analyses of individual poems,
an increase emphasized by the fact that this survey considers only a
little over half of the decade. Once again, in addition to their
illumination of particular poems, these analyses continue to demonstrate the importance and effectiveness of Cummings' expressive
techniques.

The main increase in the criticism of the seventies, however, is
in the number of major articles on Cummings. And it is in these that
the movement of the scholarship toward greater specificity is most
apparent. Only two of the major essays take a general approach. Malcolm Cowley (1973.4) combines biographical information with criticism
of Cummings' work, examining his exaltation of feeling over knowledge,
his aesthetic of the intense and personal moment, his technique, and
his development from spokesman for an age to Christian Emersonian.
William Heyen (1973.12) argues the need for a closer reading of Cummings' poems, suggests that the blunt fact of death is always his
starting point, and insists that his poems have more duplicity and
irony in them than is usually noticed. If these essays are general,
the remainder are specific. Joseph W. Mahoney (1973.17) surveys
criticism of Cummings and finds that it vibrates between two poles,
one of which defines him as an anticultural and anti-intellectual
writer, the other as an artist interpreting his culture and making
new demands on the intellect. Two essays by Richard S. Kennedy
explore specific aspects of Cummings' biography, his studies during
his years at Harvard (1976.9) and his verse, friendships, and rebel-
liousness during those same years (1977.3).

Cummings' typography is the subject of John W. Crowley's essay
(1972.9). He maintains that his typographical oddities are important
not so much for their emblematic or ideographic content as for their
exploitation of the "shift in poetry from an oral-aural to a visual-
aural mode." Linguistics approaches to Cummings are continued in
essays by Jan Aarts (1971.1), Richard Gunter (1971.12), and Tanya
Reinhart (1976.21). More important than these are several essays
which extend the attention to Cummings' most important long works,
The Enormous Room and Him, begun in the sixties. James F. Smith, Jr.
(1973.27) discusses Cummings' use in The Enormous Room of the character Jean le Nègre as an archetype of individual humanity confronting
government inhumanity. Harold T. McCarthy (1974.10) examines the
novel in terms of its hero's anomalous joy in his imprisonment and
his recognition of his suffering as a way of salvation and in terms
of Cummings' own American-patrician heritage. The mixed roles of the
narrator as artist and the artist as narrator as they are created and
developed in The Enormous Room is the subject of George S. Peek's

essay (1976.19). Jeffrey Walsh (1976.24) examines the experience recorded in The Enormous Room as the catalyst of Cummings' developing
artistic and social visions and the work itself as manifesting their
developments. Him's complex of surrealism, realism, and expression-
ism is treated in an essay by William I. Oliver (1974.16) which also
discusses the problems Cummings' play poses for a director. Marjorie
S. C. Smelstor (1974.20) examines Him and its relation to the popular
arts of the twenties.

An area of Cummings' work which had received relatively little
attention in previous decades, his paintings and drawings (only the
article by Fairfield Porter noted above is of any real importance),
is considered in three essays in the seventies. Rushworth M. Kidder
(1975.11) explores Cummings as a painter, tracing his "background in
art," his concern for the theoretical and aesthetic as well as technical aspects of painting, and his movement from abstract to representational art. The graphics Cummings drew for The Dial are the
subject of another essay by Kidder (1976.11). These, he argues,
"provide insights into the humor, economy, precision, and movement of
his poetry" and share the poetry's concern with such matters as vitality, simultaneity in the presentation of opposites, juxtapositions
of the disparate, and emphasis on "the spontaneous and intuitive."
The same drawings are discussed, as complements to the poems, by
Robert Tucker (1975.19).

As in the sixties, there are essays in the seventies which attempt
to place Cummings in context. Again, some of these show increased
specificity. Allan A. Metcalf (1970.11) discusses Cummings and Dante,
noting Cummings' use of brief explicit references to the Inferno in
the early work and larger, looser, often imagistic references to the
Paradiso in later works. This he relates to Cummings' shifting emphasis. A quite different sort of connection is suggested by James E.
Tanner (1976.22), who compares Cummings' experimental style to William
Burroughs', finding that Cummings' style is marked by deletion from
rather than addition to his cognitive content. Mary Ellen Solt
(1970.17) very briefly notes Cummings' influence on "concrete poetry."
Two other studies place Cummings in more general contexts. Paul Fort
(1976.6) locates Cummings at the center of the dialectic between aes-
theticism and energy that is typical of modern American poetry.
Renzo S. Crivelli (1972.7) examines Cummings' connections with movements in art and music: cubism and futurism in art; and the use of
sound as a coefficient of movement typical of such modern composers
as Stravinsky, Satie, and Schönberg.

Most of the essays summarized above, although generally more specific in subject and approach than those of previous decades, fall
into categories well established by the earlier criticism. But, as
the decline of New Critical domination in the fifties and sixties had
the general effect of enabling reexamination and reevaluation of Cummings' work, so the development of critical modes and approaches to
replace, supplement, or complement those of the New Criticism

generated some new areas of Cummings scholarship. We have seen the beginnings of this in the many linguistic approaches to Cummings' poems. It continues in essays by Marjorie S. C. Smelstor (1974.20), Patrick B. Mullen (1971.20), Eleanore Hombitzer (1973.13), and John M. Lipski (1976.16). The current interest in popular culture is reflected in Smelstor's discussion of Him in relation to the popular culture of the twenties (1974.20) and by Mullen's more general study of Cummings' attraction to and use of the spontaneous, unrehearsed qualities of such popular arts as burlesque, circuses, amusement parks, cartoons, and movies. Recently developed methods for applying the principles of structuralism to literary criticism are employed in Hombitzer's analysis of "a wind has blown the rain away and blown." Another application of what was originally a scientific methodology to literary study is suggested by Lipski in his use of typology, the branch of mathematics dealing with spatial properties, in a discussion of "disconnectedness" in Cummings' poetry. Further scholarship using these and other innovative methods is to be expected.

One final development in the essays of the seventies is worthy of note, the use by scholars of the Cummings materials held by Harvard's Houghton Library. Rushworth M. Kidder, in the essay on Cummings as a painter summarized above, suggests that Cummings' interest in the role of the analytical intellect in both painting and writing--as evidenced in unpublished notes in the Houghton collection--belies his frequent description as an anti-intellectual. Richard S. Kennedy, in the two biographical essays already discussed, also makes use of materials held by Harvard. In another essay (1976.12), Kidder uses manuscript pages from the Cummings Collection to describe the origin of "Buffalo Bill's" and to illuminate Cummings' process of composition in general. Future scholarship will surely continue to exploit these valuable source materials.

Significant attention to Cummings in parts of books decreased in the seventies; only three such treatments appeared. Books with Cummings as their subject continued to be published at about the rate of the previous decade. Of studies representing parts of books, Donald Barlow Stauffer's (1974.21) is a general discussion. His history of American poetry places Cummings with those avant-gardists who believed that "words are symbols that can embody concepts independently of their syntactical function," yet insists that his radically personal vision and technique prevent him from being lumped with any group. In his study of American free verse (1973.32), Walter Sutton discusses Cummings' suiting of both his traditional and experimental techniques to his largely anti-intellectual ideas. Dickran Tashjian, in a chapter of his study of the relationship of Dadaism to the American avant-garde of the teens and twenties (1975.18), maintains that Cummings does employ certain Dadaist methods "for the organic transformation of form and content in his poetry" but does not go to the Dadaist extreme of totally abandoning the denotational quality of words.

Also noteworthy is Richard S. Kennedy's introduction (1976.10) to George James Firmage's edition of the original <u>Tulips & Chimneys</u> manuscript. Kennedy traces the history of the manuscript and the history of Cummings' artistic development in the years up to its completion and maintains that the Apollonian, Satyric, and Hephaestian styles which account for most of Cummings' output are already present in these poems, although the coherent outlook on life which centers the later poems was yet to be achieved.

Two pamphlets and four books on Cummings have appeared in the seventies so far. The pamphlets are of relatively minor importance. Both (1970.6 and 1970.7) are by Wilton Eckley and are numbers in series published by the Charles E. Merrill Company. The first, a checklist, presents selected bibliographies under the categories of bibliography, biography, and scholarship and criticism. The second, an introductory essay, includes a biographical sketch, defines Cummings' technical innovations as designed to rescue language from convention and to create intensity and drama, and describes his essentially traditional and romantic theme as centered in the idea that the negative self can be transcended through love. Of the books, one is general, two are more specialized, and one is a collection of essays. Bethany K. Dumas' <u>E. E. Cummings: A Remembrance of Miracles</u> (1974.5) is comprehensive. It contains chapters on biography, the early poems, the later poems, the prose, and the plays. A concluding estimate argues that Cummings' major accomplishments are the multiplication of the poetic possibilities of the lyric and the creation of a poetic language that forces his readers to look at reality from a new angle. The linguistics studies which began in the sixties and continued in the seventies culminate in Irene R. Fairley's <u>E. E. Cummings and Ungrammar</u> (1975.5), which treats Cummings grammatical irregularities in detail, relating them to his themes, concluding that he uses them not only for the creation of particular effects in individual lines but also for the creation of larger structural patterns which become major sources of cohesiveness, and finding him, in his syntactic deviance as in his themes and other techniques, a "conservative revolutionary." Gary Lane's <u>I Am: A Study of E. E. Cummings' Poems</u> (1976.13) is introduced by an examination of Cummings' essential egocentrism, his thematic dialectic of love, and his technical striving for immediacy of effect, and lists Cummings' weaknesses as sentimentality, obscurity, and false ingenuity; but the remainder of the study is concerned with tracing, largely through close analyses of individual poems, five ideas as they develop over Cummings' career from motifs into major themes. These are: the "seduction" theme, the theme of individual and individualistic heroism, the transcendent unification of life and death, the theme of death-in-life, and the theme of love as the means to and end of transcendence. Probably the most important book on Cummings to appear in the seventies, and the last item in this survey, is <u>E. E. Cummings: A Collection of Critical Essays</u> (1972.10). Edited by Norman Friedman, this volume in Prentice-Hall's Twentieth Century Views series reprints fourteen essays, most of them significant. In his introduction, Friedman expresses his hope that it will help remedy the relative insufficiency of Cummings criticism caused by his writing a poetry of transcendence in an age dominated by the poetry of ambivalence. The essays Friedman collects, his own contributions to Cummings scholarship, and much of the other work singled out in this survey indicate that that hope is on its way to fulfillment.

It is my hope that this survey and the bibliography it introduces will facilitate that fulfillment. For if much has been done, much remains to be done. The need for a major critical biography will no doubt be filled by Richard S. Kennedy, who has already done important biographical work on Cummings and whose study of the life is due from Liveright in 1979. (Two other significant additions to the scholarship are in preparation. Temple University's Journal of Modern Literature is planning a Cummings issue in the near future, and Burt Franklin & Co. has announced that a collection reprinting critical writings on Cummings is being prepared for its The American Critical Tradition Series.) George J. Firmage's primary bibliography is in need of only minor updating. The availability and state of the texts are generally good, although a truly selective edition of the best poems would be beneficial. A complete collection of letters would be a welcome addition to the fine selection made by F. W. Dupee and George Stade. A concordance would facilitate future study of Cummings' language, imagery, and so on. As to other aspects of Cummings criticism, many areas have been studied, but many have not been studied definitively. And although this is not, I think, the place for a comprehensive list of desiderata, among those subjects needing further attention are Cummings' use of complexity, ambivalence, and irony, his "personal sign system," his treatment of and reaction to death, his use of the city, his alleged solipsism, and his use of nature as subject and theme. The question of technical and thematic development needs further and more specific consideration, and, of course, interdisciplinary studies and commentaries employing new critical methods should continue. A more accurate appraisal of his place in the modernist movement is desirable, and the frequent but at least partially contradictory description of Cummings as a thematic traditionalist and a technical modern is still in need of some clarification. Most important, however, is the need for further study of individual poems and groups of poems, because, although there have been many such studies, many of them have concentrated on a relatively small number of the poems, and because such studies are most likely to reveal Cummings' true importance in terms of his vision, craft, and development.

I have attempted to make this annotated bibliography as comprehensive as possible, including all but the most insignificant of materials insofar as I was aware of them. The foreign scholarship included is necessarily limited to that catalogued in the various quarterly, yearly, and other bibliographies published in the United States. And, because these same bibliographies are by their nature less than current, my entries for the most recent two or three years

are inevitably incomplete. It seemed sensible, nonetheless, to include what was available. Reprints and critical discussions and con-
troversies are cross referenced. Principles of indexing are outlined
in a note preceding the index. Items not actually seen are indicated
by an asterisk preceding the entry number. Annotations are descriptive of content, not judgmental. In preparing the bibliography, I
have no doubt made errors of commission and omission. I apologize
for them and would appreciate information about them.

This work owes much to many institutions and individuals. Only
the most prominent of these can be acknowledged here. A major debt
is to the compilers of earlier Cummings bibliographies, Paul Lauter,
S. V. Baum, Norman Friedman, and Wilton Eckley, and the compilers of
the Cummings entries in the <u>MLA International Bibliographies</u> and the
bibliographies in <u>American Literature</u> and <u>American Literary Scholar-
ship</u>. Professor Raymond Blois assisted with a translation of a work
in Arabic. Professors Irene R. Fairley, Norman Friedman, Richard S.
Kennedy, Akiko Miyake, and Samuel French Morse made available materials I could not otherwise have obtained. Acknowledgement is also
due the libraries of Boston College, Boston University, Brandeis University, Harvard University, Northeastern University, and Tufts University and to the Boston Public Library. My thanks to Louise
Dennett and Beverly Slayton of Northeastern's Interlibrary Loan
Department. Special thanks to Jon Lanham of Harvard's Widener
Library.

Selected List of Writings
by E. E. Cummings

1922	The Enormous Room
1923	Tulips and Chimneys
1925	& [And]
1925	XLI Poems
1926	is 5
1927	Him
1930	[No Title]
1931	W [Viva]
1933	The Red Front (translation)
1933	Eimi
1935	no thanks
1935	Tom
1937	Tulips & Chimneys (archetype edition)
1938	Collected Poems
1940	50 Poems
1944	1 X 1
1944	Anthropos: The Future of Art
1946	Santa Claus: A Morality
1950	Xaîpe: seventy one poems
1953	i: Six Nonlectures
1954	Poems: 1923–1954
1958	E. E. Cummings: A Miscellany (edited by George J. Firmage)
1958	95 poems
1959	100 Selected Poems
1963	73 poems

Selected List of Writings by E. E. Cummings

1965   <u>E. E. Cummings: A Selection of Poems</u>

1965   <u>Fairy Tales</u>

1968   <u>Complete Poems: 1923–1935</u> and <u>Complete Poems: 1936–1962</u> (two-volume British edition)

1972   <u>Complete Poems: 1913–1962</u>

1976   <u>Tulips & Chimneys</u> (typescript edition of the 1922 manuscript, edited by George James Firmage)

Writings About
E. E. Cummings, 1922-1977

1922

1   ANON. Review of The Enormous Room. The Bookman, 55, no. 5
      (July), 536.
          Brief notice asserts that the book's "flickering evi-
      dences of a sense of humor fail to make the unpleasant
      incidents less terrible."

2   ANON. Review of The Enormous Room. New York Times (29 May),
      p. 10.
          Indicts the novel and Cummings for an inaccurate and
      partial portrait of war, calls the book a failure of "real-
      ism," and considers it, and Dos Passos' Three Soldiers,
      "utterly false." Reprinted: 1962.9.

3   BISHOP, JOHN PEALE. "Incorrect English." Vanity Fair, 18
      (July), 20.
          Reviews The Enormous Room, finding behind its broken
      surface a sensitive intelligence and describing it as not
      a document of war or prison life but "a presentation of
      emotions, the tale of 'the long and difficult way' through
      which a young man had to come before he could discover the
      richness of life at its poorest." Reprinted: 1948.1.

4   CARVER, GEORGE. "The Enormous Room: A Review." The Midland,
      8 (November), 309-13.
          Describes The Enormous Room as attacking wrong through a
      startling exposition of stupidity. The effect of the book
      is conveyed by its content, its portrayal (through which
      "happening is realized"), and by the writer's gaiety in the
      face of his suffering.

5   CUMMINGS, EDWARD. "Introduction," in The Enormous Room. By
      E. E. Cummings. New York: Boni & Liveright, pp. [i]-vi.
          Reproduces some of the documents involved in securing
      Cummings' release from La Ferté Macé.

1922

6   DOS PASSOS, JOHN. "Off the Shoals." <u>The Dial</u>, 73 (July), 97-102.
      Reviews <u>The Enormous Room</u>. Dos Passos finds the novel "a distinct conscious creation separate from anything else under heaven." It approaches "the mood of reckless adventure in which men will reach the white heat of imagination needed to fuse the soggy disjointed complexity of the industrial life around us into seething fluid of creation." Cummings' material is superb; he "takes the rhythms of our American speech as the material of his prose as of his verse." Reprinted: 1943.2; 1955.7; 1962.9; 1963.9.

7   LITTELL, ROBERT. "Garbage and Gold." <u>The New Republic</u>, 30 (10 May), 320-21.
      Reviews <u>The Enormous Room</u>; discovers reading it like rooting around in garbage and finding there lumps of tarnished but precious metal. Reprinted: 1972.14.

8   MASSON, THOMAS L. "A Pilgrim's Progress in France." <u>New York Times Book Review and Magazine</u> (28 May), pp. 10, 23.
      Reviews <u>The Enormous Room</u>. Its realism is painful, its personal emphasis excessive, and its convincing portraits of women admirable. "Apart from its crudities, its mistaken disgruntled attitude and its bad writing, the book is quite worth while."

9   P., E. H. "<u>The Enormous Room</u>." <u>Current Affairs</u>, 13, no. 16 (4 September), 10, 14.
      The style of <u>The Enormous Room</u> is "most natural and unaffected"; the prose has "unmistakeable flow." The reviewer considers his reading of the book "the experience of a life time"; "it has robbed me of my last shred of altruism."

10   REDMAN, BEN RAY. "Man the Animal." <u>The Nation</u>, 114, no. 2970 (7 June), 691-92.
      Reviews <u>The Enormous Room</u>, calling it a "profoundly beautiful book" with superb portraits and marvelous poise. "It is at once an indictment and glorification of the incredible animal Man."

1923

1   ANON. Review of <u>Tulips and Chimneys</u>. <u>The Nation</u>, 117, no. 3047 (28 November), 614.
      "Mr. Cummings is a poet. One deduces that from his language, his observation, and an occasional idea that struggles across his pages. But he is also a pedant. His

typography is so perverse that the reader is scared off
before he has gone very far. The puzzle of his punctuation
is not even an amusing one; it certainly is not worth
solving."

2   CRANE, HART. "America's Plutonic Ecstasies / (With homage to
E. E. Cummings)." S₄N, Year 4, nos. 26-29 (May-August),
[54-55].
A poem making some use of Cummingsesque techniques.
Reprinted: 1948.4.

3   DUNN, EMMETT. "The Coming of Cummings." S₄N, Year 4, no. 25
(March-April), [11-13].
Responds to the appearance of "Poem, or Beauty Hurts Mr.
Vinal" in issue 23 of S₄N, arguing that Cummings is even
more guilty of clichés than the butt of his satire. (See
1923.4, 6.)

4   FREEMAN, J., G. B. MUNSON, W. R. BENET, J. P. BISHOP, D. GREEN-
HOOD, F. D. GRAB, L. GILMORE, H. D. WINNEY, R. HUNTER,
R. M. NEAL, W. W. WILLIAMS, A. A. ROSENTHAL, P. GRAY, E.
HOFFMAN, L. E. SMITH, J. CARTER, and J. L. FOWLER. "Poem:
E. E. Cummings." S₄N, Year 4, no. 25 (March-April),
[19-20].
Collects several brief comments on the appearance of
"Poem, or Beauty Hurts Mr. Vinal" in issue 23 of S₄N. The
responses range from acclaim to mild outrage. (See 1923.3,
6.)

5   GORMAN, HERBERT S. "Goliath Beats His Poetic Breast, Whilst
Critics Gape--Verses from the Left Wing of American Poetry."
New York Times Book Review (9 December), p. 1.
Reviews Tulips and Chimneys. Cummings "often reaches a
high and concentrated pitch of emotion that even his man-
nerisms cannot hide."

6   JOSEPHSON, MATTHEW. "Cummings." S₄N, Year 4, nos. 26-29 (May,
June, July, August), [94-95].
Letter notes that "Poem, or Beauty Hurts Mr. Vinal" is
"a monumental piece of social criticism." (See 1923.3, 4.)

7   JOSEPHSON, MATTHEW. "A New Poet." New York Herald-Tribune
Book Review (25 November), p. 21.
Reviews Tulips and Chimneys, praising "Puella Mea" and
finding Cummings' punctuation and typography a series of
incidental stunts clairvoyant in their use of successful
advertising techniques.

3

1923

8   MUNSON, GORHAM B.   "Syrinx."   Secession, no. 5 (July), pp. 2-
     11.
          Examines Cummings' originality and its two elements,
     accurate word choice and the development of techniques for
     the display of that accuracy.   These techniques involve the
     conversion of reorganized punctuation and typography into
     "active instruments for literary expression."   Several of
     these devices are named and described in terms of their
     effects.   Cummings' topics are the traditional ones of lyri-
     cism; his presentation renews them.   Munson finds in Cum-
     mings' anti-intellectualism a key to the open, feeling
     response his character and his ideas demand, but insists
     that this bias does not indicate an elevation of content
     over form in his work.   Indeed, Cummings marries form and
     content.   Munson discusses The Enormous Room at some length
     to demonstrate that marriage, concentrating on its techni-
     cal and organizational successes.   Reprinted: 1962.9.

                            1924

1   BLUM, W. C.   "The Perfumed Paraphrase of Death."   The Dial,
     76 (January), 49-52.
          Reviews Tulips and Chimneys, describing Cummings as an
     only superficially modern poet of love and death who satis-
     fies the lusts of the ear and of the eye, and "other old,
     often indecent, desires."

2   BROWN, SLATER.   Review of Tulips and Chimneys.   Broom, 6, no.
     1 (January), 26-28.
          Argues that Cummings has approached poetry through paint-
     ing.   "The spatial organization of color has become the
     durational organization of words, the technical problem
     that of tempo.... Logic and all its attributes of grammar,
     spelling, and punctuation, become subservient to the im-
     perial demands of form."

3   COWLEY, MALCOLM and SLATER BROWN.   "To the Editors of The
     Dial."   Broom, 6, no. 1 (January), 30-31.
          Praises Cummings and complains of The Dial's inconsis-
     tency with regard to him.

4   EDITORS, THE.   Comment.   The Dial, 76 (April), 376-79.
          Responds to Murry's treatment of Cummings (see 1924.9),
     defending his technique and commenting on his use of capi-
     talization.

                             4

5 J[EWETT], K. Review of Tulips and Chimneys. The Transatlantic
   Review, 1, no. 4 (April), 246-47.
        Describes the Cummings of Tulips and Chimneys as having
   "a tremendous ability for metaphor and paraphrase coupled
   with a startlingly original lyricism. His perverse wit
   seems to delight in stopping just short of sentimentality."

6 McCLURE, JOHN. "Tulips and Chimneys." The Double Dealer, 6,
   no. 35 (April), 121-22.
        Reviews Tulips and Chimneys, commenting on its exuber-
   ance, unevenness, promise of greatness, excessive experimentation, startling rhythms and diction, and aesthetic
   sincerity.

7 M[ONROE], H[ARRIET]. "Flare and Blare." Poetry, 23 (January),
   211-15.
        Reviews Tulips and Chimneys; finds pleasure in Cummings'
   "grand gusto" but describes his technical eccentricities as
   irritating intrusions, thus justifying her conventionalizing
   the printing of quoted poems. Reprinted: 1962.9.

8 MURRY, JOHN MIDDLETON. On Cummings, in his Discoveries: Essays in Literary Criticism. London: W. Collins Sons & Co.,
   pp. 306-10.
        Revision of 1924.9 in that Cummings is mentioned by name.

9 MURRY, JOHN MIDDLETON. On Cummings. The Yale Review, 13,
   no. 2 (January), 358-60.
        In a discussion of the Romantic cult of art as mystery,
   notes the desperate attempt of a passage by Cummings (who
   is not named) to be incomprehensible. Cummings is mentioned
   by name in a later revised edition: 1924.8. For a response, see 1924.4.

10 PARSHLEY, H. M. "A Joyful De Profundis." S4N, Year 5, no. 32
    (February), 39-44.
        Reviews The Enormous Room as an aesthetically successful
    series of characterizations. Its use of obscenity is "ro-
    bustly wholesome."

11 SELTZER, THOMAS. Review of Tulips and Chimneys. Voices, no.
    3 (March-April), pp. 56-57.
        Argues that Cummings "derives from moderns and pre-
    Elizabethans" and that the inimitable quality of his com-
    bination of "an ultra-modern system of punctuation with an
    archaic range of topic" proves that it is more than "a
    cunning stunt."

1924

12 UNTERMEYER, LOUIS. Review of Tulips and Chimneys. The Book-
      man, 69, no. 2 (April), 219-20.
          Notices Tulips and Chimneys in an omnibus review, calling
      Cummings the most interesting of the postwar artists who
      evidence "a sense of strain" in achieving their effects.
      Untermeyer dislikes the "typographical tricks" (which may
      be an attempt to disguise sentimentality), but feels that
      apart from them Cummings "communicates a genuine if disin-
      tegrated lyricism."

13 WILSON, EDMUND. "Wallace Stevens and E. E. Cummings." The
      New Republic, 38 (19 March), 102-103.
          Reviews Harmonium and Tulips and Chimneys. Unlike Ste-
      vens, Cummings is not (yet) the master of a style; his
      "style is an eternal adolescent" and he lacks the faculty
      of self-criticism. Even his best work is characterized by
      his immaturity, of which his punctuation is a symptom. His
      punctuation is ugly and his subjects are familiar, simple,
      and occasionally banal, yet Cummings is "a genuine lyric
      poet." Reprinted: 1952.19; 1962.9.

                              1925

1   KOHN, WALTER F. "The Romance of Actuality." The New Republic,
      45 (2 December), 60-61.
          Reviews XLI Poems, commenting on Cummings' disregarding
      of the "schools" and on the "inevitable and indispensable"
      quality of his experiments. In this book, actuality is
      "suddenly made romantic by being rendered in its own terms,
      without moral or artistic implications." For a response,
      see 1925.8.

2   MORLEY, CHRISTOPHER. Review of XLI Poems. The Saturday Re-
      view of Literature, 2, no. 6 (5 September), 103.
          Finds Cummings, "whether curious or indolent," always
      interesting. Of his readers, "thereareneververymany."

3   NARDI, MARCIA. "Unaccustomed Realism." New York Herald-
      Tribune Books (14 June), 5, p. 4.
          Reviews XLI Poems, emphasizing Cummings' exclusive re-
      cording of "sensuous experiences" and his "deepening in-
      clination toward complete realism."

4   RASCOE, BURTON. "Contemporary Reminiscences." Arts & Decora-
      tion, 22, no. 11 (March), 38, 70, 75.
          Recounts a meeting with Cummings at Archibald MacLeish's
      house in Paris, recalling this comment of his own on

Cummings as a lyric poet: "Uneven? Yes, I grant you! So was God." Rascoe also re-presents a Cummings monologue on the artist and comments on his conversation. Reprinted: 1929.5.

5   ROSENFELD, PAUL. "E. E. Cummings," in his Men Seen: Twenty-Four Modern Authors. New York: The Dial Press, pp. 191-200.
    Celebrates the style and theme of Cummings' The Enormous Room, especially its clear, finely modulated and accented prose and its bold submission to life. Rosenfeld finds the poems of Tulips and Chimneys less successful. Despite their musical brilliance and "native magnificence," they "suggest an impulse less robustly taut and integrated." He remarks that "Cummings may prove a formidable sport from the old Puritanic stem."

6   UNTERMEYER, LOUIS. "E. E. Cummings," in his Modern American Poetry: A Critical Anthology. Third edition. New York: Harcourt, Brace and Co., pp. 567-68.
    Introduces three Cummings poems, finding Cummings "fecund" and imaginative, but aesthetically immature because of his "distorted punctuation." These opinions alter in later editions: 1930.5; 1936.5; 1942.4; 1950.22; 1962.28.

7   VAN DOREN, MARK. "First Glance." The Nation, 121, no. 3131 (8 July), 72.
    Reviews XLI Poems as continuing the tradition established in Tulips and Chimneys. The "tricks" are unnecessary and obstructive. His future may lie in love sonnets in the grand style.

8   WESENBERG, ALICE BIDWELL. "In Defense of Mr. Cummings." The New Republic, 45 (30 December), 166.
    Responds to Kohn's review of XLI Poems (see 1925.1), emphasizing that Cummings is not an experimenter, but an innovative imitator.

9   WOOD, CLEMENT. On Cummings, in his Poets of America. New York: E. P. Dutton & Co., pp. 304-306.
    Argues, in a survey of modern poets, that "Cummings' Tulips and Chimneys reveals an authentic poet who has eaten the loco-weed miscalled modernism."

1926

1   CRAWFORD, JOHN W. "Mr. Cummings Cuts More Capers On the Parnassian Mount." New York Times Book Review (18 July), p. 8.

1926

Reviews is 5, describing Cummings as a "typographical hierophant." "He might almost be said to be a poet of improvisation rather than of achievement." Cummings has, in this book, moved closer to the "analytical complexities" of Eliot. Crawford also comments on the visual element in the poems.

2   EDITORS, THE. "Announcement." The Dial, 80 (January), 84-88.
    Announces the Dial Award for 1925 to Cummings, describing his poetry as trying "to beat the elements and the muscles and the machines at their own game--any inventions being the result of an effort to convey a new perception."

3   FITZGERALD, F. SCOTT. On The Enormous Room. Bookman, 63, no. 3 (May), 264.
    Remarks, in "How to Waste Material, A Note on My Generation," that of "all the work by the young men who have sprung up since 1920 one book survives--The Enormous Room.... It is scarcely a novel; it doesn't deal with the American scene; it was swamped in the mediocre downpour, isolated, forgotten. But it lives on." Reprinted: 1958.9.

4   HUGHES, GLENN. "A Strayed Cavalier." The Saturday Review of Literature, 3, no. 4 (21 August), 53.
    Reviews is 5; Cummings revives, with indisputable success, "the mannerisms of Marvell, Suckling, Herrick, and Carew." His typography is in need of forgiveness. Reprinted: 1934.2.

5   LESEMANN, MAURICE. "The Poetry of E. E. Cummings." Poetry, 29, no. 3 (December), 164-69.
    Reviews XLI Poems and is 5. Cummings writes poetry "of two entirely separate species," one "concerned with the external world" and its direct presentation, the other reflecting "his own inner life." Lesemann finds the "intrusion of graphic technique into an art that is essentially linear" irrelevant and notes that instead of breaking lines according to their organic rhythms, Cummings often breaks them so as "to give emphasis to images and to set off words by idea-clusters."

6   MANSFIELD, MARGERY SWETT. Review of is 5. The Bookman, 64, no. 2 (October), 231-32.
    Reviews Cummings' is 5 in an omnibus review, complaining that his refusal to punctuate causes the loss of his "fresh and lovely imagery" and joining Harriet Monroe (see 1924.7) in the experiment of "regularizing" his poems.

7   MOORE, MARIANNE. "People Stare Carefully." The Dial, 80
     (January), 49-52.
         Reviews & and XLI Poems and finds in them "a sense of
     the best dancing and of the best horticulture." Cummings
     "is fanciful, yet faithful to that verisimilitude of eye
     and rhetoric which is so important in poetry." He "shapes
     the progress of poems as if it were substance." The poems
     themselves "constitute a kind of verbal topiary-work."
     Moore complains of a lack of love in these pages but finds
     in them much verbal and figurative "glamor." Cummings has
     "created from inconvenient emotion, what one is sure is
     poetry." Reprinted: 1962.9.

8   S[TUART], H[ENRY] L[OGAN]. Review of is 5. The Commonweal,
     4, no. 19 (15 September), 452.
         is 5 shows Cummings an eminent exponent of the "new
     macaronism."

9   TAGGARD, GENEVIEVE. "Eye, Ear and Imagination." New York
     Herald-Tribune Books (25 July), 7, p. 3.
         Reviews is 5, describing Cummings as "a sensuous poet
     with an obsession for getting the darling FACT on the page
     before it entirely wilts."

10   TAGGARD, GENEVIEVE. "The Poet of the Instant." The New Re-
     public, 48, no. 614 (8 September), 76-77.
         Reviews is 5; argues that Cummings' technique is based
     on the will to choose the instant native impulse over the
     secondary "educated sense of expression.... He is a sensu-
     ous poet entirely concerned with the darling varieties of
     the verb to be." Cummings is contrasted with Keats and Amy
     Lowell.

11   VAN DOREN, MARK. Review of is 5. The Nation, 123, no. 3194
     (22 September), [274].
         In an omnibus review, describes is 5 as continuing on
     the lyric-satiric path. This path may lead Cummings into
     difficulties, for "the extreme of his foolery is meaningless
     vulgarity; the extreme of his serious work is...sentimental-
     ity."

                              1927

1   GOULD, JOE. "A Chapter from Joe Gould's Oral History." The
     Exile, no. 2, pp. 112-16.
         Comments briefly on Cummings' theory "that art is essen-
     tially the expression of personality."

1927

2   [PARK, FRANCES.] Review of <u>Him</u>. <u>Theatre Arts Monthly</u>, 11
     (December), 960.
          In an omnibus review, calls <u>Him</u> a brilliant book and
     wonders if it is a brilliant play. The reviewer feels the
     play is unproduceable under then present law and admires
     its "singular power and vitality" and its satire.

3   PRESTON, JOHN HYDE. "Drama in Extremis." <u>The Saturday Review</u>
     <u>of Literature</u>, 4, no. 21 (17 December), 453.
          Reviews <u>Him</u>, remarking Cummings' "extraordinary genius
     for language" and rebuking his lack of "regard for meaning
     and sense." Symbolism has ruined his talent. "So much for
     the man who once had the promise of an American Keats."
     For responses, <u>see</u> 1928.9 and 1928.11.

4   RIDING, LAURA and ROBERT GRAVES. On Cummings, in their <u>A</u>
     <u>Survey of Modernist Poetry</u>. London: William Heinemann Ltd.,
     pp. 9-34, 38-41, 44, 59-64, 84-88, 100, 131-34, 153, 174,
     187, 201-202, 217, 245-47, 249-50, 252, 288-89.
          In chapter one, Riding and Graves examine Cummings' "Sun-
     set" ("stinging") to demonstrate the special--and legiti-
     mate--demands the modernist poem makes upon its reader. In
     the second chapter, Cummings is briefly related to Valéry
     and to impressionism. In the third chapter, the communica-
     tive functions of his punctuation and spelling are discussed
     as part of a demonstration of the importance of the original
     punctuation and spelling to the meaning of Shakespeare's
     Sonnet 129. In chapter four, the technical devices of
     "Among" are analyzed. Chapter six contains a brief discus-
     sion of technique's relation to the making of poems in con-
     nection with Cummings' introduction to <u>is 5</u>. Many other
     minor comments are made on the pages listed above. The
     entire text of this book is reprinted in <u>The Common Asphodel</u>
     by Robert Graves, 1949.8 and 1970.8. The first chapter is
     reprinted in EΣTI: eec E. E. Cummings and the Critics,
     1962.9.

5   SAGE, ROBERT. "Roughneck Verse." <u>Transition</u>, no. 3 (June),
     pp. 169-72.
          Reviews <u>is 5</u>. Cummings is "a poetic roughneck who has
     walked into a company of correctly boring people." His
     "native elements...are perhaps the most reliable guarantee
     that american literature is not soon to lose its vitality."

6   TAGGARD, GENEVIEVE. "The Perfect Acrobat." <u>New York Herald-</u>
     <u>Tribune Books</u> (6 November), p. 2.
          Reviews <u>Him</u>, asserting that the play, "like everything
     else Cummings has written, is relating for us a permanent

preoccupation with a reality of which we are only dimly
aware," and hoping for the play "a performance as impas-
sioned, as slap-stick and as delicate as itself."

7   WILSON, EDMUND. "Him." The New Republic, 52, no. 674 (2 November), 293-94.
        Insists that Him be judged as "a dramatic poem in prose"
since it is impracticable as a play. It is full of Cummings' usual spontaneity and originality and of his usual
self-indulgence and lack of system. Reprinted: 1952.17.

8   WILSON, EDMUND. "A Preface to Persius." The New Republic,
52, no. 672 (19 October), 237-39.
        Comments on Cummings, whose behavior in an Italian res-
taurant is recorded, in relation to Persius. Both express
themselves "confusedly, inelegantly and obscenely" under
the moral anarchy of despots. "Where life is disorderly,
the poets express themselves in nonsense." Reprinted:
1952.18.

1928

1   ANON. Review of Him. Time, 11, no. 18 (30 April), 18.
        Reprints the "Warning" from Him's program and finds "par-
tially concealed in its three spasmodic acts many specimens
of acute and mordant understanding as well as a fair quantity of ribald wit." The play is an ambitious failure.

2   ANON. "A Suspect in France." The Times Literary Supplement
(26 July), p. 546.
        Reviews The Enormous Room as a "striking example of the
modernist school of writing." Its presentation is vivid
and its descriptions remarkable, but the far from normal
standards it suggests may not be ideal for one who would
fill "the quadruple role of witness, prosecuting counsel,
jury, and judge."

3   ATKINSON, J. BROOKS. "Him an' Me." New York Times (29 April),
9, pp. 1, 2.
        Responds to Dos Passos' reply (see 1928.12) to his re-
view of Him (see 1928.4), arguing that, when all considerations of its integrity of style are ended, "the dull fact
remains" that the play is a victim of self-consciousness
and is, finally, "false."

4   ATKINSON, J. BROOKS. "A Play Misunderstood." New York Times
(19 April), p. 23.

1928

> Reviews the Provincetown Theater's production of <u>Him</u> as
> a "facetious celebration." Life "regarded from mr. cum-
> mings' state of being appeared to be (1) the familiar
> tragedy of the man who had married a dumb wife and (2) a
> sophomoric burlesque show.... Imparting sensations rather
> than exposition," the play is "content with third rate
> humor and banal expression." For a reply and a response,
> <u>see</u> 1928.12 and 1928.3.

5   BENET, WILLIAM ROSE. "There's Something About <u>Him</u>." <u>New York
    Herald-Tribune</u> (29 April), 7, p. 5.
        Letter to the editor defends <u>Him</u> in particular and Cum-
    mings in general.

6   BOYD, ERNEST. Review of <u>Him</u>. <u>The Bookman</u>, 67, no. 4 (June),
    421.
        Brief notice of the Provincetown Theater's production.
    "<u>Him</u> does not provoke anger, but merely bored indifference."

7   BRACKETT, CHARLES. Review of <u>Him</u>. <u>The New Yorker</u>, 4, no. 10
    (28 April), 29-30.
        The play "contains occasional moments of exquisite po-
    etry...but Mr. Cummings has made no such paltry compromise
    as to attempt dramatic effectiveness anywhere.... I myself
    found <u>him</u> an exhaustion and a bore."

8   BROWN, JOHN MASON. Review of <u>Him</u>. <u>Theatre Arts Monthly</u>, 12
    (June), 392-93.
        Notices the Provincetown Theater's production of <u>Him</u> in
    an omnibus review, calling it the year's most ambitious
    play and reprinting in full the "Warning" given in the
    program. This warning is accurate, for it makes clear that
    <u>Him</u> "is not a play..., cannot be enjoyed...and...cannot be
    understood."

9   BROWN, SLATER. "What It Means." <u>The Saturday Review of
    Literature</u>, 4, no. 26 (21 January), 540.
        Defends <u>Him</u> against Preston's criticisms (<u>see</u> 1927.3).

10 CARB, DAVID. "<u>Him</u>." <u>Vogue</u>, 71, no. 12 (15 June), 98.
        Brief notice of the Provincetown Theater's production
    of <u>Him</u>.

11 DAMON, S. FOSTER. "Cummings' <u>Him</u>." <u>The Saturday Review of
    Literature</u>, 4, no. 25 (14 January), 522.
        Replies to Preston's review (<u>see</u> 1927.3), describing the
    play in psychological terms and as "the awful circular
    drift of the dust of reality in one skull." Damon suggests

connections with Strindberg, Joyce, Dos Passos, O'Neill, Eliot, and the Dadaists.

12 DOS PASSOS, JOHN. "Mr. Dos Passos on <u>Him</u>." <u>New York Times</u> (22 April), 9, p. 2.
      Letter responding to Atkinson's review of <u>Him</u> (<u>see</u> 1928.4). The play "might be called oblique in the sense that it attempts to generate feelings and ideas rather than put them immediately up to the understanding, and direct in that it aims to express sensations rather than to tell about them." This method panicked reviewers into judging it by alien standards. For a reply by Atkinson, <u>see</u> 1928.3.

13 GRAVES, ROBERT. "Introduction," in <u>The Enormous Room</u>. By E. E. Cummings. London: Jonathan Cape, pp. 7-15.
      Quotes T. E. Lawrence on <u>The Enormous Room</u>, explores the work's stylistically apt alternations between "'underwriting'" and "'overwriting,'" remarks on Cummings' "eye for character and significant detail," discusses the "historical truth" of the book in terms of the prison camps of World War I, and concludes with brief remarks on Cummings' poetry. Reprinted: 1930.4.

14 LITTELL, ROBERT. Review of <u>Him</u>. <u>New York Evening Post</u> (21 April), p. 27.
      <u>Him</u> is an annoying "wagonload of gargoyles and refuse." It "is neither nonsense, nor satire, nor deep stuff, nor parody, nor burlesque, nor revolt, nor art, nor dogma, nor entertainment, but simply rather painful evaluation of the contents of a weary, disordered, defeated, and uninteresting mind." Reprinted: 1934.4.

15 N[ORTH], J[ESSICA] N[ELSON]. On Cummings. <u>Poetry</u>, 31, no. 6 (March), 336.
      In a discussion of visual poetry's failings, remarks that "Cummings understands perfectly the rigid laws of phonetics and harmony." His experiments are functional, whereas many of his fellows jumble type only to "camouflage the text."

16 N[ORTH], J[ESSICA] N[ELSON]. "Out of Dreams." <u>Poetry</u>, 31, no. 6 (March), 345-46.
      Reviews <u>Him</u> as a play presenting "the struggle, not of a dual, but of a multiple personality, vision created."

17 RIDING, LAURA and ROBERT GRAVES. On Cummings, in their <u>A Pamphlet Against Anthologies</u>. London: Jonathan Cape, pp. 54-55, 173-74.

1928

Brief comments on Cummings' treatment at the hands of anthologist Louis Untermeyer.

18 SELDES, GILBERT. "The Theatre." The Dial, 85 (July), 77–81.
    Comments on the negative newspaper reviews of Him, summarizes the play, and argues that in it Cummings stands on its head the convention that the unconscious burlesques conscious life. Although Him is flawed by threats to unity and by a lack of control, it is enormously satisfying.

19 SELDES, GILBERT and OTHERS. "him" and the Critics: A Collection of Opinions on E. E. Cummings' Play at the Provincetown Playhouse. New York: The Provincetown Playhouse, 16 pp.
    Introducing excerpts from newspaper reviews of Cummings' play on stage and in book form, Seldes argues that the critics of the stage production were hysterical in their responses and failed to comprehend the play's nature. Seldes himself discusses Him as a "tragic fantasy." Portions of twenty-seven reviews, both positive and negative, are included.

20 TAGGARD, GENEVIEVE. On Him. Transition, no. 13 (Summer), pp. 243–44.
    Includes praise for Him in a letter reporting on Greenwich Village.

21 YOUNG, STARK. "Him." The New Republic, 54, no. 700 (2 May), 325–26.
    Discusses the stage production of Him, complains of the "artist's refusal to make the right concessions to the art he works in," summarizes the play's plot, and suggests places where cuts are needed. The major defect is the lack of a central image. On the other hand, the play succeeds in many ways. Reprinted: 1962.9.

22 YOUNG, STARK. On Him. The New Republic, 54, no. 702 (16 May), 382–83.
    Comments on Him. "Mr. Cummings is in debt to the theater for its endurance of his lack of craft.... The theater is in Mr. Cummings' debt because he has enriched the texture of it."

1929

1   BURKE, KENNETH. On The Enormous Room. The Bookman, 69, no. 6 (August), 465–66.

14

As part of an omnibus review of the decade's fiction, Burke describes The Enormous Room as an act of fabrication, "the romanticizing of the realistic, the documentary lie." The book's style succeeds despite its author's tendency to both hate and praise irresponsibly.

2   EASTMAN, MAX. "The Cult of Unintelligibility." Harper's, 158 (April), 632-39.
    Divides the modernist movement away from precise communication into two "tendencies": one toward "the Cult of Unintelligibility," the other toward "the cultivation of pure poetry." The former, which he dislikes, is discussed here; the latter, which he likes, in a companion piece (see 1929.3). The technical innovations of Cummings--and several others--"decrease the range, the volume, and the definiteness of communication." His "endogastric proliferation" of punctuation comes in for special castigation. "Among" is discussed as an example. Reprinted: 1931.4; 1969.9.

3   EASTMAN, MAX. "The Tendency Toward Pure Poetry." Harper's, 159 (July), 222-30.
    Companion piece to 1929.3. Here Eastman discusses the other half of the modernist movement away from precise communication: the tendency toward pure poetry, a return to poetry's roots in the magic and incantatory acts of naming. This tendency explains the modernist retreat from meaning and represents a surrender to "the mere uninterrupted qualities of existence." Among others, Cummings' "'Paris; this April sunset completely utters" and "'here's a little mouse) and" are offered as successful examples of pure poetry. Reprinted: 1931.5; 1969.10.

4   KREYMBORG, ALFRED. On Cummings, in his Our Singing Strength. New York: Coward-McCann, pp. 515-22.
    Dubs Cummings "the downeast daredevil" and describes his poetry as less eccentric than it looks. He is influenced by the "romantic rhetoricians," especially Swinburne; his paganism is a reaction against Puritanism; he is "a brilliant compound of love, romance, idealism, antipathy, realism, slang, prohibition, booze, jazz and more jazz." The three volumes after Tulips and Chimneys are even more filled with "audacities, burlesque, folderol" than it is. Kreymborg also comments on Him, which would--were it not for the obscenities--be a "masterly affair." Reprinted: 1934.3.

1929

5   RASCOE, BURTON. "A Parisian Epilogue," in his A Bookman's
    Daybook. Edited by C. Hartley Grattan. New York: Horace
    Liveright, pp. 297-305.
        Reprint of 1925.4.

6   TATE, ALLEN. On Cummings. The Bookman, 68, no. 5 (January),
    506.
        Remarks, in a survey of American poetry since 1920, that
    "Cummings is a deeply moral sensibility without moral
    ideas--a predicament which induces him to exaggerate the
    value of his perceptions."

7   TAUPIN, RENÉ. On Cummings, in his L'Influence du Symbolisme
    Français sur la Poésie Américaine (de 1910 a 1920). Paris:
    Librarie Ancienne Honoré Champion, pp. 272, 289-90.
        Asserts the influence on Cummings of such French symbol-
    ists as Gourmont, Rimbaud, and Apollinaire. In French.

                            1930

1   ANON. Review of No Title. The Saturday Review of Literature,
    7, no. 18 (22 November), 378.
        Brief notice of Cummings' untitled volume of poems,
    finding it a "peculiar mélange of satirical nonsense" which
    "seems to be a spoof at modern advertising" and which is
    "weirdly amusing."

2   BROOKER, BERTRAM. "The New Writers, VII: The Poetry of E. E.
    Cummings." The Canadian Forum: A Monthly Journal of
    Literature and Public Affairs, 10, no. 118 (July), 370-71.
        Discovers in Cummings' poetry a "fourth-dimensional
    quality" similar to that in certain abstract painting; de-
    scribes it as musical, mathematical, and metaphorical; and
    notes its swing between death and spring.

3   FERGUSSON, FRANCIS. On Cummings. The Hound & Horn, 3
    (January-March), 159-60.
        Compares Cummings with O'Neill in an attempt to place
    the latter. Him has an essential unity lacking in O'Neill's
    plays but "remains mere closet drama." Reprinted: 1951.6;
    1962.13; 1968.11.

4   GRAVES, ROBERT. "Introduction," in The Enormous Room. The
    Life and Letters Series, No. 2. London: Jonathan Cape,
    pp. 7-15.
        Reprint of 1928.13.

                            16

5   UNTERMEYER, LOUIS. "E. E. Cummings," in his <u>Modern American</u>
     <u>Poetry: A Critical Anthology</u>. Fourth edition. New York:
     Harcourt, Brace and Co., pp. 529-30.
         Introduces a larger number of Cummings poems at greater
     length, including comment on his mixture of lyric and
     satiric modes. Revised edition of 1925.6.

6   WARD, A. C. On Cummings, in his <u>The Nineteen-Twenties:</u>
     <u>Literature and Ideas in the Post-War Decade</u>. London:
     Methuen & Co., pp. 43-44, 47-50.
         Remarks Cummings' modernism in travelling "from the
     breaking-down of logical thought-sequences to the disinte-
     gration of single words." Ward admires the "creative auto-
     biography" of <u>The Enormous Room</u> but worries that the
     eccentricities of the poetry too often approach "wilful
     obscurity" and too often forget that poetry must be closer
     to speech than to print.

                                1931

1   BLACKMUR, R. P. "Notes on E. E. Cummings' Language." <u>The</u>
     <u>Hound & Horn</u>, 4 (January-March), 163-92.
         Finds that Cummings' romantic-egoistical poetry, with
     its special vocabulary, is unintelligible. Cummings makes
     a "sentimental denial of the intelligence" and asserts that
     "the unintelligible is the only object of significant ex-
     perience." The intent of both Cummings' "tough guy" poems
     and his lyrics is to replace the false abstractions of in-
     telligence, but, instead, he is himself far from the con-
     crete, substituting "one set of unnourished conventions for
     another." Thus, the meaning of his poetry, with its ex-
     treme insistence on the legitimacy of the purely private,
     can only be guessed at. From these generalizations about
     Cummings' attitudes, Blackmur moves to a discussion of
     their effects on his work. Its typographical oddities have
     "almost no reference to the <u>meaning</u> of the poems" and often
     "obscure rather than clarify the exact meaning." (Blackmur
     does admit that "the continued practice of such notation
     would produce a set of well-ordered conventions susceptible
     of general use," an idea that will be picked up and ex-
     panded by later defenders of Cummings' language.) In the
     areas of diction and imagery, Blackmur finds a debilitating
     vagueness and recurrence. He discusses Cummings' use of
     the word "flower" in demonstration. This word, and many
     others, becomes an idea and in the process is stripped of
     "its history, its qualities, and its meaning." This is
     Cummings' essential defect: "the poet's words have so far

1931

deceived him as to become ideas merely." True meaning requires contact between abstract and concrete. Cummings
moves away from this contact, away from meaning. Several
prose and verse passages are analyzed in support of Blackmur's arguments. Reprinted: 1935.5; 1937.1; 1951.2;
1952.3; 1957.1; 1962.9; 1962.10; 1968.3.

2   COATES, GRACE STONE. "'Big Liz.'" Voices, no. 61 (January),
     pp. 108-10.
          Reviews Viva; finds that Cummings "has erected his ob-
     scurity as a barricade against stupidity,...not against
     astuteness."

3   DEUTSCH, HELEN and STELLA HANAU. On Him, in their The Prov-
     incetown: A Story of the Theatre. New York: Farrar &
     Rinehart, pp. 158-62, 165, 168, 172, 174-77, 299-302.
          Comments on the Provincetown Theater's production of Him,
     on reactions to it, and on the expectation of a new Cummings
     play, and reprints the cast and scene lists from April 18,
     1922.

4   EASTMAN, MAX. "The Cult of Unintelligibility," in his The
     Literary Mind: Its Place in an Age of Science. New York:
     Charles Scribner's Sons, pp. 57-78.
          Reprint of 1929.2.

5   EASTMAN, MAX. "The Tendency Toward Pure Poetry," in his The
     Literary Mind: Its Place in an Age of Science. New York:
     Charles Scribner's Sons, pp. 79-92.
          Reprint of 1929.3.

6   GREGORY, HORACE. "An Adolescent Songster." New York Herald-
     Tribune Books (13 December), p. 22.
          Reviews Viva, dividing Cummings' poetry into two classes
     ("One is the big, blond, handsome, tough boy class. The
     other is the tender, often sentimental, Elizabethan poet
     drifting down streets lined with skyscrapers") and examining
     each. Gregory finds Cummings static but feels his best
     poetry is indestructible.

7   [KUNITZ, STANLEY J.] "E. E. Cummings," in his Living Authors:
     A Book of Biographies. New York: H. H. Wilson Co., pp. 90-
     91.
          Presents biographical information on Cummings.

8   R[OLLINS, CARL PURINGTON]. "Viva." The Saturday Review of
     Literature, 8, no. 22 (19 December), 403.

Briefly notices <u>Viva</u>, describing the book's physical appearance and commenting indirectly on its esoteric contents.

9   S., K. G. "An Experimentalist's Exhibition." <u>New York Times</u> (6 December), 2, p. 8.
Notes an exhibit of Cummings' paintings at the Painter's and Sculptor's Gallery, remarks his "startling eliminations" and "emphases," and finds him, as both painter and poet, "an intelligent experimentalist."

10 TITUS, EDWARD W. "Inglorious But Not Mute Eliots." <u>This Quarter</u>, 3, no. 4 (April–May–June), 748–49.
Argues that Blackmur's essay on Cummings' language (<u>see</u> 1931.1) fails to demonstrate that he is a Romantic or an egoist or that there is anything illegitimate in his use of the word "flower," and is therefore itself an example of "Romantic criticism." (<u>See also</u> 1931.11.)

11 TITUS, EDWARD W. On Cummings. <u>This Quarter</u>, 4, no. 1 (July–August–September), 3–10.
Includes commentary (with a letter from Richard Aldington) on the splitting of the Richard Aldington American Poetry Prize between Cummings and Walter Lowenfels. <u>This Quarter</u> prefers Cummings; Aldington concedes Cummings' importance but feels his reputation is made and that Lowenfels needs boosting. Also includes further comment on the Blackmur <u>Hound & Horn</u> essay (<u>see</u> 1931.1). (<u>See also</u> 1931.10.)

12 WALTON, EDA LOU. "More Roses and Locomotives." <u>The Nation</u>, 133, no. 3469 (30 December), 729–30.
Reviews <u>Viva</u> as presenting more "poems which are experiences in themselves, even as are roses and locomotives. In other words, E. E. Cummings remains an impressionist." His impressionism Walton discusses in some detail, and she contrasts him with Eliot.

13 ZUKOFSKY, LOUIS. On Cummings. <u>The Symposium</u>, 2, no. 1 (January), 60–61, 64, 72, 75, 77, 79.
Comments on Cummings in a survey of American poetry from 1920 to 1930. The influence of Joyce is noted, as are Cummings' "Elizabethan <u>in american</u>," his attempt to resurrect the sonnet, his musical diction, and his connotativeness.

1932

1   BEACH, JOSEPH WARREN. On Cummings, in his The Twentieth
     Century Novel: Studies in Technique. New York: The
     Century Co., pp. 399, 528.
        Notes Cummings' connection with other modern writers in-
     fluenced by post-impressionist methods in painting and his
     tendency to allude to the classical to point up the failures
     of the modern.

2   BOGAN, LOUISE. Review of Viva. The New Yorker, 7, no. 52
     (13 February), 64.
        Finds that much of Cummings "dates" but that his talent
     for self-mockery is a "saving grace."

3   COWLEY, MALCOLM. "The Last of the Lyric Poets." The New Re-
     public, 69 (27 January), 299-300.
        Describes the "esthete" atmosphere at Harvard during
     Cummings' years there, an atmosphere Cummings broke from
     after his war experiences, and reviews Viva, discussing its
     calligrammic and cryptogrammatic methods. The experimenter
     Cummings is a traditional lyric poet in an age when the
     lyric seems to have lost its vitality. Reprinted: 1967.7;
     1970.2.

4   JONES, HOWARD MUMFORD. Review of Viva. The Virginia Quarterly
     Review, 8, no. 1 (January), 144-45.
        Asserts that Cummings is "all mental trickery.... The
     method is regrettable because Mr. Cummings is really a
     satirist of depth and even dignity who has chosen to be
     known for his eccentricities rather than for his thought."

5   MEARS, HELEN. "Viva--E. E. Cummings." Fifth Floor Window, 1,
     no. 3 (February), unpaged.
        Briefly reviews Viva, emphasizing the essential serious-
     ness of Cummings' vision. A short editors' note suggests
     parallels in the languages of Cummings and Reginald Pecock.

6   RICE, PHILIP BLAIR. Review of Viva. The Symposium, 3, no. 2
     (April), 270-74.
        Discusses Viva in an omnibus review, concentrating on
     technique and commenting on Cummings' Joycean prestidigita-
     tion with words, his less frequent and more impressive
     "suiting of cadence and word texture [perfectly] to sense,"
     and his rare and most impressive welding of entire poems
     "into a unity of rhythmic form, verbal feeling and symbolic
     pattern." His attempts to "transpose musical ideas into a
     verbal medium" are, however, false.

7   TATE, ALLEN. "E. E. Cummings." <u>Poetry</u>, 39, no. 3 (March),
    332-37.
        Reviews <u>Viva</u> and finds Cummings' style inessential and
    his meaning no more than his own personality. Because of
    this, his poetry "fails to implicate the reader with the
    terms of a <u>formed</u> body of experience." Thus, the reader
    is asked to accept the origin of the poetry as more im-
    portant than the poetry itself. Reprinted: 1936.4;
    1972.10.

8   WARD, A. C. On Cummings, in his <u>American Literature: 1880-
    1930</u>. London: Methuen & Co., pp. 197-200.
        Argues that Cummings' oddities are intended to shock a
    "book-drugged audience" into attention and describes his
    poetry as "heaped with the typical phenomena of modern
    American life."

9   WILLIAMS, WILLIAM CARLOS. "<u>Viva</u>: e. e. cummings." <u>Contempo</u>,
    1, no. 21 (1 April), 1.
        Reviews <u>Viva</u>. "This seems definitely an aftermath; not
    quite in the sense of scholarship but of desire satisfied--
    not quite real any longer."

                              <u>1933</u>

1   ANON. "The Great 'I Am.'" <u>The Saturday Review of Literature</u>,
    9, no. 39 (15 April), [533,] 536.
        Reports the responses of a critic and "a distinguished
    American novelist" to <u>Eimi</u>. The former finds the book a
    witty travel story marred by an affected style, the latter
    finds it exhibitionistic.

2   ANON. "Manifesto." <u>Time</u>, 21, no. 16 (17 April), 51-52.
        Reviews <u>Eimi</u> as "a manifesto of the rights of man-as-
    artist, man-as-individual, especially man-as-e. e. cummings."

3   ASCH, NATHAN. "Descent into Russia." <u>The New Republic</u>, 74,
    no. 960 (26 April), 314.
        Reviews <u>Eimi</u>; it is more obscure and less effective than
    <u>The Enormous Room</u>.

4   BROWN, LEONARD. On Cummings. <u>Sewanee Review</u>, 41, no. 1
    (January-March), 52.
        Notes, in a review of Harriet Monroe's revised edition
    of her anthology <u>The New Poetry</u>, that Cummings, with Crane
    and Stevens, is a "belated romantic."

1933

5   C., R. M.   Review of <u>Eimi</u>.   <u>The New Yorker</u>, 9, no. 8 (8 April),
    78-79.
        Despite <u>Eimi</u>'s "too faithful" report of day to day life,
    excessive repetition, and "too rigid application of what is
    primarily a poetic technique to a prose narrative," it is
    often powerful, charming, and amusing.

6   COVICI, PASCAL.   "<u>Eimi</u>."   <u>Contempo</u>, 3, no. 11 (25 July), 2.
        Writes, in a letter to the editor, that Cummings thinks
    a novel is "almost anything."

7   DREW, ELIZABETH.   On Cummings, in her <u>Discovering Poetry</u>.
    New York: W. W. Norton & Co., pp. 71-75.
        Quotes Cummings' "among" as an example of the modern
    poetry of relativity which shackles communication in favor
    of expression.

8   GANNETT, LEWIS.   Review of <u>Eimi</u>.   <u>New York Herald-Tribune</u>
    (4 April), p. 11.
        <u>Eimi</u> is annoying and rewarding.

9   GREGORY, HORACE.   "American Values in Moscow."   <u>New York
    Herald-Tribune Books</u> (9 April), p. 6.
        Reviews Cummings' <u>Eimi</u> as "a travel diary, a Childe
    Harold's pilgrimage into a hell of his own making."   His
    "preference for America and post-War Paris is stated nega-
    tively in every line."

10 GREGORY, HORACE.   "Le Front Rouge."   <u>Poetry</u>, 42, no. 5
    (August), 281-84.
        Reviews Cummings' translation of Louis Aragon's original,
    finding both "extremely effective" and of the "quality of
    a good show to be seen, heard, or read once and then never
    to be reënacted."

11 HECHT, BEN.   "Eimi, Eimi, Meimi, Mo."   <u>The American Spectator</u>,
    1, no. 9 (June), 4.
        Review of <u>Eimi</u>, arguing that Cummings is an antirevolu-
    tionary aesthete of "the ivory-toilet set," who, as a com-
    mentator on Russia, is "deaf, dumb, and blind."

12 KREYMBORG, ALFRED.   On Cummings.   <u>The English Journal</u>, 22,
    no. 4 (April), 265-66.
        In a survey of American poetry since World War I, calls
    Cummings the "lyricist par excellence of the hard-boiled
    era..., most appealing in poems on love and death."   Kreym-
    borg notes the influences of Dada, of Lindsay, Sandburg,
    Stevens, and Moore, and--in the area of design--of Marin-
    netti, Apollinaire, and Mina Loy.

13   LESSER, SAMUEL E. "A Treatise on Evolution." Contempo, 3,
      no. 11 (25 July), 2.
          Comments on Eimi in a parodic poem.

14   MOORE, MARIANNE. "A Penguin in Moscow." Poetry, 42, no. 5
      (August), 277-81.
          Reviews Eimi as a "droll book." "In his 'enormous
      dream' about the proletarian fable, the main proficiency
      is the spry-slow suave quaintly-toddling selfsufficient im-
      perviousness to weather.... That is to say the book is a
      large poem.... And the typography...is not something super-
      imposed on the meaning but the author's mental handwriting."
      Moore complains of some of the stylistic and ideological
      excesses of the book. For example, "one is never going to
      be able to score words as one scores sounds."

15   ROSENFELD, PAUL. "The Enormous Cummings." Contempo, 3, no.
      11 (25 July), 1, 3.
          Reviews Eimi as a "comic masterpiece," "a literary ex-
      pression of...dionysiac energy," and comments on the book's
      relation to Dante's vision and on Cummings' effort to "see
      for himself" the effect of authoritarian communism on the
      individual and the artist.

16   SCHNEIDER, ISIDOR. "The Enormous Room." Contempo, 3, no. 8
      (5 April), 1, 5.
          Describes The Enormous Room as having the force of life,
      a force derived from two sources: "indignation" and "liter-
      ary energy." The book's public obscurity is accounted for
      by an affirmation out of step with contemporary pessimism.

17   STEIN, GERTRUDE. On Cummings, in her The Autobiography of
      Alice B. Toklas. New York: Harcourt, Brace and Co.,
      p. 268.
          In response to Hemingway's accusation that Cummings
      "copied everything," "Stein who had been much impressed by
      The Enormous Room said that Cummings did not copy, he was
      the natural heir of the New England tradition with its
      aridity and its sterility, but also with its individuality."

18   TROY, WILLIAM. "Cummings's Non-land of Un-." The Nation, 136
      (12 April), 413.
          Reviews Eimi, finding in its statement and style "elo-
      quent affirmations" of Cummings' "fierce individualism."
      Troy examines the book's techniques and discovers them to
      be similar to those of the poetry and similar in intention:
      a concern with the communication of sensations and percep-
      tions in all their immediacy. Troy finds these techniques

1934

successful and discusses certain of them in detail, but objects that, because of a lack of progression of action or a unifying design or pattern, "the reader's powers of instantaneous response become exhausted before he gets through very many of the 432 pages of this...'book.'" Reprinted: 1962.9.

1934

1 EMERSON, DOROTHY. "Poetry Corner: E. E. Cummings." Scholastic, 25, no. 11 (8 December), 11.
General remarks on Cummings. He causes collisions of meaning to create indefiniteness in order to suggest "more to our emotion than our intelligence can explain." "if there are any heavens my mother will" receives particular attention.

2 HUGHES, GLENN. Review of is 5, in Designed for Reading: An Anthology Drawn from "The Saturday Review of Literature" 1924-1934. Edited by Henry Seidel Canby, Amy Loveman, William Rose Benét, Christopher Morley, and May Lamberton Becker. New York: The Macmillan Co., pp. 297-300.
Reprint of 1926.4.

3 KREYMBORG, ALFRED. On Cummings, in his A History of American Poetry: Our Singing Strength. New York: Tudor Publishing Co., pp. 515-22.
Reprint of 1929.4.

4 LITTELL, ROBERT. "E. E. Cumming's Him," in The American Theatre As Seen By Its Critics, 1752-1934. Edited by Montrose J. Moses and John Mason Brown. New York: W. W. Norton & Co., pp. 326-28.
Reprint of 1928.14.

5 POUND, EZRA. "E. E. Cummings Alive." The New English Weekly, 6, no. 10 (20 December), 210-11.
Comments on Cummings as an American writer in an anti-literary milieu and describes Eimi as a new sort of literature.

6 REDMAN, BEN RAY. Review of The Enormous Room. New York Herald-Tribune Books (11 February), p. 12.
Considers The Modern Library Edition of The Enormous Room in an omnibus review, arguing that its originality is genuine for it "consists in meeting the impact of life as if no one had ever met it before, and in translating the

effects and impressions of that impact into words as though
words were a virgin medium."

7 SITWELL, EDITH. On Cummings, in her <u>Aspects of Modern Poetry</u>.
   London: Duckworth, pp. 251-64.
   Argues that at times Cummings is guilty of destroying,
   by arbitrary placement and construction, "the unexpressed
   rhythm" of the blank space on a printed page. "in the,
   exquisite;" and "Among" are discussed as examples of this
   "vice." On the other hand, Cummings also writes poems
   which have beautiful and inherent form. "You are like the
   snow only" and "After all white horses are in bed" are discussed as examples of this "virtue."

8 SPARROW, JOHN. On Cummings, in his <u>Sense and Poetry: Essays</u>
   <u>on the Place of Meaning in Modern Verse</u>. New Haven, Connecticut: Yale University Press, pp. 118-21.
   Complains of Cummings' Symbolist-influenced "substitu-
   tion of sense for meaning" and discusses "Sunset" as an
   example.

9 VAN DOREN, CARL. "Cummings, Edward Estlin," in his <u>Modern</u>
   <u>American Prose</u>. New York: Harcourt, Brace and Co.,
   p. 928.
   Brief biographical note.

<u>1935</u>

1 ABEL, LIONEL. "Clown or Comic Poet." <u>The Nation</u>, 140, no.
   3651 (26 June), 749-50.
   Reviews <u>no thanks</u>, finding only the satiric poems up to
   Cummings' previous standard and the poems on spontaneity
   lacking in spontaneity. Cummings has more in common with
   the comic performer or clown than with the comic poet.

2 ANON. "Ballet on Ice." <u>Time</u>, 26, no. 19 (4 November), 84.
   Reviews <u>Tom</u> as an imaginative updating of <u>Uncle Tom's</u>
   <u>Cabin</u> and a work free from Cummings' usual "savage wit."

3 ANON. "Buzzard of Is." <u>Time</u>, 25, no. 2 (20 May), 77.
   Reviews <u>no thanks</u>. Cummings is "a one-man poetic party"
   who is "anti-political." The reviewer is unsure about
   whether or not to take him seriously.

4 ANON. Review of <u>no thanks</u>. <u>The New Yorker</u>, 11, no. 13 (11
   May), 84.

1935

Notices the appearance of <u>no thanks</u>, finding its typography more disrupted and, perhaps, more communicative than
formerly.

5   BLACKMUR, R. P. "Notes on E. E. Cummings' Language," in his
<u>The Double Agent: Essays in Craft and Elucidation</u>. New
York: Arrow Editions, pp. 1-29.
Reprint of 1931.1.

6   BURKE, KENNETH. Review of <u>no thanks</u>. <u>The Southern Review</u>, 1,
no. 1 (Fall), 176-77.
In an omnibus review, finds the "exaggerated individualism" of <u>no thanks</u> partly compensated for by a "'oneness'
with the dramatic events of landscape and season."

7   BURKE, KENNETH. "Two Kinds of Against." <u>The New Republic</u>,
83, no. 1073 (26 June), 198-99.
Reviews <u>no thanks</u> with Fearing's <u>Poems</u>. The two have in
common "an exceptional gift for the satirically picturesque,"
the use of "vivacious" rhetorical devices, and the practice
of "suggesting the subjective through the objective." The
major difference is that Cummings is apolitical. Burke
dislikes Cummings' immature "naughtiness" and his "historical amorphousness" and holds that his "resistance to man-
made institutions of any kind serves to stimulate a romantic
sense of communion with nature" and that "the best work in
the volume is unquestionably his natural description."

8   DAMON, S. FOSTER. On Cummings, in his <u>Amy Lowell: A Chronicle,</u>
<u>With Extracts from her Correspondence</u>. Boston and New York:
Houghton Mifflin Co., pp. 255, 284, 312, 345, 363, 642, 652,
656, 687.
Occasional references to Cummings in relation to Lowell.

9   DEUTSCH, BABETTE. On Cummings, in her <u>This Modern Poetry</u>.
New York: W. W. Norton & Co., pp. 211-14, 223, 226, 228.
Asserts that for all his love lyrics, most of Cummings'
"work expresses, in carefully disrupted diction studded
with colloquialisms, the mordant post-War temper." His
techniques at times are merely decorative, at times expressive. Deutsch objects that Cummings' style is excessively
visual, "leaving the ear vacant." She compares and contrasts him with Sandburg.

10   DEUTSCH, BABETTE. "Some Rejected Addresses." <u>New York</u>
<u>Herald-Tribune Books</u> (26 May), p. 14.
Reviews <u>no thanks</u>. "Cummings' originality expresses itself as strongly in his idiosyncratic typography as in the

exercise of his fancy. But the impression left by a number
of the poems grouped together here is that they were dic-
tated by the whim of the moment."

11   FREEDLEY, GEORGE. Review of Tom. Stage, 13, no. 3 (December), 97.
    In the ballet scenario Tom Cummings has molded poetry
and prose into a prose-poetry "which catches the essential
mood of the ballet."

12   HOLMES, JOHN. Review of Tom. Boston Evening Transcript Book
Section (9 November), p. 5.
    Cummings' ballet adaptation of Uncle Tom's Cabin is
"convincing" in spite "of the almost pointless eccentricities" of his language.

13   KAUFMAN, WOLFE. "'Tom' as Ballet." Variety, 120, no. 11
(27 November), 58.
    Notices Tom, describing it as "poetry of a very high
order."

14   SCHNEIDER, ISIDOR. "E. (i.o.u.) Noncummings." New Masses,
15, no. 13 (25 June), 26-27.
    Reviews no thanks as a "literary act of suicide" which
reacts to the collapse of capitalism with "the St. Vitus
dance of hysterical individualism" instead of accepting
the revolution. "Anti-communist" poems come in for special
attack.

15   UNTERMEYER, LOUIS. Review of no thanks. The American Mercury,
35, no. 140 (August), 503-504.
    Describes no thanks in an omnibus review as "as madly
mixed a collection as this decade has seen" and prefers the
more "unacrobatic" lyrics.

1936

1   ANON. Review of Tom. The Nation, 142, no. 3680 (15 January),
82.
    Brief notice of Tom, declaring Cummings' virtuosic po-
etic prose "especially well adapted to the involutions of
the dance."

2   FINCH, JOHN. "Two Spokesmen for the Man Alone." Sewanee
Review, 44, no. 1 (January-March), 122-25.
    Reviews Cummings' no thanks with Marianne Moore's Selec-
ted Poems. Both poets choose the way of the individualist

1936

(rather than the collectivist) as their path into poetry.
The theme of "deliberate loneliness" is developed in no
thanks with new power and dignity, although the satires in
this volume are less good than in earlier ones.

3   GREGORY, HORACE. Review of Tom. Poetry, 48, no. 4 (July),
    225-26.
        Examines Tom in a survey of poets in the theatre; Cum-
    mings' dance scenario indirectly indicates "a true relation-
    ship between poetry and the stage.... Mr. Cummings sees
    the stage, and on the stage he visualizes action."

4   TATE, ALLEN. "E. E. Cummings," in his Reactionary Essays on
    Poetry and Ideas. New York: Charles Scribner's Sons,
    pp. 228-33.
        Reprint of 1932.7.

5   UNTERMEYER, LOUIS. "E. E. Cummings," in his Modern American
    Poetry: A Critical Anthology. Fifth edition. New York:
    Harcourt, Brace and Co., pp. 531-32.
        Updates previous introductions with commentary on re-
    cent volumes. Revised edition of 1925.6.

                              1937

1   BLACKMUR, R. P. "Notes on E. E. Cummings' Language," in
    Literary Opinion in America. Edited by Morton Dauwen Zabel.
    New York: Harper & Brothers, pp. 558-82.
        Reprint of 1931.1.

2   FORD, FORD MADOX. On Cummings. The Forum and Century, 98,
    no. 3 (September), 128.
        In an essay on the state of publishing, bemoans the fact
    that Cummings, with his brilliant experimentalism, even in
    the minor matter of making our alphabetic characters more
    capable of expressing shades of rhythm or voice, has no
    publisher and no readers among the general public.

3   HORTON, PHILIP. On Cummings, in his Hart Crane: The Life of
    an American Poet. New York: W. W. Norton & Co., pp. 134,
    149, 150, 156, 239, 271, 272, 325, 339.
        Brief biographical references to Cummings in relation to
    Crane and two comments on Cummings by Crane himself.

4   WINTERS, YVOR. On Cummings, in his Primitivism and Decadence:
    A Study of American Experimental Poetry. New York: Arrow
    Editions, p. 75.

Describes Cummings as a "pseudo-experimentalist...who confuses tradition with convention, and who, desiring to experiment, sees no way to escape or alter tradition save by the abandonment of convention." Reprinted: 1947.13.

1938

1   ANON. "Nobody's Poet." Time, 31, no. 25 (20 June), 55-56.
       Reviews Collected Poems, finding Cummings' treatment of "nothing" and "nobody" a national theme to which his "technical unconventionalities" are essential.

2   ANON. Review of Collected Poems. New York Herald-Tribune Books (6 March), p. 21.
       Notices, in an omnibus review, the appearance of Cummings' Collected Poems. Behind "his eccentricities there is much genuine, beautiful, and witty poetry."

3   BENÉT, WILLIAM ROSE and NORMAN HOLMES PEARSON. "E. E. Cummings," in their The Oxford Anthology of American Literature. Vol. 2. New York: Oxford University Press, pp. 1627-28.
       Brief, largely biographical commentary emphasizing Cummings' wit and his use of typography to help his readers hear "through their eyes."

4   BISHOP, JOHN PEALE. "The Poems and Prose of E. E. Cummings." The Southern Review, 4 (Summer), 173-86.
       Reviews Collected Poems and attempts to "place" Cummings' work. The early poetry is heavily influenced by the romantic tradition but already has the rapidity of movement that characterizes his work. "The influence of the romantics was soon left behind, but not the romantic attitude." Thus, Cummings defied The Poundian principles that have so influenced modern poetry and produced, as he himself would note, only "that precision which aims at creating movement." Cummings is also discussed in terms of the larger categories of romantic and classic and is found an exponent of "romantic immorality," a stance which must "return whenever civilization is found no longer an aid but a hindrance to the accomplishment of desires." Cummings' technique of immediacy is examined in terms of his concepts of the discontinuity of experience and of the mind and in terms of the influences of Ulysses and modern painting on it. Bishop finds that Cummings' personal poetry transcends mere personality in one of the two ways possible, by dramatizing "his personal desires directly." The major prose works are also discussed. Reprinted: 1948.2; 1962.9.

1938

5 BROOKS, CLEANTH, JR. and ROBERT PENN WARREN. Analysis of
    "Portrait," in their <u>Understanding Poetry: An Anthology</u>
    <u>for College Students</u>. New York: Henry Holt and Co.,
    pp. 296-98.
        Analyzes "Buffalo Bill's," defining it as a simple
    treatment of the common theme that all men--even the most
    glamorous and strong--are taken by death. What makes the
    potentially hackneyed poem fresh and alive is its unexpected
    tone: the speaker's unawed, matter-of-fact, even flippant
    attitude toward death. The poem's techniques for creating
    the impression of speed are also discussed.

6 DODSWORTH, EDMONDO. "E. E. Cummings." <u>Broletto</u>, 4 (Novem-
    ber), 19-21.
        Discusses Cummings' <u>Collected Poems</u>, classifying him as
    a poet who finds the real world characterized by irreality
    and whose poetic effort is to undermine and destroy this
    irreality in the service of a profound lyricism. The pro-
    cesses by which this service is carried out are examined,
    as are a few of Cummings' poems, especially "Memorabilia."
    In Italian.

7 FITTS, DUDLEY. "Cummings' Poetry." <u>The Saturday Review of</u>
    <u>Literature</u>, 17, no. 21 (19 March), 18.
        Reviews <u>Collected Poems</u>, finding most of the omissions
    salutary, others regrettable, and wishing that other poems
    had been dropped. Fitts argues that the volume contains
    some of the best lyrics of our time and notes Cummings'
    magic "of image, of diction, of line," and his "unflagging
    joyous delight in the fact of Being."

8 GREGORY, HORACE. "The Collected Cummings." <u>The New Republic</u>,
    94, no. 1221 (27 April), 368, 370.
        Reviews <u>Collected Poems</u>, commenting on the legitimacy of
    Cummings' "typographical diversions" as "devices of poetic
    inversion and transposition," on his place in the twenties,
    and on his wit, and recommending that Cummings accept "the
    writer's responsibility to his time and place."

9 HAYAKAWA, S. I. "Is Indeed 5." <u>Poetry</u>, 52 (August), 284-92.
        Reviews <u>Collected Poems</u>. Hayakawa finds in Cummings'
    poetry a remarkable capacity for "unaffected delight and
    wonder" and an equally remarkable lack of self-importance.
    But these qualities in Cummings were not left alone, and
    his poems on low life and war (he "has written what are
    certainly our greatest war poems") are those of a mind
    "that has been compelled to tragic adjustments." This fact
    helps explain Cummings' oddities of technique. Reprinted:
    1962.9.

10   HOLMES, JOHN.   Review of <u>Collected Poems</u>.   <u>The Atlantic Month-</u>
<u>ly</u>, 162, no. 3 (September), unpaged.
Notices <u>Collected Poems</u> in an omnibus review, discovering in it "an integrity of poetic personality, varied in
its aspect from Keatsian romanticism to willful eccentri-
city."

11   HOLMES, JOHN.   Review of <u>Tulips and Chimneys</u> and <u>Collected</u>
<u>Poems</u>.   <u>Boston Evening Transcript</u> (19 March), 3, p. 2.
Examines the archetype edition of <u>Tulips and Chimneys</u>
(1937) and <u>Collected Poems</u>.   "To think of Cummings as one
who messes up printing type is to do him an injustice; he
is one of the funniest, frankest, tenderest, most passionately ribald poets we have produced."

12   HORTON, PHILIP and SHERRY MANGAN.   "Two Views of Cummings."
<u>Partisan Review</u>, 4 (May), 58-63.
The first view, apparently Horton's, wishes for a far
more selective volume than <u>Collected Poems</u>.   It regards the
poetry as demonstrating "no technical improvement or intellectual development."   The "mingling of the trivial and
serious" and the "general confusion of values" typical of
Cummings are "a result of his deliberate rejection of
knowledge, whether of himself or of life at large."   The
second view, apparently Mangan's, finds that Cummings' special miracle persists in the <u>Collected Poems</u>.   His faults
are those of his virtues "--gusto, abundance, magnilo-
quence--" and some of the critical animus against him results from his derivation from French poetry.   This view
also lists the usual critical charges against Cummings--
failure in precise communication, "pretentiousness, exec-
rable taste, and limitation of subject"--and responds to
each.   Reprinted: 1962.9.

13   HUMPHRIES, ROLFE.   "Anarchist--Poet--Advertiser."   <u>New Masses</u>,
27, no. 3 (12 April), 23-25.
Reviews <u>Collected Poems</u>.   Cummings is a poet caught in
the struggle within himself between advertising man and
anarchist.

14   JACK, PETER MONRO.   "The Private Exercise of Poetry."   <u>New</u>
<u>York Times Book Review</u> (26 June), p. 2.
Reviews <u>Collected Poems</u>, concentrating on Cummings' rejection of ideology and his persistence in writing as a
"nature poet."

15   LEACH, HENRY GODDARD.   Review of <u>Collected Poems</u>.   <u>The Forum</u>
<u>and Century</u>, 99, no. 4 (April), 256.

1938

Brief notice of <u>Collected Poems</u>. It is "a rare collector's item for the many, a book of horse laughter for some, a treasure of fierce beauty for the few."

16 MACNEICE, LOUIS. On Cummings, in his <u>Modern Poetry: A Personal Essay</u>. London: Oxford University Press, pp. 71, 97, 187.
Brief comments on Cummings, on poetry as act, on his sentimentality, and on an image from <u>The Enormous Room</u>.

17 RODMAN, SELDEN. "E. E. Cummings," in his <u>A New Anthology of Modern Poetry</u>. New York: Random House, p. 419.
A biographical note calling Cummings a "first-rate humorist" and "one of the most original lyrical talents at work today." Reprinted: 1946.17.

18 ROSENFELD, PAUL. "The Brilliance of E. E. Cummings." <u>The Nation</u>, 146, no. 13 (26 March), 360, 362-63.
Reviews <u>Collected Poems</u>, the archetype edition of <u>Tulips and Chimneys</u>, and the recording <u>Seven Poems</u>. Cummings is modern because of his similarity to the fauves and cubists and because of his incorporation of the baroque and romantic traditions.

19 ROSKOLENKO, HARRY. "Collected Circus." <u>Voices</u>, no. 94 (Summer), pp. 43-45.
Reviews <u>Collected Poems</u>, discussing Cummings' part in the "obscurantist revolution" of modern poetry and connecting him with other American "artists and clowns."

<u>1939</u>

1 EASTMAN, MAX. On Cummings, in his <u>Enjoyment of Poetry, With Other Essays in Aesthetics</u>. New York: Charles Scribner's Sons, pp. 142-43.
Uses Cummings as an example of a modern poet "so earnestly striving not to be romantic" as to "have almost a neurotic aversion to emotional congruity," but, on grounds of a personal anecdote, finds Cummings' auditory acuteness "the sure proof of a poet."

2 FINCH, JOHN. "New England Prodigal." <u>The New England Quarterly</u>, 12, no. 4 (December), 643-53.
Avers that the nineteenth-century romantic stance of rejecting external authority in favor of internal authority at the center of Cummings' poetry is "tragically out of date." His "platform of moral isolation...does offer

certain advantages.... From it...he can speak with a
private intensity; he can muster a heady indignation....
But...the danger is that one may forget what is going on
outside, how men speak to each other and what happens to
men together." This is likely the source of Cummings'
obscurity.

3   WINTERS, YVOR. Review of Collected Poems. American Litera-
    ture, 10 (January), 520-22.
        Examines Collected Poems. Cummings' subject matter is
    simple; he writes either sentimentally or smuttily about
    love. His regular poems are inexpert, his innovations have
    little to recommend them. His typographical experiments
    are based on incorrect theory. Cummings lacks the artistry
    of other modern experimenters, and the romantic ideas which
    marred their works are carried to extremes in his to produce
    "a more or less infantile exhibitionism, at once mildly un-
    pleasant and infinitely tedious." Reprinted: 1962.9.

1939-1940

1   ROSENFELD, PAUL. "The Enormous Cummings." Twice a Year, 3-4
    (Fall-Winter, Spring-Summer), 271-80.
        Discusses Cummings' The Enormous Room and Eimi as "serio-
    comic" revivals "of the impulse for freedom." Both books
    initiate a new literary genre, the antithesis of the novel.
    Rosenfeld sees the books as a recapitulation of the Thoreau,
    Emerson, Whitman tradition, but considers most important
    their expression of the "prophetic feeling of the affirma-
    tive will of Creation in reference to human freedom."
    Reprinted: 1962.9.

1940

1   DREW, ELIZABETH and JOHN L. SWEENEY. On Cummings, in their
    Directions in Modern Poetry. New York: W. W. Norton &
    Co., pp. 57, 69, 200, 232-33, 253, 255, 257, 263, 264.
        Describes Cummings as "essentially romantic," a malad-
    justed ironist. His speech and punctuation "may enforce a
    new angle of discernment," but more often such patterns are
    "overassertive." His vocabulary is dominated by eccentri-
    city. Cummings' use of synaesthesia and metaphysical jux-
    taposition is noted.

2   MILLETT, FRED B. On Cummings, in his Contemporary American
    Authors: A Critical Survey and 219 Bio-Bibliographies.
    New York: Harcourt, Brace and Co., pp. 145, 310-11.

1940

Calls Cummings a superficial experimenter with an insatiable "passion for freakishness." His real talents are a fresh response to beauty and bold metaphors. Includes a biographical sketch and primary and secondary bibliographies.

3 UNTERMEYER, LOUIS. On Cummings. The Virginia Quarterly Review, 16, no. 3 (Summer), 401-402.
In a survey of modern American poetry, finds that two usually separate modern tendencies--the antirealistic and the superrational and surrealistic--meet in Cummings. His technique is equally paradoxical. His "work presents a lavish (or confusing) disorganization, a refusal (or failure) to integrate."

4 VAN DOREN, CARL. On Cummings, in his The American Novel, 1789-1939. Revised and Enlarged edition. New York: The Macmillan Co., pp. 323, 334.
Emphasizes the success of The Enormous Room, calling it superior to Lewis's 100% and Dos Passos' Three Soldiers, but insists that it is not a novel.

5 WELLS, HENRY W. On Cummings, in his New Poets From Old: A Study in Literary Genetics. New York: Columbia University Press, pp. 85, 141, 149, 152-53, 232-38.
Notes Cummings' use of New York street slang, his easy use of traditional forms, and his imitative typography. Wells comments specifically on the use of speech rhythms in "'next to of course god america i" and particular attention is given to Cummings' "conscious debt to the masters of the Renaissance lyric of sentiment." Reprinted: 1964.25.

6 ZABEL, MORTON DAUWEN. On Cummings. The Southern Review, 5, no. 3 (Winter), 594-96.
In a survey of poetry from 1937 through 1939, credits Cummings with realizing "that when handling the most original themes or unconventional crudities of subject matter, one must respect the same accuracy of rhythmic form and language that is implicit in the strictest lyric classicism."

1941

1 AIKEN, CONRAD. "Poetry as Entertainment." The New Republic, 104 (16 June), 830-32.
Discusses Cummings along with MacNeice and Elizabeth Bishop. Cummings has two styles, an eccentric one which

conceals sentimentality and an archaic, poetic one which is made by lack of punctuation to appear adventurous. Reprinted: 1958.1

2   BLACKMUR, R. P. Review of 50 Poems. The Southern Review, 7 (Summer), 201-205.
    Admires Cummings' continuing immediacy and energy, but with three reservations: first, that Cummings is not an experimental poet; second, that his vocabulary is excessively general--although this view is held less extremely than before (see 1931.1); and third, that a large portion of his scatology fails to reach the levels of disgust or gesture. Blackmur also attends to new developments in these poems: "the use of prepositions, pronouns, and the auxiliary verbs in the guise of substances, and in general the rich use of words ordinarily rhetorical--mere connectives or means of transition in their ordinary usage--for the things of actual experience." Reprinted: 1972.10.

3   BOGAN, LOUISE. Review of 50 Poems. The New Yorker, 17, no. 3 (1 March), 57.
    Criticizes the book as "irrevocably stuck in the past" and often "very malicious."

4   BROWN, RAY C. B. Review of 50 Poems. Voices, no. 106 (Summer), pp. 49-51.
    Reviews 50 Poems, describing Cummings as "a self-conscious poetic virtuoso, seemingly interested only in topiary eccentricities."

5   DEUTSCH, BABETTE. "e. e. cummingsesq." The Nation, 152 (17 May), 591.
    Reacts to 50 Poems in a parodic poem which complains of Cummings' lack of development in subject and style. Reprinted: 1962.9.

6   FITTS, DUDLEY. Review of 50 Poems. The Saturday Review of Literature, 23, no. 25 (12 April), 14.
    Reviews Cummings' 50 Poems as part of an omnibus review; it continues his "same marvelous tricks and ribald twitches and occasional socking of the topmost bell."

7   HART, JAMES D. "Cummings, E[dward] E[stlin]," in his The Oxford Companion to American Literature. New York: Oxford University Press, p. 172.
    Brief encyclopedia entry gives biographical material and comments on Cummings' subjects and styles, particularly his use of technique as a means to resist sentimentality. Revised editions: 1948.8; 1956.8; 1965.13.

1941

8   HEALY, J. V. Review of 50 Poems. Accent, 1, no. 4 (Summer),
        252.
            Describes the Cummings of 50 Poems as worshipping "affec-
        ted naiveté, irresponsibility, and baby talk." His "emo-
        tions are self-generated, without either objective sanction
        or imaginative sanction."

9   JACK, PETER MONRO. "Fifty New Poems by E. E. Cummings."
        New York Times Book Review (13 April), p. 10.
            Reviews 50 Poems, remarking a "kind of New England in-
        tegrity and willfulness in Cummings' poetry, whether it is
        denying...or affirming...the existence of a moral order in
        the world."

10 KEES, WELDON. "A Supplement from Cummings." Poetry, 59, no.
        3 (December), 162-64.
            Reviews 50 Poems; notes Cummings' typical unevenness and
        his lack of "'progression,'" and connects that lack with
        his preservation of self in a violent, changeful world.

11 NEMEROV, HOWARD. "Undeniably the Same." New York Herald-
        Tribune Books (2 March), p. 24.
            Reviews Cummings' 50 Poems, concluding that there "can
        be no complaint against his new book except this," that
        "while he has produced something undeniably pleasing and
        undeniably workmanlike, he has also produced something un-
        deniably the same."

12 POORE, CHARLES. "Books of the Times." New York Times (2
        April), p. 21.
            Examines 50 Poems in an omnibus review. It includes
        "crazy capers" and "good poems."

13 SPENCER, THEODORE. Review of 50 Poems. Furioso, 1, no. 4
        (Summer), 55-56.
            Explores Cummings' effort "to make the order of his
        words as close to his subject as he can, so that the order
        of the poem will be a reflection of the shape of the ex-
        perience," and his "technique of surprise."

14 SWEENEY, JOHN L. Review of 50 Poems. The Yale Review, 30,
        no. 4 (June), 819.
            Notices 50 Poems in an omnibus review, finding that Cum-
        mings' "most striking effects have been achieved by an
        economy of means." The early poetry "was rich in simple
        but surprising feats of expression. In his latest poems,
        the simplicity and surprise have degenerated into fussiness
        and clutter."

1942

15 TATE, ALLEN. Review of 50 Poems. Partisan Review, 8, no. 3
     (May-June), 242-43.
         In an omnibus review, complains of the critical neglect
     of 50 Poems and asserts that some of Cummings' poems "are
     among the best work of our time."

1942

1 KAZIN, ALFRED. On Cummings, in his On Native Grounds: An
     Interpretation of Modern American Prose Literature. New
     York: Reynal & Hitchcock, pp. 324-27.
         Discusses The Enormous Room. It expresses the new sen-
     sibility of what would be called the lost generation. Cum-
     mings saw reality as "composed of brutal sensations and
     endured only by a fiercely desperate courage and love; it
     was so anarchical that all attempts to impose order on it
     were motivated by either ignorance of chicanery. What re-
     mained to the artist...was the pride of individual self-
     knowledge and the skill that...gave all its devotion to
     the integrity of art."

2 KUNITZ, STANLEY J. and HOWARD HAYCRAFT. "Cummings, Edward
     Estlin," in their Twentieth Century Authors: A Biographi-
     cal Dictionary of Modern Literature. New York: The H. W.
     Wilson Co., p. 339.
         Encyclopedia entry argues that Cummings' "endeavor is to
     represent direct experience by the very form of his work as
     well as by its meaning."

3 SCHLAUCH, MARGARET. On Cummings, in her The Gift of Tongues.
     New York: Viking Press, pp. 247, 249-51.
         Briefly notes Cummings' technique of juxtaposing words
     from "two different realms of physical sense," his use of
     a kind of pseudo-phonetic notation, and his vivisection of
     words to make them conform to his rhythmic desires. Re-
     printed: 1955.29.

4 UNTERMEYER, LOUIS. "E. E. Cummings," in his Modern American
     Poetry: A Critical Anthology. Sixth edition. New York:
     Harcourt, Brace and Co., pp. 547-48.
         Updated and expanded introduction, concluding that it
     "is a likely irony that Cummings will finally be appraised
     ...as a thinly disguised and wholly unashamed romantic
     poet." Revised edition of 1925.6.

1943

1 ARTHOS, JOHN. "The Poetry of E. E. Cummings." American
    Literature, 14 (January), 372-90.
        An overview of Cummings' poetry to date. Cummings is
    atypical in his pagan, anti-Puritan celebration of the life
    of the senses, but this paganism is "corrupted" with the
    idea "that the casual experience of the senses provides a
    sufficient truth for living." This attitude Arthos finds
    one with "a common American trait, a way of refusing to be
    affected by experience." Examining Cummings' technique,
    Arthos comments on his tendency to treat abstract words
    like material ones, on his economy and concreteness, and on
    his skillful use of the languages of slang and jazz. His
    use of punctuation and typography is also examined. Arthos
    concludes by noting that Cummings "is a Platonist, absorbed
    in the discipline of contemplation and devoted to the per-
    ception of being."

2 DOS PASSOS, JOHN. "Off the Shoals," in The Shock of Recogni-
    tion. Edited by Edmund Wilson. New York: Doubleday,
    Doran and Co., pp. 1247-53.
        Reprint of 1922.6.

3 TATE, ALLEN. On Cummings, in his Recent American Poetry and
    Poetic Criticism: A Selected List of References. Washing-
    ton: The Library of Congress, p. 3.
        Brief comment on Collected Poems in which Cummings is
    described as "one of our best poets." His "typographical
    innovations have obscured his solid achievements."

4 WELLS, HENRY W. On Cummings, in his The American Way of
    Poetry. Columbia Studies in American Culture, No. 13,
    edited by Harry J. Carman, Merle E. Curti, John A. Krout,
    and Herbert W. Schneider. New York: Columbia University
    Press, pp. 4, 192, 208, 228, 230, 231, 235.
        Quotes Hart Crane's description of Cummings as an im-
    pressionist who at times makes brilliant organic use of
    calligraphy and slang and notes in passing Cummings' dynam-
    ic use of American language, his typically American non-
    conformity, and his recognition of the role of blacks in
    the development of American speech rhythms.

5 WILLIAMS, ORLO. On Cummings. The National Review, 121, no.
    729 (November), 390, 393.
        Notes that Cummings' syntax deliberately increases the
    difficulty of his poems.

1944

1   ANON. Review of <u>1 X 1</u>. <u>The New Yorker</u>, 20, no. 6 (25 March), 99.
        Brief notice of <u>1 X 1</u>. Cummings is at his best when he abandons "his trick style."

2   ANON. "Yunnuhstan?" <u>Newsweek</u>, 23, no. 11 (13 March), 78, 80.
        Comments on the one-man show of Cummings' oils and water-colors at New York's American British Art Center and the about to be published <u>1 X 1</u>, describing both paintings and poems as essentially traditional.

3   AXELROD, JOSEPH. "Cummings and Phonetics." <u>Poetry</u>, 65, no. 2 (November), 88-94.
        Analyzes "applaws)" to demonstrate that Cummings' unorthodox typography "is the result of a direct concern with sound, as well as with visual design." Axelrod's phonetic discussion concludes that Cummings' "'eccentric' spelling and arrangement have resulted in certain subtleties of accent, rhythm, sound quality, and juncture which could scarcely have emerged in a traditional typography."

4   D[E VRIES], P[ETER]. "To Be." <u>Poetry</u>, 64, no. 3 (June), 158-64.
        Reviews <u>1 X 1</u>, finding that in it Cummings' grammatical liberties have reached the point where they can be accepted not as tricks but as his "natural kind of vocabulary," as speech. His tendency to make nouns of verbs and other parts of speech is a key to his essential desire "to express...the fact and experience of <u>being</u>." Cummings' resistance to the scientific, analytic, conforming impulses of the modern world is also remarked.

5   GREGORY, HORACE. Review of <u>1 X 1</u>. <u>The Saturday Review of Literature</u>, 27, no. 49 (2 December), 48, 50.
        In an omnibus review, finds <u>1 X 1</u> in the lyric tradition and praises its "revival of courtly music and compliment, of poetic wit, and the art of burlesque that Italian players brought into being with the Commedia del Arte."

6   JACK, PETER MONRO. "'nonsun blob a'--and Other Poems by ee cummings." <u>New York Times Book Review</u> (26 March), p. 5.
        Reviews Cummings' <u>1 X 1</u> as "a reassertion of the individual, of the subjective integrity of man and the need of its preservation.... There is a passion of love in the poems, and there is a passion of hate and satire. But the one is complementary to the other."

1944

7   KOCH, VIVIENNE. Review of 1 X 1. *Maryland Quarterly*, 1, no.
     3 (Summer), 165-66.
          Comments, in an omnibus review, that the three sections
     of 1 X 1 are concerned with images of Society, Love (in-
     cluding Art) and Nature respectively and remarks that Cum-
     mings' hatred is only for what "in conduct and in language
     is cant."

8   LECHLITNER, RUTH. Review of 1 X 1. *New York Herald-Tribune*
     Weekly Book Review (9 April), p. 9.
          Reviews Cummings' 1 X 1 in an omnibus review. "In spite
     of an almost phonographic repetition, his love songs remain
     surprisingly fresh; and his continued attacks upon civilized
     'manunkind'...lose none of their bite. The essential merit
     of his form lies in its precision and economy, its emphasis
     by arrangement."

9   MATTHIESSEN, F. O. Review of 1 X 1. *The Kenyon Review*, 6
     (Autumn), 688-90.
          Reviews 1 X 1. Despite his constant concern with growth,
     Cummings' themes and techniques remain essentially un-
     changed. He is as concerned with and as incapable of the
     organic principle as was Emerson. Both conceive of life as
     consisting "entirely of inspired moments" and so are "with-
     out the basic requirement for growth--continuity." In
     spite of Cummings' "capacity for exuberant renewal," this
     leads to solipsism and monotony. Reprinted: 1952.11;
     1962.9.

10   MIZENER, ARTHUR. Review of 1 X 1. *Partisan Review*, 11, no. 3
     (Summer), 358-59.
          Notices 1 X 1 in an omnibus review, describing Cummings
     as "still unconvinced that the unique exquisiteness of
     living in general and of loving in particular can be con-
     veyed without resort to verbal displacement."

11   MOORE, MARIANNE. "One Times One." *Nation*, 158 (1 April), 394.
          Reviews 1 X 1 as Cummings' "book of masterpieces,...a
     book of wisdom that knowledge cannot contradict,...an apex
     of positiveness and of indivisible, undismemberable joy."
     Reprinted: 1955.25.

12   SPENCER, THEODORE. "E. E. Cummings." *The New Republic*, 110,
     no. 14 (3 April), 475-76.
          Reviews 1 X 1 as reinforcing Cummings' rank as a poet.
     "By concentrating with complete honesty on his own response
     to individual objects and emotions he has not merely per-
     fected a personal idiom, but in his best poems he has
     achieved a special depth and insight."

13   SWALLOW, ALAN. Review of <u>1 X 1</u>. <u>The New Mexico Quarterly</u>
      <u>Review</u>, 14, no. 4 (Winter), 482.
         Examines <u>1 X 1</u> in an omnibus review, arguing that al-
      though there is little thematic change from earlier works,
      there are two "important advances in method...: (1) An
      attempt to achieve greater complexity, especially with the
      pun.... (2) Greater use of interruption and qualification
      to the argument."

14   WARREN, ROBERT PENN. Review of <u>1 X 1</u>. <u>Accent</u>, 4, no. 4
      (Summer), 251-53.
         Discusses <u>1 X 1</u>; argues that the purer "soft" and "hard"
      poles of the earlier poems have in the later work "been
      drawn into more elaborate combinations and fused under
      greater pressure." The poems succeed when the two elements
      are both involved. Warren finds the distinction of this
      volume its lyrics and generalizes that Cummings' problem
      "has always been to find a subject."

15   WEISS, T. Review of <u>1 X 1</u>. <u>Quarterly Review of Literature</u>,
      1, no. 4 (Summer), 328-31.
         Notices <u>1 X 1</u>, describing Cummings as the "arch-bombard-
      ier of stuffiness" and his poems as "ruthlessly stript."
      Weiss also comments on Cummings' use of speech idioms, his
      craft, his lack of a "profoundly integrating intelligence,"
      his love lyrics, and his failure to change.

                                <u>1945</u>

1   SHAPIRO, KARL. On Cummings, in his <u>Essay on Rime</u>. New York:
      Reynal & Hitchcock, pp. 20-21.
         Discusses Cummings in verse, describing him as an "ex-
      ponent" of Cubism "concerned with the component/Integers of
      the word...// And their arranged derangement." Shapiro
      praises Cummings' mind and his ability "to delight, amuse
      and anger," but wonders if it is wise to "atomize the lan-
      guage" and "adulate the alphabet."

2   TATE, ALLEN. "Edward Estlin Cummings," in his <u>Sixty American</u>
      <u>Poets: 1896-1944</u>. Washington: The Library of Congress,
      pp. 25-27.
         The headnote to the Cummings bibliography asserts that
      he is "one of the half dozen best" poets of his generation.
      The bibliography concerns itself almost exclusively with
      primary works and lists recordings. Revised edition:
      1954.28.

<u>1946</u>

1   ANDREWS, DONALD H. "E. E. Cummings: Algebraic Poet." <u>Johns</u>
<u>Hopkins University Literary Magazine</u>, 1; 15-19.
      Argues that Cummings is at the opposite pole from Dadaist
efforts at nonmeaning because "his poems are at first reading obscure not because of a vacuum, but because of an
over-dense condensation of meaning." This condensation is
related to the symbolic condensations of algebra.

2   ANON. "No Takers?" <u>Time</u>, 48, no. 26 (23 December), 91.
      Reviews <u>Santa Claus: A Morality</u>, summarizing the "play-
let" and noting that it is without Cummings' typical "stunt-
ing with language."

3   BARZUN, JACQUES. "E. E. Cummings: A Word about <u>Him</u>." <u>The</u>
<u>Harvard Wake</u>, no. 5 (Spring), pp. 55-[56].
      Comments on his, and others', reactions to <u>Him</u>'s produc-
tion, arguing that Cummings not only absorbed much of the
linguistic audacity and subversive buffoonery of the
twenties but also remained aware of his own and the world's
imperfections.

4   BREIT, HARVEY. "The Case for the Modern Poet." <u>New York</u>
<u>Times Magazine</u> (3 November), pp. 20, 58, 60, 61.
      Responds to Coblentz's strictures against modern poetry
(<u>see</u> 1946.5). In the particular case of Cummings, Breit
notes his "beautiful lyrics" and remarks briefly on the
rationale of his innovations. For another reply to Coblentz, <u>see</u> 1946.7.

5   COBLENTZ, STANTON A. "What Are They--Poems or Puzzles?" <u>New</u>
<u>York Times Magazine</u> (13 October), pp. 24, 50, 51, 53.
      Accuses Cummings and other modern poets of ignoring "the
fundamental purposes and values of poetry." For replies,
<u>see</u> 1946.4 and 1946.7.

6   DOS PASSOS, JOHN. On Cummings. <u>The Harvard Wake</u>, no. 5
(Spring), p. 64.
      Praises Cummings for his "workmanlike skill" and inven-
tiveness.

7   FRANKENBERG, LLOYD. "Fuller Explanation." <u>New York Times</u>
<u>Magazine</u> (3 November), p. 24.
      Responds to Coblentz's use of a section of Cummings'
"r-p-o-p-h-e-s-s-a-g-r" as an example of the disaster of
modern poetry (<u>see</u> 1946.5) by commenting briefly on the
signifying functions of the poem's techniques. For another
response to Coblentz, <u>see</u> 1946.4.

8 FRANKENBERG, LLOYD. "Nothing as Something as One." The
   Harvard Wake, no. 5 (Spring), pp. 46-54.
       Argues that Cummings writes poetry in praise of an aris-
   tocracy that has to do not with government, class, hierarchy, or qualitative comparison, but with anyone alive and
   individual. Frankenberg discusses Cummings' opposition of
   "anyone" and "mostpeople" in detail and concludes that what
   "is most permanent about his poems is a kind of transiency:
   their ability to catch what is perpetually on the move."
   His method for achieving this special sort of transiency is
   based in his gift of emotional interpenetration. Reprinted:
   1947.5.

9 FRANKENBERG, LLOYD. On Cummings. The Saturday Review of
   Literature, 29, no. 12 (23 March), 6, 56.
       Comments, in a discussion of meaning in modern poetry,
   on the precise artistry of Cummings' "what a proud dreamhorse pulling" and on the success of his line "spring is
   like a perhaps hand."

10 GREGORY, HORACE and MARYA ZATURENSKA. "E. E. Cummings:
    American Poet of the Commedia dell' Arte." The Harvard
    Wake, no. 5 (Spring), pp. 65-74.
        Asserts that Cummings' central theme is that of courtly
    love and that his central character is the young lover.
    His impatience with the world is that of the young lover
    and it is from this angle that much of his criticism is
    addressed. The terms of that criticism are those of bur-
    lesque (which has its roots in the commedia dell' arte),
    not of satire. Reprinted: 1946.11; 1962.9; 1969.16.

11 GREGORY, HORACE and MARYA ZATURENSKA. On Cummings, in their
    A History of American Poetry, 1900-1940. New York: Har-
    court, Brace and Co., pp. 336-47.
        Reprint of 1946.10.

12 JONSSON, THORSTEN. "Cummings, Med Några Kommentarer," in his
    Sidor av Amerika: Intryck och Resonemang. Stockholm:
    Albert Bonniers Förlag, pp. 255-89.
        Examines in a general way Cummings' themes and techniques
    and comments on several particular poems. The examination
    and commentary is interspersed among translations of twenty-
    nine Cummings poems into Swedish (two "untranslatable" poems
    are reprinted in English). Jonsson concentrates on Cum-
    mings' combined role of mystical lyricist and social critic
    and notes his similarity to Finland's Gunnar Björlings as
    well as his relationships with many American and British
    writers. Comment on specific poems frequently presents
    context and summarizes. In Swedish.

1946

13   KREYMBORG, ALFRED. "A First and Lasting Impression." The
        Harvard Wake, no. 5 (Spring), pp. 58-60.
            Comments on his continuing sense of Cummings' "fresh-
        ness."

14   LEVIN, HARRY. "Of Birds and Books." The Harvard Wake, no. 5
        (Spring), pp. 61-63.
            Suggests that, in Cummings' terms, poetry might be de-
        fined as "the vain attempt of books to emulate birds," and
        describes Cummings as "a disaffected traditionalist." Levin
        also comments briefly on influences on Cummings and on his
        influence on others.

15   MOORE, MARIANNE. On Cummings. The Harvard Wake, no. 5
        (Spring), p. 24.
            Calls Cummings "a concentrate of titanic significances.
        ... He does not make aesthetic mistakes."

16   PORTER, FAIRFIELD. "The Paintings of E. E. Cummings." The
        Harvard Wake, no. 5 (Spring), pp. 75-76.
            Discusses "the variety of Cummings' paintings," their
        "accurate observation of selected detail," and their inter-
        est in "external phenomena.... The phenomena are...the
        impact of the whole of something in sensuous instead of
        conceptual terms." Porter contrasts Cummings with Picasso
        and compares him with Marin. His media are light and tex-
        ture, his concern is with motion instead of weight.

17   RODMAN, SELDEN. "E. E. Cummings," in his A New Anthology of
        Modern Poetry. New York: The Modern Library, p. 444.
            Reprint of 1938.17.

18   ROSENFELD, PAUL. "The Voyages." The Harvard Wake, no. 5
        (Spring), pp. 31-44.
            Asserts that Eimi qualifies Cummings as a soldier of
        liberty and a guardian of the nation's spiritual life.
        Rosenfeld describes the various effects of the book's ex-
        periments with prose technique, defines its main symbol as
        "the absurd contradiction of an expectation by an event,"
        and compares it to The Divine Comedy and the comedies of
        Aristophanes. The central difference between Eimi and the
        Ionian's work is that the latter is informed by a negative
        vision, the former by a positive, idealistic one. Rosen-
        feld discusses this "Idealist vision" at length, compares
        Eimi with The Enormous Room, and--in terms of the economic
        and political developments of the 1930's--describes it as
        the "equilibration of the Swing to the Left." Reprinted:
        1972.10.

19   SHAPIRO, KARL.   "The Bohemian."   The Harvard Wake, no. 5
        (Spring), p. 45.
            Remarks that Cummings' consistency over a period of
        twenty-five years "may be the pursuit of an ideal or merely
        a lack of development." Shapiro prefers to believe the
        former, but feels Cummings ended "by becoming a snob."

20   SPENCER, THEODORE.   "Technique as Joy: Observations on the
        Poetry of E. E. Cummings."   The Harvard Wake, no. 5 (Spring),
        pp. 25-29.
            Argues that Cummings "is for the individual human being
        against mechanical regimentation." His technique is a di-
        rect result of this attitude. "The living object, the
        living moment, being so desirable, so much an occasion of
        delight, the poet's job is to...re-create it in permanent
        form as actually as possible." To do this, Cummings de-
        velops means for destroying the time content of language
        and replacing it with simultaneity. The poem "1 oo k-" is
        analyzed in demonstration. Spencer also discusses the de-
        velopment of Cummings' recent poetry and his increasingly
        mature use of the sonnet. Reprinted: 1953.15; 1953.16;
        1962.9. Revised version: 1950.21.

21   TATE, ALLEN.   A Letter.   The Harvard Wake, no. 5 (Spring),
        p. 30.
            A letter to Cummings, arguing that, over the war years,
        he was the "one American poet who kept his humanity and his
        poetry."

22   TRILLING, LIONEL.   On Cummings.   The Harvard Wake, no. 5
        (Spring), p. [57].
            Considers that Cummings' long partisanship for life, and
        for the life of words, is the mark "of a truly developing
        talent."

23   WILLIAMS, WILLIAM CARLOS.   "Lower Case Cummings."   The Harvard
        Wake, no. 5 (Spring), pp. 20-23.
            Stresses Cummings' creation of a language with "a peculi-
        arly unhistoric, historical new world character.... He
        avoids the cliché first by avoiding the whole accepted modus
        of english. He does it...to reveal, to disclose, to free a
        man from habit." Reprinted: 1954.31; 1969.34; 1972.10.

1947

1   ADAMS, ROBERT M.   "Grasshopper's Waltz: The Poetry of E. E.
        Cummings."   Cronos, 1, no. 3 (Fall), [1]-7.

Explores Cummings' apparent technical radicalism and his
theme of individualism. His unorthodox devices are used
largely for the precise control of tempo and for the expression of the chaos of reality. His theme of self-reliance
is limiting, for it rejects man and the world and seems, at
times, merely self-centered. This makes clear that Cummings' style is not radical but a substitute for a subject.

2   ANON. Review of <u>Santa Claus: A Morality</u>. <u>The New Yorker</u>,
22, no. 48 (11 January), 87.
Brief notice of <u>Santa Claus</u>, finding it presents "a
theme of love vs. death, hate, 'science,' and 'the mob' in
terms simplified to the point of parody."

3   FLETCHER, JOHN GOULD. On Cummings. <u>The Georgia Review</u>, 1,
no. 2 (Summer), 159.
Asserts, in a survey of poetry from 1937 through 1947,
that Cummings "has conducted his unique exploration into
the resources of language with brilliant results." Reprinted: 1947.4.

4   F[LETCHER], J[OHN] G[OULD]. On Cummings, in <u>10 Eventful Years:
A Record of Events of the Years Preceding, Including, and
Following World War II, 1937 through 1947</u>. Volume 3. Edi-
ted by Walter Yust. Chicago: Encyclopedia Britannica,
p. 586.
Reprint of 1947.3.

5   FRANKENBERG, LLOYD. "Introduction," in <u>1 X 1</u>. By E. E. Cummings. London: Horizon, pp. [9-20].
Reprint of 1946.8.

6   FRANKENBERG, LLOYD. "Setting an Abstraction to Catch an Abstraction." <u>New York Times Book Review</u> (6 April), p. 26.
Reviews Cummings' <u>Santa Claus</u> as illuminating the "logical, emotional and necessary connection between what his
satire ridiculed and what his lyrics celebrated."

7   HUMPHRIES, ROLFE. "A Lower-Case Santa Claus." <u>The Nation</u>,
164, no. 3 (18 January), 78.
Reviews <u>Santa Claus</u> as "one of the author's less happy
efforts." It is "too simple and too ecclesiastical."

8   LEARY, LEWIS. "[Cummings, E. E.]," in <u>Articles on American
Literature Appearing in Current Periodicals, 1920-1945</u>.
Durham, North Carolina: Duke University Press, p. 192.
Lists criticism on Cummings published between 1933 and
1944.

9   MATTHIESSEN, F. O. On Cummings. The Sewanee Review, 55, no.
    1 (January–March), 47–48.
        In a survey of American poetry from 1920 to 1940, de-
    scribes Cummings as "a lyricist of romantic love, who is
    also a romantic anarchist in the New England tradition, and
    believes that a poem is an inspired moment breaking through
    the bars of syntax." Reprinted: 1948.10; 1953.10; 1963.15;
    1974.11.

10 MAYO, ROBERT D. "Cummings' 'Chansons Innocentes, (I).'"
    English "A" Analyst, no. 2 (May), unpaged.
        Describes the poem, on the literal level, as a spring
    song which presents the world as seen through the eyes of
    a child. All the poem's details are used to create the
    child's world. On a symbolic level, the identification of
    the "balloonman" with Pan links the spring world of the
    modern child with the ancient and eternal spirit of the
    spring; it also suggests the natural paganism and animal
    enthusiasms of childhood. These two levels, the first de-
    scending, the second ascending, intersect at the twentieth
    line. Reprinted: 1952.12; 1955.23; 1968.20.

11 RASCOE, BURTON. On Cumming, in his We Were Interrupted.
    Garden City, New York: Doubleday & Co., pp. 185, 188–89,
    192.
        Anecdotal reminiscences of Cummings in Paris and of his
    brilliant monologues.

12 WHITELY, MARY N. S. "Savagely a Maker." Poetry, 70, no. 4
    (July), 211–17.
        Reviews Anthropos: The Future of Art as emphasizing
    "the idea of negative plurality and positive individuality."
    A detailed summary is provided.

13 WINTERS, YVOR. On Cummings, in his In Defense of Reason:
    Primitivism and Decadence: A Study of American Experimental
    Poetry; Maule's Curse: Seven Studies in the History of
    American Obscurantism; The Anatomy of Nonsense; The Signi-
    ficance of "The Bridge" by Hart Crane, or What Are We to
    Think of Professor X? Denver, Colorado: Alan Swallow,
    p. 86.
        Reprint of 1937.4.

14 WOODBURN, JOHN. "Much in Little." The Saturday Review of
    Literature, 30, no. 1 (4 January), 16–17.
        Reviews Santa Claus as a morality play, the structure of
    which is "fronded with irony and bitter wisdom."

1948

1   BISHOP, JOHN PEALE. "Incorrect English," in his <u>The Collected</u>
     <u>Essays of John Peale Bishop</u>. Edited by Edmund Wilson. New
     York: Charles Scribner's Sons, pp. 243-45.
     Reprint of 1922.3.

2   BISHOP, JOHN PEALE. "The Poems and Prose of E. E. Cummings,"
     in his <u>The Collected Essays of John Peale Bishop</u>. Edited
     by Edmund Wilson. New York: Charles Scribner's Sons,
     pp. 83-95.
     Reprint of 1938.4.

3   CLURMAN, HAROLD. "Theatre: The Underground." <u>New Republic</u>,
     119, no. 6 (9 August), 26-27.
     Reviews the revival of <u>Him</u> by the "interplayers" at the
     Provincetown Playhouse, contrasting the present response to
     the play with the original one, remarking on the tired tame-
     ness of the current theatre, and summarizing Cummings'
     themes.

4   CRANE, HART. "America's Plutonic Ecstasies," in <u>Hart Crane:</u>
     <u>A Biographical and Critical Study</u>. By Brom Weber. New
     York: The Bodley Press, pp. 390-91.
     Reprint of 1923.2.

5   DICKINSON, PATRIC. Review of <u>1 X 1</u>. <u>Time and Tide</u>, 29, no. 5
     (31 January), 120.
     Describes the Cummings of <u>1 X 1</u> as "traditional, almost
     mid-nineteenth century (despite his typograbatics)."

6   FRANKENBERG, LLOYD. "The Poetry of E. E. Cummings." <u>Twice a</u>
     <u>Year</u>, nos. 16 and 17, pp. 273-300.
     Argues that Cummings' poems "celebrate individuals....
     To this central conception everything in his work is ad-
     dressed: his experimental techniques; his resurrecting of
     language from the dead box of grammar; his reanimation of
     the cliché and the colloquial; his concern with the look of
     a poem, how it lies on the page, as well as with the shape
     it makes in the ear; his audible punctuation, double-duty
     negatives and all the devices he employs, such as between
     statement (an aside from an aside) and parenthetically dis-
     persed words, for achieving immediacy and simultaneity.
     This accent on individuals accounts too for his satire."
     Frankenberg evidences these generalizations by lengthy ex-
     aminations of poems, plays, and prose works. Partially
     reprinted in 1949.7.

1948

7 [FRIEDMAN, NORMAN.] "The Poetry of E. E. Cummings: A Critical Appreciation." Essay submitted for the Bowdoin Prize,
   Harvard University, 51 pp.
       Submitted under the pseudonym of Michael Lee, the essay
   examines Cummings' "depth of insight, skill of execution,
   and power of communication." It contains the seeds of some
   of the approaches and ideas in Friedman's later work on
   Cummings (see especially 1960.8 and 1964.9). A typescript
   is held by the Harvard University Archives.

8 HART, JAMES D. "Cummings, E[dward] E[stlin]," in his The Oxford Companion to American Literature. Second edition.
   New York: Oxford University Press, pp. 172-73.
       Slightly updated entry. Revised edition of 1941.7.

9 LE BRETON, MAURICE. On Cummings, in his Anthologie de la
   Poésie Américaines Contemporaine. Paris: Les Editions
   Danoël, pp. 57, 297.
       Briefly considers Cummings as a modern and comments on
   his technical effort to achieve freshness and immediacy,
   while introducing an anthology of modern American poems
   translated into French. A headnote to the Cummings' poem
   presented, "when god lets my body be," notes his relationship to the dadaists "and other poetic acrobats" and remarks
   on the poem's "connection" with Kilmer's "Trees." In
   French.

10 MATTHIESSEN, F. O. On Cummings, in Literary History of the
   United States. Edited by Robert E. Spiller, Willard Thorp,
   Thomas H. Johnson, and Henry Seidel Canby. Vol. 2. New
   York: The Macmillan Co., 1351-52.
       Reprint of 1947.9.

11 O'CONNOR, WILLIAM VAN. On Cummings, in his Sense and Sensi-
   bility in Modern Poetry. Chicago: The University of
   Chicago Press, pp. 60-61, 76, 116, 124, 158-59, 183, 217-18,
   230, 248.
       Briefly notes Cummings' attempts "to catch the surface
   effects of physical actuality as they appear to him," his
   use of typography to capture those effects and to suggest
   the cadences of speech, his use of verbs and subordinate
   parts of speech as nouns, his use of color to express exub-
   erance, his ironic examinations of society, his opposition
   of the individual to the state, and his attack on the idea
   of political control. Reprinted: 1970.14.

12 PHELAN, KAPPO. "Him." The Commonweal, 48, no. 23 (17 September), 547.

1948

Describes the Provincetown Playhouse revival of <u>Him</u> as
hilarious if slightly dated.

13   POUND, EZRA. "E. E. Cummings," in his <u>If This Be Treason</u>.......
Siena, Italy: Tip. Nuova, pp. 3-9.
Comments on Cummings printed from a rough draft of one
of Pound's Rome radio broadcasts. <u>Eimi</u> is placed in the
company of works by Joyce and Wyndham Lewis. (<u>See also</u>
1948.14.)

14   POUND, EZRA. "E. E. Cummings /examind.," in his <u>If This Be</u>
<u>Treason</u>....... Siena, Italy: Tip. Nuova, pp. 9-15.
Comments on Cummings printed from a rough draft of one
of Pound's Rome radio broadcasts. Cummings is put in the
line of James, Thoreau, and Whitman; <u>Eimi</u> is classed with
Joyce's <u>Ulysses</u> and Lewis' <u>The Apes of God</u>. (<u>See also</u>
1948.13.)

15   RAIZISS, SONA. "E. E. Cummings," in her <u>La Poésie Américaine</u>
<u>"Moderniste," 1910-1940</u>. Translated by Charles Cestre.
Paris: Mercure de France, pp. 107-116.
A brief introductory discussion of Cummings as a romantic innovator, with comment on his sentimentality, his
typography, his connections with Villon and Marvell, his
images, and his diction. In French.

16   WELLS, HENRY W. On Cummings. <u>Word Study</u>, 24, no. 2 (December), 2.
Notes, in an essay on modern American poetic diction,
that if some of Cummings' experiments become dull upon
repetition, "others helped to fashion a glowing and an in-
gratiating lyric style."

<u>1949</u>

1   ALDRIDGE, JOHN W. "America's Young Novelists: Uneasy Inheri-
tors of a Revolution." <u>The Saturday Review of Literature</u>,
32, no. 7 (12 February), 6-8, 36-37, 42.
Points out that unlike such novelists of World War I as
Cummings, Hemingway, and Dos Passos, the writers of World
War II are not innovators of new methods. Aldridge suggests
that the revolt of the earlier writers had to do with the
then uniqueness of their experience and with the fact that
they were part of a language experiment which sought to
throw off past restraints and find a mode of expression
fit to a "younger, more realistic time."

2   ANON. "'As I Go Along.'" Time, 53, no. 23 (6 June), 69-70.
       Reviews a Manhattan exhibit of Cummings' paintings,
     calling him "a poet who is generally at odds with the world,
     and a painter who is at peace with nature." The paintings
     are "sunny, splashy," and "done with slapdash delight....
     Compared with his writings, Cummings' art seems as soft and
     wholesome as fresh butter."

3   ANON. "Cummings in Russia." Newsweek, 33, no. 7 (14 Febru-
       ary), 81-82.
       Notices Sloane's reissue of Eimi, finding it personal
     rather than political and its "acute observation, wit, and
     sensibility" obscured by its style. Still, it illuminates
     "corners of everyday Soviet life" often overlooked.

4   ANON. "Russia Revisited." Time, 53, no. 7 (14 February),
       100, 103.
       Reviews the reissue of Eimi; although the book's obscuri-
     ties still seem unnecessary, its scenes and events grow
     increasingly impressive and pertinent.

5   BREIT, HARVEY. "Comrade Cummings." New York Times Book Re-
       view (20 February), p. 15.
       Notices Sloane's reissue of Eimi, calling it perhaps
     "the most personal travel book ever written."

6   BROOMELL, MYRON H. Review of "tw." Variegation: A Free
       Verse Quarterly, 4, no. 4 (Autumn), 18.
       Notices the poem's appearance in the February 1949 Par-
     tisan Review, describing its form and noting its "series of
     liquid and murmurous syllabifications."

7   FRANKENBERG, LLOYD. "Cummings Times One," in his Pleasure
       Dome: On Reading Modern Poetry. Boston: Houghton Mifflin
       Co., pp. 157-94.
       An opening section entitled "To Be, As a Transitive
     Verb" reprints part of 1948.6. The second section, "The
     Metaphor-Poem," describes Cummings' development of an "in-
     ternal mimicry...not so much related to the philosopher's
     'idea' as...to the 'significant form' of the painter."
     Several poems are discussed as examples. In section three,
     "Algebra of the Heart," Frankenberg discusses Cummings'
     ideas of individual love and aliveness and his hatred of
     abstraction, compared here to ideas in Erich Fromm's Man
     for Himself. The final section, "The Whole Idea," discusses
     Cummings' use in Him and especially in Santa Claus of "stock
     figures to project in dramatic form his feelings about the
     world." Reprinted: 1962.9.

1949

8   GRAVES, ROBERT. On Cummings, in his <u>The Common Asphodel:</u>
    <u>Collected Essays on Poetry, 1922-1949</u>. London: Hamish
    Hamilton, pp. 61-72, 75-76, 84-86, 92-93, 96-98, 116-18,
    125, 134, 160.
        Reprint of 1927.4.

9   P[RESTON], S[TUART]. "Poet-Painter." <u>New York Times</u>, 2,
    p. 12.
        Reviews Cummings' one-man show at the American British
    Art Center, describing his paintings as "unpretentious,
    oddly moving evocations" infused with the "romantic feeling"
    of his early poems.

10 RIGOR, CONRADO B. "Whim: A Poetic Technique, Observations on
    the Poetry of E. E. Cummings." <u>12th Street</u>, 2, no. 3 (Win-
    ter), [95]-102.
        Argues that the ideas and techniques of Cummings' poetry
    are characterized by "joyous whim." Several poems are dis-
    cussed in support of this argument and comment is made on
    Cummings' connections with the avant-garde of the twenties
    and on his critical reputation.

11 SHAPIRO, KARL. "Prosody as the Meaning." <u>Poetry</u>, 73 (March),
    336-51.
        Debunks the critical assumption that art appeals to the
    understanding other than indirectly. Using the conclusions
    of an earlier essay, "A Farewell to Criticism," Shapiro
    sets out to prove his points by presenting a lengthy analy-
    sis of Cummings' "applaws" (poem VIII in <u>1 X 1</u>). Reprinted:
    1962.9.

12 STEINBERG, JACK. "Cummings' '1 X 1.'" <u>The Explicator</u>, 8,
    no. 3 (December), Item 17.
        Analyzes "1 X 1," finding in it a compact pattern of
    "parallel and simultaneous sound and sense rhythms" which
    creates a visual design. The artificiality of rules and
    systems is contrasted with "traditional natural beings."
    The poem creates a new arithmetic which has human love
    hurdle the "limits of time, space, and reason," and its
    rushing movement through linked stanzas supports this idea.
    Reprinted: 1966.43.

                                1950

1   ANDREWS, DONALD H. "Cummings and Communication." <u>The Hopkins</u>
    <u>Review</u>, 3, no. 4 (Summer), 36-37.
        Reviews <u>Xaîpe</u>, calling Cummings "frugal and fugal." At
    a time when principles of communication are being precisely

formulated, his book is important not only as poetry but as communicative pattern, for Cummings' oddities and obscurities are carefully contrived and part of an integral idea.

2   ANON. "Self Tail and All." The Times Literary Supplement
     (7 July), p. 422.
         Reviews Xaîpe, commenting that Cummings' apparent arbitrariness of form is due not so much to a concern with "purely typographical composition" as to "the far deeper" one of "representing experience exactly."

3   ARMS, GEORGE and JOSEPH M. KUNTZ. Explications of Poems by
     Cummings, in their Poetry Explication: A Checklist of Interpretation since 1925 of British and American Poems Past
     and Present. New York: The Swallow Press and William
     Morrow & Co., pp. 51-[52].
         A checklist of explications. Revised edition: 1962.19.

4   BARROWS, HERBERT C. JR. and WILLIAM R. STEINHOFF. "Cummings'
     'Anyone Lived in a Pretty How Town' (50 Poems, 29)." The
     Explicator, 9, no. 1 (October), Item 1.
         Explicates the way in which Cummings reworks the language and exploits sound and sense in this poem to force "simple, familiar words to produce beautiful and sharply arresting effects." This technique gives distinction to the poem's contrasting of natural and unnatural responses to life. See 1952.4 and 1964.24. Reprinted: 1954.2;
     1966.3.

5   BOGAN, LOUISE. Review of Xaîpe. The New Yorker, 26, no. 13
     (20 May), 113-14.
         Argues that the "deletion of the tragic makes Cummings' joy childish and his anger petulant."

6   BREIT, HARVEY. "Talk with E. E. Cummings." New York Times
     Book Review (31 December), p. 10.
         Records a visit with Cummings after his receipt of a fellowship from the Academy of American Poets. Cummings comments on such matters as his use of the lower-case "i" and the importance of intensity in art. Reprinted: 1956.3.

7   DAICHES, DAVID. Review of Xaîpe. The Yale Review, 40, no. 2
     (December), 354-55.
         Reviews Xaîpe as part of an omnibus review, finding it "a rich and fascinating volume" of a poet who is "the master of several styles" and who handles the short and long lines with equal effectiveness. Daiches asserts that Cummings "is a major modern poet," prefers his lyrics to his satires, and calls him the best love poet of this century.

1950

8   DEUTSCH, BABETTE. "Poetry at the Mid-Century." The Virginia
    Quarterly Review, 26, no. 1 (Winter), 67-75.
        In a broad discussion of modern American poetry's rela-
    tion to Whitman, Dickinson, and Poe, notes in passing Cum-
    mings' debt to Leaves of Grass and his connection with
    Dickinson.

9   FERGUSSON, FRANCIS. "When We Were Very Young." The Kenyon
    Review, 12 (Autumn), 701-705.
        Comments on the reissue of Eimi. "The passage of time
    has confirmed and documented Cummings' essential vision of
    the 'unworld' of Marxian totalitarianism" yet has not dimmed
    the brilliance of his portrait. Fergusson agrees with Troy
    (see 1933.18) on the successes of the book's techniques and
    its lack of a unifying center, and he recommends that the
    book be read in small, one might say lyric, doses. Fergus-
    son also discusses the persona of the book and the creed-
    lessness of Cummings' encounter with and criticism of Soviet
    Russia. Reprinted: 1962.9.

10 FRANKENBERG, LLOYD. "An Obligation to be Gay." New York Times
    Book Review (2 April), pp. 5, 36.
        Reviews Xaîpe; describes Cummings as a major lyric poet
    and notes the "natural piety" beneath his pyrotechnics, his
    liberation of language, his functional typography, his
    rhythms combining song and dance, the centrality of the
    satires to his vision, and his "affirmative expressions."

11 FREEMANTLE, ANNE. Review of Xaîpe. The Commonweal, 52, no.
    15 (21 July), 370.
        Comments on Xaîpe in an omnibus review, remarking on
    Cummings' compression and his concern with "the mortal
    things that touch the mind."

12 HUMPHRIES, ROLFE. Review of Xaîpe. The Nation, 171, no. 4
    (22 July), 91.
        Reviews Xaîpe in an omnibus review, finding the poems a
    little "otiose," a little too persistently gay.

13 JARRELL, RANDALL. Review of Xaîpe. Partisan Review, 17, no.
    7 (September-October), 728-30.
        After tracing Cummings' reputation, describes his poems
    as "the popular songs of American intellectuals" and com-
    plains that their exclusion of the tragic leaves both their
    joy and anger trivial. The poems are often attractive (he
    has been true to himself), but there is a moral vacuum at
    their heart (he has been false to others and the world).
    Reprinted: 1953.6.

14 MORGAN, FREDERICK. Review of Xaîpe. The Hudson Review, 3,
    no. 3 (Autumn), 463-64.
        Examines Cummings' Xaîpe in an omnibus review; it con-
    tinues his typical successes and failures. Morgan takes
    special delight in Cummings' ear for sound and is especially
    disturbed by his egocentric oversimplifications.

15 MOSELEY, EDWIN M. "Cummings' 'These Children Singing in Stone
    A' (50 Poems, 37)." The Explicator, 9, no. 1 (October),
    Item 2.
        Examines Cummings' description of "a sculpture of singing
    children wreathed in flowers," noting that it "winds words
    and rhythms around each other as if they were the children
    and the singing and the flowers interwoven into a single
    figure." The poem presents the sculpture as catching love-
    liness without making it merely static. It also implies
    Cummings' frequently opposed themes of the natural intuitive
    perceptions of children and the insensitive nonperceptions
    of adults. See 1955.11. Reprinted: 1966.34.

16 OLSON, CHARLES. On Cummings. Poetry New York, no. 3, pp. 19-
    20.
        Notes, in the essay "Projective Verse," the influence of
    Cummings, and others, on field composition, remarking his
    use of the typewriter in composing and considering his spe-
    cial contribution the technique of suspending a word or
    syllable at the end of a line. Reprinted: 1959.21;
    1960.18; 1965.20; 1967.26; 1973.20.

17 POUND, EZRA. On Cummings, in his The Selected Letters of Ezra
    Pound: 1907-1941. Edited by D. D. Paige. New York: Har-
    court Brace Jovanovitch, pp. 201-202, 223, 227-28, 244-45,
    265, 266, 268-69, 277, 290-91, 292, 301, 325, 327, 328.
        Contains letters to Cummings and letters which mention
    him. Both types are generally concerned with matters of
    publication and what might be called literary gossip. Re-
    printed: 1971.22.

18 ROSENTHAL, M. L. Review of Xaîpe. New Republic, 123, no. 12
    (18 September), 18-19.
        Comments on Xaîpe, forgiving Cummings his sentimentality
    "because the colloquial impudence and emotional freshness
    of his style help restore our faith in the importance of our
    own experience." Rosenthal considers the satiric verse in-
    ferior to the lyric and discusses Cummings' occasionally
    racist lapses.

1950

19 SCOTT, W. T. Review of <u>Xaîpe</u>. <u>The Saturday Review of Litera-</u>
    <u>ture</u>, 33, no. 52 (30 December), 8.
        Briefly notices <u>Xaîpe</u>, calling Cummings our finest lyri-
    cist and most "captivating inventor of phrase."

20 SOUTHWORTH, JAMES G. "E. E. Cummings," in his <u>Some Modern</u>
    <u>American Poets</u>. Oxford: Basil Blackwell, pp. [135]-47.
        Surveys Cummings' verse, finding it without growth and
    marred by novelties that are merely "technical swagger."
    His attitudes are consistently adolescent and escapist; he
    is "almost entirely a creature of the senses; he is a snob."

21 SPENCER, THEODORE. "Technique as Joy: Observations on the
    Poetry of E. E. Cummings," in <u>Modern American Poetry</u>.
    Focus Five. Edited by B. Rajan. London: Dennis Dobson,
    pp. 118-26.
        A slightly expanded reprint of 1946.20.

22 UNTERMEYER, LOUIS. "E. E. Cummings," in his <u>Modern American</u>
    <u>Poetry</u>. Mid-Century Edition. New York: Harcourt, Brace
    and Co., pp. 508-509.
        Slightly updated headnote to a selection of Cummings'
    poems. Revised edition of 1925.6.

23 VOWLES, RICHARD B. "Cummings' 'Space Being...Curved' (<u>Collec-</u>
    <u>ted Poems</u>, 196)." <u>The Explicator</u>, 9, no. 1 (October),
    Item 3.
        Presents the scientific principles which the poem attacks
    and explicates its anti-intellectual images. "The poem is
    an attack, in Cummings' naive bombast, on the physical sci-
    entist's approach to a godlike but empty omnipotence."
    Reprinted: 1966.48.

24 WELLS, HENRY W. "Cummings in His Own Footsteps." <u>Voices</u>, no.
    143 (Autumn), pp. 48-50.
        Reviews <u>Xaîpe</u>, finding the writing in it "considerably
    more sustained and less forced than in some of the preceding
    books." Cummings "has grown more and more a philosophical
    poet devoted to refinement (or repetition) of a relatively
    few ideas and to variations on comparatively few rhythmical
    patterns and imagistic themes."

1951

1 ALDRIDGE, JOHN W. On Cummings, in his <u>After the Lost Genera-</u>
   <u>tion: A Critical Study of the Writers of Two Wars</u>. New
   York: McGraw-Hill Book Co., pp. 13-16, 88, 107, 113, 115.

Connects Cummings with other members of the "lost generation," especially Hemingway and Dos Passos, in his sense of
rebellion and his breaking of new stylistic ground to express the lessons of the war. Reprinted: 1958.2.

2   BLACKMUR, R. P. "Notes on E. E. Cummings' Language," in
    Literary Opinion in America. Second edition. Edited by
    Morton Dauwen Zabel. New York: Harper & Brothers,
    pp. 296-314.
        Reprint of 1931.1.

3   BOGAN, LOUISE. On Cummings, in her Achievement in American
    Poetry, 1900-1950. Chicago: Henry Regnery, pp. 76-77.
        Asserts that Cummings' career-long use of "youthful ty-
    pographical oddities tended...to become tiresome" and that
    "his failure to mature, emotionally and intellectually,
    finally introduced a note of peevishness into his work as
    a whole."

4   COWLEY, MALCOLM. On Cummings, in his Exile's Return: A Liter-
    ary Odyssey of the 1920s. New York: The Viking Press,
    pp. 38, 42-43, 114, 123, 133, 151, 158-59, 176, 186, 191,
    204, 251, 254, 283.
        Passing anecdotal and critical references to Cummings as
    a member of the literary generation of the twenties.

5   C[UMMINS], V[IRGINIA KENT]. On Cummings. The Lyric, 31, no.
    2 (Spring), 59-60.
        Considers Cummings' poetry largely meaningless. (For a
    response, see 1952.7.)

6   FERGUSSON, FRANCIS. On Cummings, in Literary Opinion in Ameri-
    ca. Second edition. Edited by Morton Dauwen Zabel. New
    York: Harper & Brothers, pp. 519-21.
        Reprint of 1930.3.

7   G[LAUBER], R[OBERT] H. Review of Xaîpe. The Beloit Poetry
    Journal, 1, no. 3 (Spring), 27.
        Reviews Xaîpe, complaining of Cummings' failure to move
    on to new problems rather than stay with his old skills and
    themes.

8   HAINES, GEORGE IV. "::2:1 The World and E. E. Cummings." The
    Sewanee Review, 59 (Spring), 206-27.
        Describes Cummings' work as divisible into one part
    loathing and one part love. "It is abstraction he loathes
    and in that loathing his expression is often most concrete,
    his love finds as often only abstraction by means of which

to express itself." The apparent contradictoriness of this statement Haines resolves by defining the two sorts of abstraction involved. The first is the application of the laws of mechanical science to human life. This occurs in a concrete world and so Cummings' rejection of it is concrete. His alternative to it, the second abstraction, his metaphysic--"ultimately the transcendence of individuality through love"--finds its expression in abstraction because men and women can never be one in the concrete world. The technique through which the metaphysic is expressed is typified by its preservation of "the quality of individuality in the phraseology of the universal and the abstract." Haines discusses both metaphysic and technique at length, with supporting analyses. He also relates Cummings' ideas and craft to expressionist aesthetics and to nineteenth-century romanticism. Cummings includes and goes beyond these, for he does not distinguish merely between feeling and thinking, but between feeling and unfeeling, creative thinking and destructive thinking. Reprinted: 1972.10.

9   HAUSER, JACOB. "Academies of the Perverse." The Lyric, 31, no. 2 (Spring), 63-64.
        Argues that the award to Cummings of a $5,000 prize by The Academy of American Poets demonstrates that academies are no longer academic but are engaged in pursuit of the "different." Hauser considers modern art a fake and quotes from Cummings to make his point: "Is such work worth five thousand dollars or even five cents?"

10   HUTCHINSON, PEARSE. On Cummings. Envoy, 5, no. 18 (May), 39, 45-46.
        Comments on Cummings in a survey of American poets, according his poems about sex and about prostitutes high praise.

11   HYNES, SAM. "Cummings' 'Collected Poems, 276.'" The Explicator, 10, no. 2 (November), Item 9.
        Analyzes the grasshopper poem, calling it "an attempt to deal with words visually, and to create art as a single experience, having spatial, not temporal extension: to force poetry toward a closer kinship with painting and the plastic arts, and away from its kinship with music." Reprinted: 1966.26.

12   JACKINSON, ALEX and OTHERS. "Anti-Semitism and E. E. Cummings." Congress Weekly, 18 (20 August), [11]-13.
        A discussion by seven writers and critics of anti-Semitic content in Cummings' work, occasioned by controversy over

the awarding to him of The Academy of American Poets Award
for 1951. Jackinson opens the discussion. He admits the
presence of anti-Semitic content in the poems but argues
that specific "deprecations shock only until...woven into
the fabric of his entire work." What "really counts is the
intent behind an allegedly offensive slur" and Cummings' intent is not vicious. So Jackinson acquits Cummings of the
charge of anti-Semitism and examines the infamous "kike"
passage from page 46 of Xaîpe to demonstrate that "far from
being anti-Semitic in intent, the lines are pointedly and
effectively anti anti-Semitic." Ludwig Lewisohn argues that
Cummings "can in his amused and amusing universal disgruntle-
ment be made out anything--fascist, anti-Semite, what you
will. Fundamentally, he is nothing. The charm of his work
is in the sprightly dexterities of his use of language."
Stanton A. Coblentz finds Cummings "an affected mouther of
inanities" who is viciously anti-Semitic and socially and
politically base. A comparison with Goebbels is suggested.
Charles I. Glicksberg admits that he dislikes Cummings' poetry, but he finds the whole issue of anti-Semitism in it
a failure to see the work as a whole and, therefore, "a
mare's nest." Leslie A. Fiedler considers anti-Semitic ut-
terances of all kinds "effectively evil" and notes that Cummings never presents any other than a stereotyped portrait
of a Jew. But Cummings is a good writer, who like most men
combines evil and goodness but who unlike most men is an
artist. Harry Roskolenko finds the source of Cummings'
anti-Semitism in his "confused origins" as a satirist. His
satire "insists on indelicacy, mostly for the purposes of
shock. But it stems from a divided sensitivity" and in the
anti-Semitic poems the method becomes cheap and trite. Yet
even in these, the matter is complex, for "they are of two
minds, going in two directions." William Carlos Williams
applauds the award to Cummings and asserts that the question
of anti-Semitism is irrelevant since it ignores the requirement that the artist be free to say "Whatever He Chooses to
Say." (For another response see 1952.7.) Reprinted:
1962.9.

13   MILES, JOSEPHINE. On Cummings, in her "The Primary Language
      of Poetry in the 1940's." University of California Studies
      in English, 19, no. 3 (February), 385, 389, 391, 392, 393,
      439, 440-42, 444-45, 457, 476, 516, 517, 521.
         Comments on characteristics of the language of Cummings'
      poetry of the forties. Miles provides information on such
      matters as adjectival emphasis, proportions of speech parts,
      use of verbs and "cognitive abstractions and constructions,"
      line length, the juggling of speech parts, especially in

1951

"nonsun blob a" and "pity this busy monster, manunkind,"
the persistent use of the verb "I am," and so on. Reprinted: 1965.18.

14   RANSOM, JOHN CROWE. On Cummings. <u>The Kenyon Review</u>, 13, no.
     3 (Summer), 451-52.
         In a discussion of poetry from 1900-1950, tentatively
     ranks Cummings, with such writers as Williams, Pound, Moore,
     and Crane, as a "Minor Poet," one who will survive "for not
     a few half-centuries."

15   STRAUMANN, HEINRICH. On Cummings, in his <u>American Literature</u>
     <u>in the Twentieth Century</u>. London: Hutchinson House,
     p. 159.
         Notes that Cummings' poetry reveals both the positive
     and negative aspects of the experimental method and a
     "preference for the themes of love and death." Reprinted:
     1962.27; 1965.26.

16   WHICHER, GEORGE F. On Cummings, in <u>The Literature of the</u>
     <u>American People: An Historical and Critical Survey</u>. Edited
     by Arthur Hobson Quinn. New York: Appleton-Century-Crofts,
     Inc., pp. 964-66.
         Notes Cummings' connection with surrealist painting,
     comments on the romantic sensibility beneath the orthodox
     surface of his poems, and describes him as having written
     "the best abstract verse of the period."

1952

1   ANON. Headnote. <u>Life</u>, 33, no. 21 (24 November), 104.
         Headnote to Cummings' "mortals)," reprinted as part of
     an article on <u>Poetry</u> magazine's fortieth anniversary, as-
     serts that Cummings is one of the "most original of American
     poets."

2   B[ENTLEY], E[RIC]. "<u>Him</u> (1927)," in <u>From the Modern Reper-</u>
     <u>toire: Series Two</u>. Edited by Eric Bentley. Denver, Colo-
     rado: University of Denver Press, pp. 485-94.
         Notes on this anthologizing of <u>Him</u>. Bentley comments on
     his own 1950 production of the play in Salzburg and repro-
     duces, in English, the summarizing and tentatively inter-
     preting program notes from that production. Bentley also
     includes an interpretation of the play by Theodore Hoffman,
     one of his Salzburg colleagues. Hoffman finds in <u>Him</u> paral-
     lels to Attic comedy, suggesting that Cummings seeks modern
     remnants of ancient fertility rites in our own society,

finding its imagery in burlesque and the circus and its
ritual in psychoanalysis. Hoffman then briefly summarizes
the play in terms of these ideas.

3   BLACKMUR, R. P. "Notes on E. E. Cummings' Language," in his
    Language as Gesture: Essays in Poetry. New York: Har-
    court, Brace and Company, pp. 317-40.
        Reprint of 1931.1.

4   CARR, ARTHUR. "Cummings' 'Anyone Lived in a Pretty How Town.'"
    The Explicator, 11, no. 2 (November), Item 6.
        Argues that the poem is both a "love-story" and an "un-
    love"-story. The first "praises the happy and successful
    isolation of two lovers who keep innocence and naturalness."
    The second "tells the 'really truly' story of the loss of
    innocence and of love that is the common lot of children
    growing up." See 1950.4 and 1964.24. Reprinted: 1966.7.

5   CRANE, HART. On Cummings, in his The Letters of Hart Crane.
    Edited by Brom Weber. New York: Hermitage House, pp. 85,
    96, 108, 120, 133, 167, 182, 213, 251, 307, 310-11, 321,
    324, 349, 354-55, 375.
        Brief references to Cummings as a member of the New York
    literary scene, comments on his poetry, and suggestions of
    his influence.

6   DEUTSCH, BABETTE. On Cummings, in her Poetry in Our Time.
    New York: Henry Holt and Co., pp. 85, 111-16, 325-54, 369.
        Asserts that Cummings exemplifies the principles of the
    imagists in his use of "private punctuation" and "unique
    typography." He is akin to Apollinaire in his "attempt to
    do with print what Hopkins tried to do by his peculiarities
    of diction, to present the 'inscape' of things." Deutsch
    partially reverses her objection in This Modern Poetry
    (1935.9) that Cummings' technique is excessively visual by
    noting his feeling for "aural values." Reprinted: 1956.5;
    1963.8. (The latter of these is a revised edition, but the
    Cummings entry is unchanged.)

7   FRIEDMAN, NORMAN. "Poem vs. Slogan: In Defense of E. E.
    Cummings." The Reconstructionist, 18, no. 1 (22 February),
    18-23.
        Responds to Virginia Kent Cummins (see 1951.5) and to
    certain contributors to the Congress Weekly symposium on
    Cummings and anti-Semitism (see 1951.12), commenting on the
    confusion between aesthetic and moral values that undercuts
    such discussions, examining the "evidence" against Cummings,
    and demonstrating that Cummings eschews sloganeering and
    fights stereotypes rather than subscribing to either.

1952

8   FRIEDMAN, NORMAN. "The Why of E. E. Cummings." Thought, 4,
     no. 27 (5 July), 10–13.
          Argues that Cummings' theme and forms are concerned with
     the "tension between collective and individual authority."
     In terms of this generalization, Friedman examines his sub-
     jects and structures, his connections with Whitman, Dickin-
     son, and Thoreau, and his "triumphant humanism." Reprinted:
     1957.12.

9   HUTCHENS, JOHN K. "A Note on the Nineteen Twenties," in The
     American Twenties: A Literary Panorama. Edited by John K.
     Hutchens. Philadelphia: J. B. Lippincott Co., pp. 11, 20.
          Notes that Cummings made creative use of post-World War I
     disillusion and comments very briefly on The Enormous Room
     and the lyric poems.

10   JONES, HOWARD MUMFORD. On Cummings, in his The Bright Medusa.
     Urbana: The University of Illinois Press, pp. 12–14.
          Classes The Enormous Room with other important books of
     the twenties as emphasizing the self as an ultimate in art
     and value.

11   MATTHIESSEN, F. O. Review of 1 X 1, in his The Responsibili-
     ties of the Critic. New York: Oxford University Press,
     pp. 119–20.
          Reprint of 1944.9.

12   MAYO, ROBERT D. "Cummings' 'Chansons Innocentes (I),'" in
     Introduction to Literature. Second edition. Edited by
     Louis G. Locke, William M. Gibson, and George Arms. New
     York: Rinehart and Co., pp. 238–41.
          Reprint of 1947.10.

13   [NORMAN, CHARLES.] "Personality." Time, 60, no. 18 (3 Novem-
     ber), 67.
          An anecdotal, biographical essay, describing Cummings at
     Patchin Place and at his farm in New Hampshire.

14   PEARCE, ROY HARVEY. On Cummings. The Yale Review, 41, no. 3
     (March), 432–36.
          Comments on Cummings as part of an examination of "The
     Poet as Person," suggesting that he, like Williams, is de-
     voted to the word and "marked by obsession with personal-
     ity.... Cummings' mode is the lyric." His achievement has
     been the technical attempt "to rescue abstract language from
     the abstractness that deadens it." Reprinted: 1959.22.
     Revised version: 1961.10.

15 RAIZISS, SONA. On Cummings, in her <u>The Metaphysical Passion:</u>
    <u>Seven Modern American Poets and the Seventeenth-Century</u>
    <u>Tradition</u>. Philadelphia: University of Pennsylvania Press,
    pp. 16, 43, 53, 120, 129, 141, 155, 162, 168, 286n.
        Brief comments on Cummings in relation to twentieth-
    century poetry's use of the metaphysical tradition.

16 TURNER, W. PRICE. "Immediacy of Precision: E. E. Cummings--
    An Appreciation." <u>The Poet</u>, no. 2 (Spring), pp. 3-5.
        Rejects criticism of Cummings' innovative techniques and
    celebrates his debunking "of all pomp and sham," his "un-
    canny ability to catch a likeness," and his affirmative
    stance.

17 WILSON, EDMUND. "E. E. Cummings' <u>Him</u>," in his <u>The Shores of</u>
    <u>Light: A Literary Chronicle of the Twenties and Thirties</u>.
    New York: Farrar, Straus and Young, pp. 382-85.
        Reprint of 1927.7.

18 WILSON, EDMUND. "A Preface to Persius," in his <u>The Shores of</u>
    <u>Light: A Literary Chronicle of the Twenties and Thirties</u>.
    New York: Farrar, Straus and Young, pp. 267-73.
        Reprint of 1927.8.

19 WILSON, EDMUND. "Wallace Stevens and E. E. Cummings," in his
    <u>The Shores of Light: A Literary Chronicle of the Twenties</u>
    <u>and Thirties</u>. New York: Farrar, Straus and Young, pp. 49-
    53.
        Reprint of 1924.13.

1953

1   BENTLEY, ERIC. On <u>Him</u>, in his <u>In Search of Theater</u>. New York:
    Alfred A. Knopf, pp. 106-107, Plate IV.
        Comments on Bentley's own production of <u>Him</u> in 1950 in
    Salzburg. "Above all, <u>Him</u> represents a deeply American at-
    tempt at...reanimating...the theater." With three photo-
    graphs.

2   BUDD, LOUIS J. "Cummings' 'Buffalo Bill's Defunct.'" <u>The</u>
    <u>Explicator</u>, 11, no. 8 (June), Item 55.
        Rejects Brooks' and Warren's reading of the poem (<u>see</u>
    1938.5) and argues that "Cummings regards the hero as a dis-
    tressingly revered caricature of genuinely human actions and
    values, an avatar of stillborn sentience." Reprinted:
    1966.6.

1953

3   BURNS, DAVID. "First Person Singular." The Yale Review, 43,
     no. 2 (December), 306-308.
         Reviews i: Six Nonlectures as "an honest attempt at
     autobiographical self-discovery" of interest not only to
     readers of the poetry but also to "all who concern them-
     selves with the place of the individual in a mass society."

4   FITTS, DUDLEY. "An Esthetic Striptease." New York Times Book
     Review (15 November), p. 34.
         Reviews i: Six Nonlectures, noting that Cummings is "a
     rebel in the good Yankee conservative fashion," summarizing
     the nonlectures' contents, and describing their author as
     an "artist in love with this world and the art of worlds
     hidden."

5   GROSSMAN, D. JON and ALAIN BOSQUET. "Note des Traducteurs:
     La Poésie de E. E. Cummings est-elle traduisible?" Profils,
     no. 2 (January), pp. [32]-33.
         Examines the special difficulties of translating Cum-
     mings' poetry into French. In French.

6   JARRELL, RANDALL. On Cummings, in The New Partisan Reader,
     1945-1953. Edited by William Phillips and Philip Rahv.
     New York: Harcourt, Brace and Co., pp. 418-21.
         Reprint of 1950.13.

7   KILBY, CLYDE S. "Cummings' 'Memorabilia.'" The Explicator,
     12, no. 2 (November), Item 15.
         Analyzes the poem's contentual and sonic satire of
     American tourists abroad and suggests possible allusions to
     Browning's poem of the same title. See 1954.14 and 1963.3.
     Reprinted: 1966.28.

8   KOVAL, ALEXANDER. "Bemerkungen zur Übersetzung der Gedichte
     von E. E. Cummings." Perspektiven, no. 2 (January),
     pp. [33]-36.
         Comments on the traditional and experimental aspects of
     Cummings' work in an essay on the difficulties of translat-
     ing his poems into German. In German.

9   LAUTER, PAUL. "The Poetry of E. E. Cummings: An Index,
     Bibliography, and Check-List." Carbon copy of the type-
     script of appendices to the author's honors thesis, donated
     to Harvard University Library. New York: New York Univer-
     sity, 39 pp.
         An alphabetical index to first lines of Cummings' poems,
     giving places of original and subsequent publication, with
     a bibliography of works by and about Cummings. Revised

edition: 1955.17. Revised edition reprinted: 1971.13; 1976.14; 1977.4.

10 MATTHIESSEN, F. O. On Cummings, in Literary History of the United States. Second edition. Edited by Robert E. Spiller, Willard Thorp, Thomas H. Johnson, and Henry Seidel Canby. New York: The Macmillan Co., pp. 1351-52. Reprint of 1947.9.

11 MILLER, MARTHA M. "The Discovery of Me: E. E. Cummings Reflects on a Year at Harvard as Norton Professor." Harvard Alumni Bulletin, 55, no. 15 (9 May), 610, [612], 614, 633.
    Discusses Cummings' Norton Lectures as occasions and in terms of their content.

12 QUASIMODO, SALVATORE. "Nota alle traduzione delle poesie di E. E. Cummings." Prospetti, 2 (January), [80]-81.
    Comments on the difficulty of translating Cummings into Italian and argues that his novelty is not in his technique but in his "furious search for the real." In Italian. Reprinted: 1958.22; 1964.22.

13 ROLO, CHARLES J. Review of i: Six Nonlectures. The Atlantic, 192, no. 6 (December), 95.
    Notices i: Six Nonlectures as "an aesthetic self-portrait and a definition of Mr. Cummings' 'stance' as a writer.... The central motifs are the importance of feeling...and 'the eternal fight of selfhood against mobism.'"

14 SCOTT, WINFIELD TOWNLEY. "e. e. cummings, Who Believes in Love, Spring, Freedom." New York Herald-Tribune Book Review (29 November), p. 3.
    Reviews i: Six Nonlectures, finding a touch of coyness here, as elsewhere in Cummings' work, "a minor blemish amidst a fresh independence which wars not really against intellectualism but against the extensions of intellectualism substituting for feeling."

15 SPENCER, THEODORE. "Poetik der Freude." Perspektiven, no. 2 (January), pp. [25]-32.
    Reprint in German of 1946.20.

16 SPENCER, THEODORE. "Technique as Joy: Observations on the Poetry of E. E. Cummings." Perspectives USA, no. 2 (Winter), pp. [23]-29.
    Reprint of 1946.20.

1953

17 WHICHER, STEPHEN E. "Cummings' 'What If a Much of a Which of
      a Wind.'" The Explicator, 12, no. 2 (November), Item 14.
        Suggests that the poem affirms man's capacity to value
      in the present as consolation for the annihilation of the
      world rather than affirming a belief in future immortality.
      Whicher also outlines areas of continuing difficulty in the
      poem. Reprinted: 1966.50.

1954

1 BALLIET, WHITNEY. "The Author." The Saturday Review, 37,
      no. 51 (18 December), 10.
        A biographical headnote to David Burns' review of Poems:
      1923-1954 (see 1954.9).

2 BARROWS, H. C., JR. and W. R. STEINHOFF. "Critique," in The
      Case for Poetry: A New Anthology. Edited by Frederick L.
      Gwynn, Ralph W. Condee, and Arthur O. Lewis, Jr. Englewood
      Cliffs, New Jersey: Prentice-Hall, pp. 79-80.
        Reprint of part of an analysis of "anyone lived in a
      pretty how town," 1950.4.

3 BAUM, S. V. "E. E. Cummings: The Technique of Immediacy."
      The South Atlantic Quarterly, 53 (January), 70-88.
        Reacts to a critical tendency to separate Cummings' form
      and technique from his content. Baum sees Cummings' techni-
      cal denial of authority as an expression of his thematic
      concern with individualism. His reduction of moral stand-
      ards to the two categories of affirmative and negative has
      required him to develop techniques allowing the presentation
      of simultaneous, momentary perception in spite of the neces-
      sarily historical nature of conventional syntax. Baum cata-
      logues Cummings' fresh use of punctuation and typography to
      demonstrate that his disorders contain an orderly notation--
      a new set of conventions--for such presentation. In addi-
      tion, Baum gives three poems, "ta," "a thrown a," and "!
      blac," detailed explication in support of his argument.
      Reprinted: 1972.10.

4 BELOOF, ROBERT LAWRENCE. "E. E. Cummings: The Prosodic Shape
      of his Poems." Ph.D. dissertation, Northwestern University.
        Examines Cummings' prosody in terms of "stress prosody,
      free verse in metaphysical form, pictograms, syllabic pros-
      ody, oral verse in visual (non-pictorial) form, dramatic
      free verse, [and] foot prosody." The question of Cummings'
      originality and development is also explored, again from a
      prosodic point of view.

5   BERTHOFF, WARNER. Review of i: Six Nonlectures. The New
     England Quarterly, 27, no. 1 (March), 106-108.
         Remarks on Cummings' Charles Eliot Norton Lectures for
     1952-1953.

6   BOGAN, LOUISE. "Verse." The New Yorker, 30 (11 December),
     198-202.
         Reviews Poems: 1923-1954 and The Collected Poems of
     Wallace Stevens. Cummings brought into American poetry a
     "bittersweet mixture of satire and sentiment." His typo-
     graphical experiments now seem less important than his per-
     sistent attempt to reintroduce "into formal verse vital
     material that Victorian taste had outlawed." It is his
     satire that remains his "main contribution to the reinvigor-
     ation of modern verse." Stevens is, on the other hand, the
     pure contemplative poet. We should be grateful for both.
     Reprinted: 1962.9.

7   BRINNIN, JOHN MALCOLM. On Cummings, in New World Writing.
     Fifth Mentor Selection. New York: The New American
     Library of World Literature, p. 231.
         Mentions Cummings as one of several American poets who
     have transcended the limitations of Imagism and "expanded
     its insights."

8   BROWN, JOHN. On Cummings, in his Panorama de la Littérature
     Contemporaine Aux États-Unis. Paris: Librairie Gallimard,
     pp. 101, 138, 146, 248, 283-85.
         Comments on Cummings as a war novelist, as a poet com-
     bining sentimental lyricism with harsh speech, and as one
     of the many exploiters of the ideas introduced by Whitman.
     A brief discussion of Cummings' poems notes his debt to
     Apollinaire, his accurate depiction of the twenties, his
     defense of the individual against the mass, his themes, and
     his special vocabulary. In French.

9   BURNS, DAVID. "Antique Virtues in Modern Dress." The Saturday
     Review, 37, no. 51 (18 December), 10-11.
         Reviews Poems: 1923-1954, calling Cummings "one of the
     finest lyric poets and social satirists America has yet
     produced," explaining his experiments with diction and
     typography as attempts to shock surfeited senses and sensi-
     bilities into awareness, and commenting on his celebration
     of the "antique virtues" of love, nature, and the individual
     in his "modern-antique songs."

10   CHAMBERLAIN, JOHN. "ee cummings: His Spontaneous Song, His
     Undying Belief in Man." New York Herald-Tribune Book Review
     (26 December), p. 1.

1954

Reviews <u>Poems: 1923-1954</u>, concentrating on the sound
values of Cummings' poems and commenting on his theme of
spontaneity and his belief in man the nonabstraction.

11   CUNLIFFE, MARCUS. On Cummings, in his <u>The Literature of the
     United States</u>. London: Penguin Books, pp. 224, 264, 282,
     304, 311, 315-17, 318, 361.
        Brief general remarks on Cummings as an amusing if not
     profound innovator. Reprinted: 1961.5 and 1967.8.

12   FREEMANTLE, ANNE. "The Pilgrimage of an American Poet." <u>The
     Commonweal</u>, 59, no. 20 (19 February), 503-505.
        Reviews <u>i: Six Nonlectures</u>, finding them filled with an
     atmosphere of piety and almost Confucian sweetness, and in
     them the iconoclastic poet-painter become the hierarchical,
     conservative preacher.

13   GRAVES, ROBERT. "Review of <u>i: Six Nonlectures</u>." <u>The New
     Statesman and Nation</u> (12 June), pp. 761-62.
        Notes Cummings similarity to Vachel Lindsay, summarizes
     the autobiographical content of the "nonlectures," and re-
     marks on Cummings' didacticism. Reprinted: 1955.10;
     1956.7; 1972.10.

14   GRIFFITH, BEN W., JR. "Cummings' 'Memorabilia.'" <u>The Explica-
     tor</u>, 12, no. 7 (May), Item 47.
        Rejects Kilby's reading (<u>see</u> 1953.7) of the word "Cin-
     cingondolanati" as a jest at the tourists' experimenting
     with Italian and suggests instead that the poet is speaking
     and is using "his familiar technique of interspersing such
     words as 'signore' and 'gondola' as a contrapuntal theme to
     demonstrate the sounds of the city.... In order that the
     counterpoint may be heightened to the extreme, the word
     'gondola' is placed in the middle of Cincinnati...." <u>See</u>
     1963.3. Reprinted: 1966.19.

15   HARRINGTON, MICHAEL. "Modern Idiom, Traditional Spirit." <u>The
     Commonweal</u>, 61, no. 10 (10 December), 294-95.
        Reviews <u>Poems: 1923-1954</u>. The basic fact about Cum-
     mings' work is the "paradox of the popular revolutionary
     image and the conservative reality." The unconventional ar-
     rangements are largely irrelevant and the best poems are
     lyric in Valéry's sense, "the development of an exclamation,"
     but there "is a serious lack of depth in cummings' romanti-
     cism." (For replies to this review, <u>see</u> 1955.19 and
     1955.30.)

16   HOOD, EDWARD M. Review of <u>i: Six Nonlectures</u>. <u>Shenandoah</u>,
      5, no. 2 (Spring), 74-78.
           Examines <u>i: Six Nonlectures</u>, summarizing them and sug-
      gesting that the only criticism to be raised against them
      is an over-adroitness of language pleasing to a lecture
      audience but distracting to a reader.

17   JARRELL, RANDALL. "A Poet's Own Way." <u>New York Times Book</u>
      <u>Review</u> (31 October), p. 6.
           Reviews <u>Poems: 1923-1954</u> and finds it a "formidable col-
      lection," but complains of Cummings' excessive pride, his
      monotony of subject, tone, mood, melody, and technique, and
      his tendency to split man "into a delicate unique Ariel...
      and...a Brooklyn Caliban." Reprinted: 1962.9.

18   KAZIN, ALFRED. "E. E. Cummings and His Fathers." <u>The New</u>
      <u>Yorker</u>, 24, no. 46 (2 January), 57-59.
           Reviews <u>i: Six Nonlectures</u>. Kazin comments on Cummings'
      sentimentality, describes his dual character as traditional-
      ist and clown, and discusses his autobiographical remarks
      in terms of that character and of his relationship to cer-
      tain transcendentalists and other American originals. Re-
      printed: 1955.15; 1962.9; 1972.10.

19   LEARY, LEWIS. "Cummings, Edward Estlin," in his <u>Articles on</u>
      <u>American Literature: 1900-1950</u>. Durham, North Carolina:
      Duke University Press, pp. 65-66.
           A bibliography of Cummings scholarship published between
      1922 and 1950.

20   MOORE, GEOFFREY. "E. E. Cummings," in his <u>The Penguin Book of</u>
      <u>Modern American Verse</u>. London: Penguin Books, pp. [177]-
      79.
           Discusses Cummings' themes and techniques in general
      terms in a headnote to a selection of his poems.

21   MORSE, SAMUEL F. "A Man and His Work." <u>Hartford Courant Maga-</u>
      <u>zine</u> (7 November), p. 19.
           Reviews <u>Poems: 1923-1954</u>; finds that, if their initial
      shock has worn off, "the staggering typography, the aston-
      ishing verbal virtuosity, and the often-amazing subject
      matter have acquired substance and persuasiveness, the au-
      thority of rightness."

22   NORMAN, CHARLES. "A New Nonanthology." <u>Saturday Review</u>, 37,
      no. 5 (30 January), 18.
           Notices <u>i: Six Nonlectures</u> as reminding us of the "deep-
      ly serious side" of a "dedicated man" who is "so completely

1954

creative that even his lectures...offer new esthetic experiences."

23   REDMAN, BEN RAY. "Ground Breaker." Saturday Review, 37, no.
      27 (3 July), 19.
           Reviews 1 X 1. "Like our nuclear physicists, Cummings
      employs fission and fusion: he breaks the familiar down
      into unfamiliar fractions and he fuses elsewhere elements
      of experience that have not met before."

24   ROSENTHAL, M. L. On Cummings, in Symbols and Values: An
      Initial Study. Thirteenth Symposium of the Conference on
      Science, Philosophy and Religion. Edited by Lyman Bryson,
      Louis Finkelstein, R. M. Maciver, and Richard McKeon. New
      York: The Conference on Science, Philosophy and Religion
      in their Relation to the Democratic Way of Life, pp. 336-37.
           In a discussion of the recurrent symbolic situation in
      modern American poetry of the sensibility outraged by a
      regimented world, notes Cummings' "hedonistic placing of
      value-sources and delight in the imagery of nature."

25   SAROYAN, WILLIAM. "There Ought to Be More." The Nation, 178,
      no. 9 (27 February), 177-78.
           Reviews i: Six Nonlectures, summarizing thus: "what a
      book, what a poet, what a man."

26   SICKELS, ELEANOR M. "The Unworld of E. E. Cummings." American
      Literature, 26, no. 2 (May), 223-38.
           Argues that, although Cummings' lyric poetry has in-
      creased in effectiveness in his later poems, the satiric
      has become "less effective as either propaganda or art" be-
      cause of "a nihilism, a near solipsism, which is the re-
      ductio ad absurdum of what is in itself a virtue--his indi-
      vidualism." These matters Sickels traces through Cummings'
      career, concluding that satire must include a tragic sense
      of human dignity as well as "sharp amusement and bitter in-
      vective" and that Cummings' does not.

27   STALLMAN, R. W. and R. E. WATTERS. "An Interpretation of E. E.
      Cummings' 'Anyone Lived in a Pretty How Town,'" in their The
      Creative Reader: An Anthology of Fiction, Drama, and Poet-
      ry. New York: The Ronald Press Co., pp. 885-87.
           Describes the poem as "simple to understand." "Cummings
      uses language 'reflexively,' every word being counterpointed
      against another." At the literal level, there is a narra-
      tive plot. "What makes the poem seem so strange or seeming-
      ly incomprehensible is its uncommon arrangement of common
      words, its wrenched syntax, and its coining of new words

from old ones by reconverting their dictionary meaning and usage." These matters are discussed in some detail.

28   TATE, ALLEN. "Edward Estlin Cummings," in his <u>Sixty American Poets: 1896-1944</u>. Washington: The Library of Congress, pp. 19-21.
        The Cummings entry is slightly updated in this revision of 1945.2.

29   TYLER, PRISCILLA. "Critique," in <u>The Case for Poetry: A New Anthology</u>. Edited by Frederick L. Gwynn, Ralph W. Condee, and Arthur O. Lewis, Jr. Englewood Cliffs, New Jersey: Prentice-Hall, pp. 80-81.
        Analyzes grammar as a poetic device in "anyone lived in a pretty how town."

30   WILLIAMS, WILLIAM CARLOS. "E. E. Cummings' Paintings and Poems." <u>Arts Digest</u>, 29 (1 December), 7-8.
        Comments on Cummings as a painter, giving special credit to his watercolors, and as a poet.

31   WILLIAMS, WILLIAM CARLOS. "Lower Case Cumming," in his <u>Selected Essays of William Carlos Williams</u>. New York: Random House, pp. 263-67.
        Reprint of 1946.23.

<u>1955</u>

1   BODE, CARL. "E. E. Cummings: The World of 'Un.'" <u>Poetry</u>, 86, no. 6 (September), 358-63.
        Reviews <u>i: Six Nonlectures</u> and <u>Poems: 1923-1954</u>, agreeing with Blackmur's criticisms of Cummings' language (<u>see</u> 1931.1), finding the verse without development and in <u>i: Six Nonlectures</u> "nothing new," and concluding that "briskly vibrating sound and verbal paradox" are not enough to make poetry. Paired with a different view by Logan (<u>see</u> 1955.20). Revised: 1961.2.

2   BRINNIN, JOHN MALCOLM. On Cummings, in his <u>Dylan Thomas in America: An Intimate Journal</u>. Boston: Little, Brown, and Co., pp. 26-27.
        Recounts a meeting between Thomas and Cummings at the latter's home.

3   CARRUTH, HAYDEN. Review of <u>Poems: 1923-1954</u>. <u>Perspectives USA</u>, no. 12 (Summer), pp. 139-40.

1955

> Notices <u>Poems: 1923-1954</u>, in an omnibus review, as "a monumental testimony to the experimental impulse." Too often, however, the experiments are superficial, the typography is an obstruction, and "the first objective of experimentalism--an ultimate precision of language--" is lost sight of.

4   CIARDI, JOHN. "The Seductiveness of E. E. Cummings." <u>The Nation</u>, 180, no. 7 (12 February), 142.
> Reviews <u>Poems: 1923-1954</u>, noting Cummings' integrity and artistry and finding his world oversimplified.

5   COLE, THOMAS. Review of <u>Poems: 1923-1954</u>. <u>Imagi</u>, 6, no. 4, [13].
> Discusses <u>Poems: 1923-1954</u>, worrying that Cummings' achievements are too often static but asserting that his "love and nature poems are certain to endure."

6   DEUTSCH, BABETTE. Review of <u>Poems: 1923-1954</u>. <u>Accent</u>, 15, no. 1 (Winter), 73-77.
> Examines <u>Poems: 1923-1954</u> in an omnibus review; finds that, if Cummings has not matured, he has kept his "verve." His successful poems translate into his idiom "the assault of experience." His mark is his love of movement and his skill in recording it. Deutsch also comments on Cummings' lapses into sentimentality, vulgarity, or self-repetition, his conceptual vocabulary, tendency toward allegory, mastery of rhythm, and unevenness, and compares him with the Irish poet James Stephens.

7   DOS PASSOS, JOHN. "Off the Shoals," in <u>The Shock of Recognition</u>. Second edition. Edited by Edmund Wilson. New York: Farrar, Straus and Cudahy, pp. 1247-53.
> Reprint of 1922.6.

8   FELHEIM, MARVIN. "Cummings' 'In Just--.'" <u>The Explicator</u>, 14, no. 2 (November), Item 11.
> Describes the poem as having "three movements, each built about the refrain of the balloonman's whistle; each movement has a spatial as well as a tonal quality; both qualities are quite definitely suggested by the placement of words on the page.... The three movements explore the phenomenon of spring in time and space and sound; all three convey the sense of wonder in terms of a simple design (a horizontal line, a circle, a vertical line...) and in terms of simple sound." <u>See</u> 1965.29. Reprinted: 1966.13.

9   FRASER, G. S. "The Aesthete and the Sensationalist." <u>Partisan Review</u>, 22, no. 2 (Spring), [265]-72.

Reviews Cummings' Poems: 1923-1954 with The Collected
Poems of Wallace Stevens, discussing the two poets in a mock
dialogue and a more conventional essay. Fraser finds Cummings' use of language "sensationalist" and argues that,
when judged by the highest standards, his poetry is missing
something central, "the complex personal relationships of
men and women." For this theme he substitutes "a celebration of the sexual appetites and achievements of the hearty
male animal" and "of a kind of mystical attitude toward life
in general." Fraser also lists "marks of permanent adolescence" in Cummings' work, notes that he is a "lyrical"
rather than a "tragic" or "comic" writer, praises the readability and documentary value of his poems, and comments on
his philosophy. Reprinted: 1957.8.

10   GRAVES, ROBERT. "The Essential E. E. Cummings, A Review of
Six Nonlectures," in his The Crowning Privilege: Collected
Essays on Poetry. London: Cassell and Co., pp. 161-65.
Reprint of 1954.13.

11   HENRY, NAT. "Cummings' 'These Children Singing In Stone A.'"
The Explicator, 13, no. 8 (June), Item 51.
Expands on Moseley's reading (see 1950.15). Henry suggests that Cummings is more conventional in this poem than
usual and "rewrites" the poem to demonstrate his point. He
also suggests that "Cummings has indeed captured in words
the instant of beauty unchanging forever in stone." Reprinted: 1966.22.

12   HOFFMAN, FREDERICK J. On Cummings, in his The Twenties:
American Writing in the Postwar Decade. New York: The
Viking Press, pp. 62-66, 220-21.
Considers The Enormous Room and Eimi as examples of the
peculiar influence of World War I on postwar attitudes "toward those who continued to live and believe 'conventionally.'" Hoffman also comments on Him, calling it the "most
remarkable American experiment in the expressionist drama."
Reprinted: 1965.14.

13   HONIG, EDWIN. "'Proud of His Scientific Attitude.'" The
Kenyon Review, 17, no. 3 (Summer), 484-91.
Reviews Poems: 1923-1954, calling Cummings "the expressionist par excellence." He writes three kinds of poems, on
love, on hating, and on nature, and his "fastidious syntactical distortions are so well-contrived they suggest something of the manner and formal qualities of the heroic
couplet; but in effect they often cloak attitudes that are
cantankerous or juvenile." Comparing Cummings to his

contemporaries, Honig argues that, unlike them, "he derives little from symbolism or imagism, and despite his verbal and typographic eccentricities he is very close to a traditional poet like Frost." He also comments on Cummings' connection with Pound and with other users of conversational and idiomatic speech and explores his "assertive Puritan" and essentially American stance.

14 JACKINSON, ALEX. "E. E. Cummings: The Lark and the Larrikin." Olivant Quarterly, 1 (Second Quarter), 137-42.
Comments on Cummings' "hates and his likes," on his attempting "to do with words what the abstractionists do with the brush," on his relationships to the literary scene of the twenties, and on his desire to achieve that "precision which creates movement."

15 KAZIN, ALFRED. "E. E. Cummings and His Fathers," in his The Inmost Leaf: A Selection of Essays. New York: Harcourt, Brace and Co., pp. 191-96.
Reprint of 1954.18.

16 KUNITZ, STANLEY J. and VINETA COLBY. "Cummings, Edward Estlin," in their Twentieth Century Authors: A Biographical Dictionary of Modern Literature, First Supplement. New York: The H. W. Wilson Co., pp. 250-51.
Encyclopedia article updates previous entry (see 1942.2), with biographical, critical, and bibliographical material.

17 LAUTER, PAUL. E. E. Cummings: Index to First Lines and Bibliography of Works By and About the Poet. Denver, Colorado: Alan Swallow, 46 pp.
Revised publication of appendices to author's thesis, originally available in carbon copy of typescript. With a revised introduction, ten new poems indexed, and the index rearranged to present publication information chronologically. Added sections give places of publication of uncollected poems, appearances of art works by Cummings in periodicals, and partially descriptive bibliographies of Cummings' books. The checklist of news stories, miscellaneous articles, and critiques and reviews is updated and expanded. Revision of 1953.9. For supplements, see 1955.18 and 1957.14. Reprinted: 1971.13; 1976.14; 1977.4.

18 LAUTER, PAUL and S. V. BAUM. "E. E. Cummings Bibliography-- Supplement One." Available from the authors, 3 pp. Mimeographed.
Supplement to 1955.17. Updates and corrects the earlier bibliography. See also 1957.14.

19 LOGAN, JOHN. "E. E. Cummings." The Commonweal, 61, no. 15
    (14 January), 409-410.
        Replies, in a letter to the editors, to Harrington's
    review of Poems: 1923-1954 (see 1954.15), complaining that
    it damns with faint praise and commenting on Cummings' sense
    of language, his use of the lyric, and his relation to
    Eliot's ideas about tradition and the individual talent.
    (See also 1955.30.)

20 LOGAN, JOHN. "Six of One and Six Hundred of the Other."
    Poetry, 86, no. 6 (September), 353-58.
        Reviews i: Six Nonlectures and Poems: 1923-1954,
    stressing Cummings' rejection of tyranny and his compassion.
    i is discussed as an act of self-transcendence and a cele-
    bration of the human spirit. In commenting on Poems: 1923-
    1954, Logan notes Cummings' development and discusses his
    typographical, orthographical, and grammatical inventions.
    Cummings' accomplishment in general is described as "monu-
    mental" and "prodigious." Paired with a different view by
    Bode (see 1955.1).

21 MAURER, ROBERT EDWARD. "E. E. Cummings: A Critical Study."
    Ph.D. dissertation, University of Wisconsin.
        Argues that more than any other modern author Cummings
    "consistently and forcefully maintains that his work is
    himself." "In studying Cummings' life, one inevitably be-
    comes conscious of the unifying theme that underlies his
    career and is reflected in every facet of his writing: the
    isolation of the individual artist-human being from soci-
    ety." This theme, as it was developed and expressed in
    Cummings' life and work over the course of his career, is
    discussed in detail.

22 MAURER, ROBERT E[DWARD]. "Latter-Day Notes on E. E. Cummings'
    Language." The Bucknell Review, 5 (May), 1-23.
        Partially rebuts Blackmur's essay on Cummings' language
    (1931.1). Maurer agrees that Blackmur's points are somewhat
    valid in relation to the early poetry, but argues that Cum-
    mings' use of language has grown in the later poems, espe-
    cially in terms of his technique of employing certain
    concrete or abstract words as a "metaphorical shorthand for
    concepts." In the later poems, Cummings' metonymical lan-
    guage often provides the thrills of uniqueness and compre-
    hension and becomes increasingly precise. His technique in
    creating new uses for favorite words "is to accumulate mean-
    ings for each of them that total up to the same kind of
    positive and negative oppositions that are set against each
    other throughout his work." "In a way he is creating an

easy cipher of meaning, penetrable but not completely so at
first sight. And is this not also the case of any author
who utilizes a few dominant symbols in order to express his
special insight into experience, who must make each use of
a symbol function in its context and yet adds to its meaning
with each repeated use?" Maurer also points out that Cummings' rhythmic skills are increasingly developed in the
later poems. Reprinted: 1972.10.

23 MAYO, ROBERT D. "Cummings' 'Chanson Innocente, I,'" in Read-
ing Modern Poetry: A Critical Anthology. Edited by Paul
Engle and Warren Carrier. Chicago: Scott, Foresman and
Co., pp. 133-36.
Reprint of 1947.10.

24 MOORE, MARIANNE. "Humility, Concentration and Gusto," in her
Predilections. New York: The Viking Press, pp. 12-21,
passim.
Remarks that "little man in a hurry" (254, no thanks)
indicates precise emphasis by "the ordering of words" rather
than by punctuation. Reprinted: 1956.12 and 1965.19.

25 MOORE, MARIANNE. "One Times One," in her Predilections. New
York: The Viking Press, pp. 140-43.
Reprint of 1944.11.

26 POORE, CHARLES. Review of Poems: 1923-1954. New York Times
(3 February), p. 21.
Reviews Poems: 1923-1954 with Stevens' collected poems,
noting Cummings' fine ear for rhythm, his music and wit,
and his "permanent iconoclasm."

27 RUS, LOUIS C[ALVIN]. "Structural Ambiguity: A Note on Meaning
and the Linguistic Analysis of Literature with Illustrations
from E. E. Cummings." Language Learning, 6, nos. 1 and 2,
62-67.
Comments on Cummings' poem 19 from 50 Poems and "in" to
evidence the argument that linguistic analysis of such matters as structural ambiguity can be a form of literary
criticism if and when the linguistic facts are shown to be
meaningful within the literary work. Reprinted from
1955.28.

28 RUS, LOUIS CALVIN. "Structural Ambiguity in the Poetry of
E. E. Cummings." Ph.D. dissertation, University of Michigan.
Explores "structural ambiguities in Cummings' poetry,
relating them to the typographical elements and the meanings

of the poems." Linguistic method and analysis are employed
to these ends. A portion of the dissertation is reprinted:
1955.27.

29 SCHLAUCH, MARGARET. On Cummings, in her The Gift of Language.
    New York: Dover Publications, pp. 247, 249-51.
        Reprint of 1942.3.

30 SCHOECK, R. J. "E. E. Cummings." The Commonweal, 61, no. 22
    (4 March), 585-86.
        Replies to Logan's response (see 1955.19) to Harrington's
    review of Poems: 1923-1954 (see 1954.15) by quoting several
    negative or mixed criticisms of Cummings' work.

31 VON ABELE, RUDOLPH. "'Only to Grow': Change in the Poetry of
    E. E. Cummings." PMLA, 70, no. 5 (December), 913-33.
        Rebuts the frequent charge that Cummings' poetry is with-
    out development by evidencing its growth through three
    periods in three technical and two thematic categories. The
    periods are 1913-1926, 1926-1935, and 1935-1950. The tech-
    niques are typographical rhetoric, syntactic dislocation,
    and word-formation. The themes are romantic love and the
    satire of science and intellect. In technique and in theme,
    Cummings has moved from impressionist presentation and evo-
    cation to a more abstract concern with asserting, remon-
    strating, and defining. These matters are discussed in
    detail.

32 WEBSTER, HARVEY CURTIS. "The Poetry of E. E. Cummings." The
    New Leader, 38, no. 25 (20 June), 23-24.
        Reviews Poems: 1923-1954, finding Cummings' view of life
    more a matter of hope than of belief and admiring his quali-
    ties of anger and ecstasy.

1956

1 BOSQUET, ALAIN. On Cummings, in his Anthologie De La Poésie
   Américaine: Des Origines a Nos Jours. Paris: Librairie
   Stock, pp. 9, 27, 31, 298-99.
       Defines Cummings as a key figure in the post-World War I
   rupture of American from English verse. His reorderings of
   words, rhythm, and syntax are integral; his concentrated
   poems are powerfully evocative in both visual and aural
   modes. With a biographical note. In French.

2 BRADLEY, SCULLEY, RICHARD CROOM BEATTY, and E. HUDSON LONG.
   "E. E. Cummings," in their The American Tradition in

1956

Literature. Vol. 2. New York: W. W. Norton & Co., 1202-
1203.
Brief headnote introduces a selection of Cummings' poems,
presenting biographical information and commentary on his
experimental techniques and traditional themes. Revised
editions: 1961.3; 1967.3; 1974.2.

3   BREIT, HARVEY. "E. E. Cummings," in his The Writer Observed.
Cleveland, Ohio: The World Publishing Co., pp. 159-61.
Reprint of 1950.6.

4   BROOKS, VAN WYCK and OTTO L. BETTMANN. On Cummings, in their
Our Literary Heritage: A Pictorial History of the Writer
in America. New York: E. P. Dutton & Co., pp. 233, 237.
Describes Cummings as "an enemy of clichés, pomposity
and cant," behind whose "mockery lay a sense of the infinite
worth of the individual...menaced by a standardized world."

5   DEUTSCH, BABETTE. On Cummings, in her Poetry in Our Time.
New York: Columbia University Press, pp. 85, 111-16, 352-
54, 369.
Reprint of 1952.6. Revised: 1963.8.

6   FRANKENBERG, LLOYD. On Cummings, in his Invitation to Poetry:
A Round of Poems from John Skelton to Dylan Thomas, Arranged
with Comments. New York: Doubleday & Co., pp. 73-74, 257-
60, 280-82.
Commentary on three Cummings poems. "no man, if men are
gods; but if gods must" is an arc refracting the opposites
of Apollonian order and Dionysian abandon. "what a proud
dreamhorse" creates movement, realism, and an affectionate
tone and uses the Pegasus myth to expand the dimensions of
its description. "darling! because my blood can sing" is
a "dancing song" which "brings together two strands often
separate in his poetry: the lyric and the satiric." Reprinted: 1968.13.

7   GRAVES, ROBERT. "The Essential E. E. Cummings, A Review of
Six Nonlectures," in his The Crowning Privilege: Collected
Essays on Poetry. Garden City, New York: Doubleday & Co.,
pp. 166-70.
Reprint of 1954.13.

8   HART, JAMES D. "Cummings, E[dward] E[stlin]," in his The Ox-
ford Companion to American Literature. Third edition. New
York: Oxford University Press, pp. 172-73.
Slightly updated entry. Revised edition of 1941.7.

9   LIPTON, LAWRENCE. On Cummings. Departure, 3, no. 9 (Spring),
     9.
          Remarks, in an essay on "Disaffiliation and the Art of
     Poverty," that Cummings is "the most uncompromising and
     alienated" of American poets and connects his lyrics of
     social protest with those of Kenneth Patchen and with the
     poetry of Burns and Blake.

10   LLOYD, DONALD J. and HARRY R. WARFEL. On Cummings, in their
     American English in its Cultural Setting. New York:
     Alfred A. Knopf, p. 328.
          Describes Cummings as having "most deliberately used
     language the way a sculptor uses stone" and sets "Portrait
     VIII" ("Buffalo Bill's") in phonemic notation as an example
     of that notation's value as a tool for observation.

11   MAURER, ROBERT E. "E. E. Cummings' Him." The Bucknell Review,
     6 (May), 1-27.
          Discusses the negative critical reaction to the Province-
     town Playhouse's production of Cummings' expressionist play
     and examines the play in detail to demonstrate that its
     point was badly missed. Maurer argues that the techniques
     of Him are informed by Cummings' desire to create active
     versus static works of art, and he describes and paraphrases
     the play's actions and nonactions to demonstrate its drama-
     tic experimentation and its treatment of the "problem of the
     artist" in relation to his self, his society, and his loved
     one. Maurer also briefly relates Him to other expressionist
     dramatic experiments of the twenties. Reprinted: 1972.10.

12   MOORE, MARIANNE. "Humility, Concentration and Gusto," in her
     A Marianne Moore Reader. New York: The Curtis Publishing
     Co., pp. 123-30, passim.
          Reprint of 1955.24.

13   [RUSSELL, PETER.] Review of i: Six Nonlectures. Nine, 4,
     no. 2 (April), 61.
          Notices the publication of Cummings' Norton "nonlectures,"
     considering them a "most useful general introduction to Mr.
     Cummings' life and works."

14   SCHLAUCH, MARGARET. On Cummings, in her Modern English and
     American Poetry: Techniques and Ideologies. London: C. A.
     Watts & Co., pp. 32, 37, 65-67.
          Comments briefly on Cummings' word coinage by prefix,
     his use of "pure repetition," and his shifting of speech
     parts. This last, which makes "concretes express abstract
     ideas," is used excessively.

1956

15 WATSON, BARBARA. "The Dangers of Security: E. E. Cummings'
    Revolt against the Future." The Kenyon Review, 18, no. 4
    (Autumn), 519-37.
        Argues that Cummings has been in constant rebellion
    against "the future now arriving," agrees with Allen Tate
    (see 1946.21) that he is one of the only modern poets to
    retain his humanity and his poetry, and examines the ques-
    tion this raises of how Cummings has better related to his
    world and the artist's place in it than his more directly
    socially concerned fellows. Watson answers this question
    by discussing Cummings in relation to his contemporaries,
    by describing his rejection of "the intellectualizing, de-
    vitalizing, and neutering of emotion" which enables the
    development of mass societies, and by outlining his revital-
    izing of the lyric impulse for the modern world. She ex-
    plains the method of this revitalization and discusses
    Cummings' untheoretical theory of feeling, impulse, and
    inclination. "Growth and risk emerge as the cardinal prin-
    ciples of Cummings' anarchistic freedom." This freedom is
    not a principle of disorder, but a special kind of order,
    one which a man cannot control or fully know, but with which
    he must flow in willing risk. "Cummings' own poetry is
    true to this theory." These attitudes help explain Cum-
    mings' lack of development in the sense of progress toward
    an increasingly accurate portrayal of the world. Reprinted:
    1972.10.

1957

1 BLACKMUR, R. P. "Notes on E. E. Cummings' Language," in his
    Form and Value in Modern Poetry. Garden City, New York:
    Doubleday & Co., pp. [287]-312.
        Reprint of 1931.1.

2 BRAUER, GEORGE C. "Cummings' '(one!).'" The Explicator, 16,
    no. 3 (December), Item 14.
        Expands Rus's interpretation (see 1957.20), emphasizing
    further the way in which grammatical and descriptive details
    in the poem express the theme of unity. Reprinted: 1966.4.

3 BREKKE, PAAL. On Cummings, in his Amerikansk Lyrikk. Oslo:
    H. Aschehoug & Co. (W. Nygaard), pp. 146-48.
        Briefly presents biographical, bibliographic, and criti-
    cal material to supplement the translation of seven Cummings
    poems into Norwegian. In Norwegian.

1957

4   BROOKS, VAN WYCK. On Cummings, in his Days of the Phoenix:
    The Nineteen-Twenties I Remember. New York: E. P. Dutton
    & Co., pp. 10, 30-31, 67, 155.
        Occasional references to Cummings as a literary figure
    of the twenties, describing him as "the last of the Yankee
    come-outers" and a disillusioned romantic.

5   COFFMAN, STANLEY K. On Cummings. Books Abroad, 31, no. 1
    (Winter), 11.
        In a survey of American poetry from 1927 to 1952, de-
    scribes Cummings as having ventured beyond imagism and
    objectivism to consistently assert "the ultimate value of
    the life of the individual." This individualism is often
    "a little unreal" because oversimplified.

6   COPLEY, FRANK O. On Cummings, in his Gaius Valerius Catullus:
    The Complete Poetry. Ann Arbor: The University of Michigan
    Press, pp. viii-ix, xiv.
        Comments on Cummings in a discussion of Catullus' use of
    persons, his allusiveness, and his pioneering innovations.
    (The translations of Catullus given here make use of many
    of Cummings' techniques.)

7   DE FORD, SARA. "E. E. Cummings," in her Lectures on Modern
    American Poetry. [Tokyo:] Hokuseido Press, pp. [133]-44.
        A general examination of Cummings' poetry emphasizing his
    experimental techniques and conventional themes. "when god
    lets my body be," "Sunset" ("stinging"), and "Chanson Inno-
    cente, I" are discussed in some detail. Slightly revised
    from lectures delivered at Tokyo University and Tsuda
    College.

8   FRASER, G. S. "E. E. Cummings and Wallace Stevens," in
    Literature in America. Edited by Philip Rahv. New York:
    Meridian Books, pp. 350-57.
        Reprint of 1955.9.

9   FREEDMAN, MORRIS. On Cummings. Southern Folklore Quarterly,
    21, no. 4 (December), 194.
        Notes, in an essay on natural jazz rhythms in folk songs,
    the presence of jazz rhythms in Cummings' poems.

10 FRIED, ERICH. "E. E. Cummings oder Die Sprache, in der man
    nicht lügen kann." Texte und Zeichen, 2, no. 15 (15 Septem-
    ber), 496-511.
        Comments briefly and generally on Cummings in preface to
    renderings of four poems--"the moon is hiding in," "anyone
    lived in a pretty how town," "my father moved through dooms

81

of love," and "Impression--IV"--into German. Each of the translated poems receives a brief introductory comment. In German.

11   FRIEDMAN, NORMAN. "Diction, Voice, and Tone: The Poetic Language of E. E. Cummings." PMLA, 72, no. 5 (December), 1036-59.
Rejects Blackmur's strictures on Cummings' language (see 1931.1) and argues that the poet's style is "mixed." At its center is a vocabulary of a certain sort which can be described as his "neutral mode." This "may be defined as a modified romantic style--romantic because of the quality and quantity of certain 'sweet,' 'soft,' 'warm,' and 'moist' words...and modified because of the frequent intrusion of antipathetic or 'plain,' 'hard,' 'cool,' and 'dry' words." This mode's juxtaposition "allows Cummings either to intensify or modify certain traditional associations of certain traditional words." The "clash of vocabularies" this suggests is the crucial fact of Cummings' style and is rooted in his vision of life which, "although transcendental, begins in an early and never-failing sensuous delight in the physical world." Varying to the right of the norm of the neutral mode "produces a purely serious, archaic, reverential, and formal style, while varying to the left creates a purely vulgar, violent, burlesque, and mock style." In addition to the three relatively pure styles of neutral, formal, and burlesque is Cummings' previously mentioned "mixed" style in which the three come together in a "compound of voices and tones." Friedman also comments on Cummings' development of a "conceptual vocabulary" by the transformation of other parts of speech into nouns. This essay appears in slightly revised form as chapter 3, "Voices," of Friedman's E. E. Cummings: The Art of His Poetry, 1960.8.

12   FRIEDMAN, NORMAN. "The Why of E. E. Cummings." The University of Connecticut Fine Arts Festival Magazine and Connecticut Writer, pp. 2-5.
Reprint, with minor changes, of 1952.8.

13   HARPER, MR. "Bard in Boston." Harper's Magazine, 215, no. 1288 (September), [86]-87.
Comments on Cummings' performance at the 1957 Boston Arts Festival.

14   LAUTER, PAUL and S. V. BAUM. "E. E. Cummings Bibliography--Supplement Two." Available from the authors, 4 pp. Mimeographed.

1957

Supplements to 1955.17 and 1955.18. Updates, expands,
and corrects the earlier bibliography and its first supplement.

*15   LEHMAN, BETTE. "Interpreter of the Moment." The Stylus, 2
        (Spring), 7-10.
            Cited in Baum, 1962.9.

16   LEVIN, HARRY. On Cummings, in his Contexts of Criticism.
        Cambridge: Harvard University Press, pp. 166, 167, 231,
        240, 243.
            Notes Cummings' "temperamental kinship" with Hemingway,
        his counterpointing of slogans against weather, and the
        Marxist response to his work.

17   NIST, JOHN. "E. E. Cummings Speaks to the Academic World."
        Artesian, 2, no. 4 (May-June), 9.
            Reports on a talk and reading given by Cummings at the
        University of Michigan.

18   OLIVER, EGBERT S. "E. E. Cummings." Literary Criterion, 3
        (Summer), 1-12.
            A general introduction to Cummings. The "force and
        weight of his poetic effort and poetic achievement have been
        toward experience and away from mere craftsmanship." He
        "exalts the individual--the living self--above the group,
        the mass, the state."

19   RIZZARDI, ALFREDO. "Un Clown del Nostro Tempo." Letterature
        Moderne, 7, no. 4 (July-August), 402-21.
            Argues that the distance between Cummings' public and
        critical reputations has to do with his resistance of the
        dominant metaphysical mode of his generation and his crea-
        tion and celebration of a kind of anarchic moralism, a
        sensory, clownish, clowning poetry of joy and affirmation.
        Several poems are discussed from this angle. In Italian.
        Reprinted: 1959.26.

20   RUS, LOUIS C. "Cummings' '(one!).'" The Explicator, 15, no.
        6 (March), Item 40.
            Finds the poem to consist "of three descriptive sentences
        which are united by overlapping language structures," ana-
        lyzes the "resulting grammatical ambiguities," and discovers
        that those ambiguities both unite the poem in its theme of
        unity and demonstrate the operation of the creative process.
        See 1957.2. Reprinted: 1966.36.

1957

21 WEALES, GERALD. On Cummings, in his "The Poet as Player," in
    New World Writing, No. 11. New York: The New American
    Library, pp. 238-39.
        Briefly describes the precision of a public reading by
    Cummings.

22 WILLIAMS, WILLIAM CARLOS. On Cummings, in his The Selected
    Letters of William Carlos Williams. Edited by John C.
    Thirlwall. New York: McDowell, Obolensky, pp. 64, 191,
    327-28.
        Contains a letter to James Laughlin in which Cummings is
    described--with Pound--as one of the two most distinguished
    American poets, and a letter to Cummings about the Art Di-
    gest essay Williams was to write on Cummings' poems and
    paintings (see 1954.30).

                              1958

1   AIKEN, CONRAD. On Cummings, in his A Reviewer's ABC: Collec-
    ted Criticisms of Conrad Aiken from 1916 to the Present.
    New York: Meridian Books, pp. 285-88.
        Reprint of 1941.1.

2   ALDRIDGE, JOHN W. On Cummings, in his After the Lost Genera-
    tion: A Critical Study of the Writers of Two Wars. New
    York: The Noonday Press, pp. 13-16, 88, 107, 113, 115.
        Reprint of 1951.1.

3   ANON. "The Latest from E. E. Cummings." Time, 72, no. 15
    (13 October), 104.
        Briefly notes the appearance of 95 poems, describing it
    as continuing Cummings' celebration of the life of feeling
    and demonstrating the "attention holding" quality of his
    typography.

4   ANON. "Shy But Richly Comic." Newsweek, 51, no. 22 (2 June),
    92.
        Reviews E. E. Cummings: A Miscellany, finding the col-
    lection of prose pieces uneven but various evidence of
    Cummings' "superb eye for whatever vibrating scene is be-
    fore him." The reviewer considers the art criticism "highly
    perceptive."

5   CECIL, DAVID and ALLEN TATE. "E(dward) E(stlin) Cummings," in
    their Modern Verse in English 1900-1950. New York: The
    Macmillan Co., pp. 648-49.
        Brief biographical and bibliographic note.

6 CROWDER, RICHARD. "Cummings' '48.'" The Explicator, 16, no.
   7 (April), Item 41.
        Analyzes the details of this poem ("floatfloaflof1f")
   "about the dance in general and Paul Draper in particular,"
   with special attention to the ways in which "Cummings' cus-
   tomary play with letters and marks of punctuation is especially suitable to this subject." Reprinted: 1966.9.

7 DEUTSCH, BABETTE. "Legerdemain and Wonder." New York Herald-
   Tribune Book Review (12 October), p. 3.
        Reviews 95 poems as employing Cummings' "customary tech-
   niques" and reiterating "his usual themes."

8 FIRMAGE, GEORGE J. "Introduction," in E. E. Cummings: A Miscellany. Edited by George J. Firmage. New York: The
   Argophile Press, pp. ix-x.
        Briefly explains sources of some of the fugitive Cum-
   mings' pieces collected in this volume. Revised edition:
   1965.10.

9 FITZGERALD, F. SCOTT. On Cummings, in his Afternoon of an
   Author. New York: Charles Scribner's Sons, pp. 120-21.
        Reprint of 1926.3.

10 FRIEDMAN, NORMAN. "The Poetic Mask of E. E. Cummings: Character and Thought of the Speaker." The Literary Review, 2,
   no. 1 (Autumn), 124-44.
        Asserts that Cummings' persona is a man apart from men
   and discusses the values of that persona. The persona
   dwells apart as "the servant of one cause only--freshness
   of response and accuracy in its expression--," the chief
   obstacle to which is submission to mass life. Cummings'
   speaker resists the latter and achieves the former. "The
   moral and philosophical values which this speaker entertains
   as a consequence of having such a character derive basical-
   ly, therefore, from this position of transcendence which he
   assumes." His morality is pre-lapsarian, and so "his reaction to suffering and evil is, since they are wholly man-
   made, hate unalloyed with pity." On the other hand, the
   state of beatitude may be achieved here and now and without
   divine intervention. Thus, his joy. It is in terms of
   these ideas that the speaker examines the areas of human
   thought and experience which concern him: love, death, and
   time; the natural and the artificial; society and the individual; and dream and reality. Love transcends death and
   time; the natural, the artificial; the individual, society;
   dream, reality. Friedman also discusses in some detail the
   conceptual vocabulary Cummings developed to deal with these

1958

ideas. Reprinted as part of chapter 1, "Vision," of Friedman's E. E. Cummings: The Art of His Poetry, 1960.8.

11   GRAVES, ROBERT. "Corn Can Sparkle Like a Star." New York
      Times Book Review (26 October), p. 59.
          Reviews 95 poems, commenting on Cummings' slow matura-
      tion, his uniqueness, and the sonic notation of his
      typography.

12   GREEN, PHILIP. "an unessay on ee cumMing$_S$." The New Republic,
      138, no. 20 (19 May), 24-26.
          A parodic essay, finding that Cummings is solipsistic
      when excessively unconventional and succeeds when he merges
      "the best features of innocence with convention."

13   GUNN, THOM. Review of 95 poems. The Yale Review, 48, no. 2
      (December), 299-300.
          Notices 95 poems in an omnibus review; Cummings' poetry
      is marred by vagueness, didacticism, and cliché, and "by
      now rather wearisome tricks." He does, however, have a
      talent for humorous and sentimental poems.

14   HESSE, EVA. "Nachwort," in her E. E. Cummings: Gedichte.
      Munich: Langewiesche-Brandt, unpaged.
          Six-page afterword to a translation of Cummings' poems
      into German presents general commentary on his longer prose
      works and on the themes and techniques of his poems. With
      a brief bibliography. In German.

15   HICKS, GRANVILLE. "The Intransigent E. E. Cummings." Saturday
      Review, 41, no. 47 (22 November), 14.
          Compares, in a review of Norman's biography, Cummings'
      radical individualism to Thoreau's and discusses it in re-
      lation to the judgments of the thirties and subsequent eras.

16   LAUTER, PAUL. "The Lyric Verse of E. E. Cummings." The New
      Leader, 41, no. 45 (8 December), 24-25.
          Reviews 95 poems. Cummings "continues to hold out
      against the organizational blandishments of contemporary
      Dagons. To Cummings, Love's still the only god, and Spring
      is his prophet." There has been no real "poetic growth" for
      Cummings because his integrity has made him "reject the
      changing world...asserting in its place the ultimate valid-
      ity of his own perceptions." Unfortunately, "the fog at the
      center of Cummings' language" has made these perceptions
      unknowable.

17   LEVIN, GERALD. "Cummings' 'Poem' ('Love's function...')."
      The Explicator, 17, no. 3 (December), Item 18.
          Explicates the poem in terms of Cummings' idea "that the
      self maintains its individuality even as it eternally ap-
      proaches union with nature through love." Reprinted:
      1966.30.

18   MAURIN, MARIO. "E. E. Cummings, 'le poeté maudit' de Greenwich
      Village nous parle de l'Europe, d'Apollinaire et de lui-
      même." Le Figaro Litteraire (5 July), p. 12.
          Describes Cummings' Greenwich Village home as prelude to
      an interview. The interviewer intersperses Cummings' com-
      ments with explanatory remarks of his own. In French.

19   NORMAN, CHARLES. The Magic-Maker: E. E. Cummings. New York:
      The Macmillan Co., 416 pp.
          A biographical study of Cummings' life, works, and en-
      vironments. Norman discusses Cummings' parents, his home
      life at Cambridge and Joy Farm, his years at Harvard, his
      life in Greenwich Village and Paris during the twenties,
      his trip to Russia, and--in less depth--the more or less
      public events of his career through 1955. He also provides
      factual and atmospheric background on the making of Eight
      Harvard Poets and The Enormous Room, on the events leading
      to Cummings' release from La Ferté Macé, on his reading, on
      his relationship with The Dial, on the details surrounding
      the publication of several of his volumes of poems, on his
      public readings, on his Boston Arts Festival performance,
      and on the Norton lectureship. There are chapters on Cum-
      mings as a playwright and a painter. Norman also includes
      much material--factual, anecdotal, and otherwise--difficult
      or impossible to obtain elsewhere; for example, he reprints
      Pound's review of Eimi from the New English Weekly and sug-
      gests (on information from Cummings' sister) a possible
      source for "in Just-." There are frequent and generous
      quotations from contemporary reviews of Cummings' works.
      The biography also contains a fair amount of critical com-
      ment, largely adulatory. With illustrations. Reprinted:
      1972.19; 1972.20. Revised: 1964.21; 1967.25.

20   PAGNINI, MARCELLO. "E. E. Cummings, Poeta Dell' Impressione
      Dell' Analisi." Studi Americani, 4; [343]-61.
          Discusses Cummings as a lyric poet concerned with captur-
      ing moments of primary perception and impression in all
      their simultaneity and comments on him in terms of such
      writers as Apollinaire and such movements as Symbolism,
      Imagism, and Futurism. In Italian.

1958

21   PRESS, JOHN. On Cummings, in his <u>The Chequer'd Shade: Re-
      flections on Obscurity in Poetry</u>. London: Oxford Univer-
      sity Press, pp. 15, 169-70.
          Suggests that Cummings has approached the kind of system
      of notation that would allow poetry to be read as though it
      were music which Hopkins contemplated but never effected.
      Press also notes Cummings' "dazzling vividness" of imagery
      and his "sophisticated orchestration" of musical themes,
      compares these aspects of his work to similar ones in Sit-
      well's, and offers "jake hates" as example.

22   QUASIMODO, SALVATORE. "Introduzione alle poesie di E. E.
      Cummings," in his <u>E. E. Cummings: Poesie Scelte</u>. Milan:
      All' Insegna del Pesce d' Oro, pp. 5-8.
          Reprint of 1953.12.

23   REDMAN, BEN RAY. "Pot-Boilers With Ideas." <u>New York Times
      Book Review</u> (15 June), p. 4.
          Reviews <u>E. E. Cummings: A Miscellany</u>, finding that many
      of the pieces are "pot-boilers," but that many of them are
      also "loaded with ideas and amusement, and that there is
      hardly one of them that does not tell us something of the
      man and mind from which the poetry has sprung."

24   SITWELL, EDITH. "E. E. Cummings," in her <u>The Atlantic Book of
      British and American Poetry</u>. Boston: Little, Brown and
      Co., pp. 911-12.
          Discusses "you are like the snow only" as an example of
      Cummings at his best. The poem's "delicate rhythm...is ob-
      tained not only by the varying length of the lines, but by
      the absence of external rhymes, coupled with the use of
      assonances and an occasional rhyme or dissonance placed...
      <u>within</u> the lines."

25   WIDMER, KINGSLEY. "Timeless Prose." <u>Twentieth Century Litera-
      ture</u>, 4, nos. 1-2 (April-July), [3]-8.
          Discusses <u>The Enormous Room</u> as a member of a peculiarly
      American prose tradition of works with the following "pre-
      dominant characteristics: a conscious violation and avoid-
      ance of traditional prose forms; the attempt to turn
      narrative prose into lyric poetry without the traditional
      formal order of poetry; the mixture of aesthetic functions--
      documentary, autobiographical, fictional, and poetic; and
      the experimentation with logical, causal and temporal rela-
      tionships in the effort to achieve different kinds of aes-
      thetic experience." <u>The Enormous Room</u> is discussed under
      these categories, especially the last. Widmer concludes
      that the "fragmentation of chronological time and the

subjective eternalizing of rhetorical time" in the "novel"
cannot give it coherence. Thus, at least intermittently,
Cummings provides novelistic time order. In Eimi, where
this last is abandoned, "timelessness...becomes a treadmill
to tedium."

<u>1958-1959</u>

1   BENTON, RICHARD P. "Explaining E. E. Cummings' 'One X.'"
    <u>Exercise Exchange</u>, 6 (December-February), 20-23.
        Suggests an exercise for demonstrating to students the
    aesthetic effect of Cummings' technique in "One X" ("death
    is more than").

<u>1959</u>

1   ANON. Additional Cummings' Drawings and Prints, in <u>The Dial</u>
    <u>and The Dial Collection</u>. Edited by the Worcester Art Museum.
    Worcester, Massachusetts: Worcester Art Museum, p. 102.
        Lists thirty-nine of Cummings' works included in <u>The Dial</u>
    collection, but not in the present exhibition.

2   ANON. Cummings' Drawings and Prints in <u>The Dial</u> Exhibition,
    in <u>The Dial and The Dial Collection</u>. Edited by the Worces-
    ter Art Museum. Worcester, Massachusetts: Worcester Art
    Museum, p. [90].
        Lists five Cummings' pen and ink drawings included in
    the exhibition.

3   ANON. Cummings' Paintings in <u>The Dial</u> Exhibition, in <u>The Dial</u>
    <u>and The Dial Collection</u>. Edited by the Worcester Art Mu-
    seum. Worcester, Massachusetts: Worcester Art Museum,
    p. 64.
        Comments briefly on Cummings' connection with <u>The Dial</u>
    and on his oil painting, "Sound," included in the exhibition.

4   BAKER, SHERIDAN. "Cummings and Catullus." <u>Modern Language</u>
    <u>Notes</u>, 74, no. 3 (March), 231-34.
        Examines how Cummings' use of a line from an allusive
    poem of Catullus intensifies the wry irony of his satire
    on progress, "o pr."

5   BEACH, SYLVIA. On Cummings, in her <u>Shakespeare and Company</u>.
    New York: Harcourt, Brace and Co., pp. 127-28.
        Notes the appearance of a selection from <u>The Enormous</u>
    <u>Room</u>, translated into French by George Duplaix, in the all-
    American number of Adrienne Monnier's <u>Le Navire d'Argent</u>.

1959

6   BERRYMAN, JOHN.   Review of 95 poems.   The American Scholar, 28,
        no. 3 (Summer), 388, 390.
            Suggests that Cummings' dependence on the parenthesis has
        to do with his attempt to achieve simultaneity and informal-
        ity, but may also be a defense against one of his worst
        faults, "hollow rhetoric."   Berryman finds sentimentality
        behind Cummings' "satirical and tough-guy attitudes" and
        finds it especially in 95 poems, a volume below Cummings'
        usual standard.

7   BOULTENHOUSE, CHARLES.   "Poems in the Shapes of Things."   Art
        News Annual, 28; 64-87, 178.
            Comments briefly on Cummings' "birds(" as a "shape poem."

8   BRITTON, JOHN.   "Cummings' 'Pity this Busy Monster, Manunkind.'"
        The Explicator, 18, no. 1 (October), Item 5.
            Explicates the poem and finds it a more successful pre-
        sentation of the theme of "Space being (don't forget to
        remember) Curved," that is, that modern man is trapped un-
        awares in a closed world of empty materialism.   See 1961.7
        and 1969.21.   Reprinted: 1966.5.

9   CANDELARIA, FREDERICK H.   "Cummings and Campion."   Notes and
        Queries, 204, no. 4 (April), 134-36.
            Examines Cummings' "what if a much of a which of a wind"
        as an "answer" to Thomas Campion's "what if a day, or a
        month, or a yeare."   Campion's poem "underscores the insig-
        nificance of man; Cummings answers with a statement of the
        magnificence of man."   Candelaria notes in conclusion that
        Cummings' allegiance, unlike that of most of his contempor-
        aries, is to the "Elizabethan poets of song" rather than to
        the Metaphysicals.

10   CHURCHILL, ALLEN.   On Cummings, in his The Improper Bohemians:
        A Re-creation of Greenwich Village in Its Heyday.   New York:
        E. P. Dutton & Co., pp. 120, 277, 290-92, 329.
            Notes Cummings' appearance in the Pagan, his place in the
        composite figure of the young man in Ernest Boyd's "Aesthete:
        Model 1924" in American Mercury (1 January 1924), responses
        to the Provincetown's production of Him, and his continua-
        tion of early Bohemian days in his home in Patchin Place.

11   DE JOUVENAL, RENAUD.   "Edward Estlin Cummings."   Europe, 37,
        nos. 358-359 (February-March), 132-33.
            Describes Cummings, in a headnote to several of his poems
        in French translation, as a poet who combines sentimental
        emotion with cynical realism and a technique based in typo-
        graphical distortion.   De Jouvenal discusses the difficulty

of translating Cummings, demonstrating the problems in the poem "(fea." In French.

12 DICKEY, JAMES. Review of 95 poems. The Sewanee Review, 67, no. 3 (July-September), 511-16.
     Examines 95 poems in an omnibus review. Because he believes Cummings' books are all alike, Dickey's approach is general. Cummings' poetry is seriously flawed, yet he constantly restores his work "to an eminence which seals the critic's mouth and changes him into a more perceptive being." In attempting to explain this paradox, Dickey explores those aspects of Cummings he most admires: not his "techniques," but his "quirky, indignant sharpness of observation," his "devotion to a spontaneous, outward-going... view of the world," his "personal daring with diction and image," his "personal and incorruptible relation to the English language," his "immediacy and intensity," and his constant effort "to establish and consecrate the moment." Reprinted: 1964.6; 1968.5; 1971.5.

13 DONOGHUE, DENIS. "Drame À Thèse: Auden and Cummings," in his The Third Voice: Modern British and American Verse Drama. Princeton, New Jersey: Princeton University Press, pp. 70-75.
     Summarizes and comments on the agon, protagonist, and antagonist of Cummings' Santa Claus, complimenting Cummings for recognizing that the stark terms of his thesis drama were suited to the conventions of a Morality play. Donaghue also notes that much "of the thought of Santa Claus is Wordsworthian in its concern for Understanding in preference to Knowledge, for Love in preference to Big Business."

14 HOLLANDER, JOHN. Review of 95 poems. Partisan Review, 26, no. 1 (Winter), 142-43.
     Notices 95 poems, in an omnibus review, as "a weak book, containing fewer interesting or charming poems than Xaîpe."

15 HOOD, EDWARD M. Review of 95 poems. Shenandoah, 10, no. 3 (Spring), [49]-53.
     Reviews 95 poems. Much of Cummings' famous obscurity is no more than camouflage for clichés. Because Cummings rejects the social quality of language, the only "vital context" of his poetry is in his own mind, "which remains, for us, permanently unknowable."

16 LOEB, HAROLD. On Cummings, in his The Way It Was. New York: Criterion Books, pp. 98, 108, 167-68, 169, 198.
     Brief references to Cummings, some in relation to the little magazine Broom, others anecdotal.

1959

17 LOGAN, JOHN. "The Advent of E. E. Cummings." The Commonweal,
   70, no. 9 (29 May), 233-35.
       Reviews 95 poems, commenting on Cummings' typical combin-
   ation of visual and auditory art, on Blackmur's remarks on
   his language (see 1931.1), and on Norman's biography (see
   1958.19), and arguing that Cummings' mentality "not only
   takes us back to the Pythagoreans" but also "forward to the
   Existentialists." Logan also comments on Cummings' relation
   to the Beat poets and compares him briefly to the other
   major figures of his generation.

18 MAURER, ROBERT. "Of, By, and For E. E. Cummings." The Antioch
   Review, 19, no. 2 (Summer), 281-87.
       Notices 95 poems, E. E. Cummings: A Miscellany, and
   Norman's The Magic-Maker: E. E. Cummings. Maurer comments
   on the anachronism of Cummings' intense personalism in an
   era when poets have struggled to extinguish personality,
   finds A Miscellany a convenience of largely documentary interest, and comments on Cummings' continuation of lyricism
   in 95 poems, particularly in those poems which sing "joy-
   ously of natural phenomena."

19 MILLS, RALPH J., JR. "The Poetry of Innocence: Notes on E. E.
   Cummings." The English Journal, 48, no. 8 (November), 433-
   42.
       Examines Cummings' opposition of "'civilized' scientific
   method" with the appraisal of being and becoming, the alter-
   nation of tradition and innovation in his early poetry, and
   his plotting--from his understanding of the infinite possi-
   bility of man--of "the two courses of satire and lyricism in
   his poetry." Cummings' techniques are the result of his
   concern with "the appearances and events of the world," and
   it is therefore not surprising that "he tries to approximate
   what he sees." His lyric poetry stems from "a trust in
   feeling rather than intellect." The satire "exists as the
   reverse of the lyric poems and indirectly reinforces the
   poet's claims for love, beauty, and the rights of the person." Mills also comments on Cummings' love poems and on
   his faith, describing him as an "outspoken, heterodox
   preacher."

*20 NIST, JOHN. On Cummings, in his "Critical Sketches in Anglo-
   American Literature." São-Paulo, Brazil: University of
   São-Paulo, pp. 9-11. Mimeographed.
       Cited in Baum, 1962.9. Professor Nist indicates that the
   work is unavailable.

21 OLSON, CHARLES. On Cummings, in his Projective Verse. New
    York: Totem Press, pp. 7-8.
        Reprint of 1950.16.

22 PEARCE, ROY HARVEY. On Cummings, in Interpretations of Ameri-
    can Literature. Edited by Charles Feidelson, Jr. and Paul
    Brodtkorb, Jr. New York: Oxford University Press, pp. 379-
    82.
        Reprint of 1952.14.

23 REXROTH, KENNETH. On Cummings. Translated by J.-J. Fol and
    P. Gavarry. Europe, 37, nos. 358-59 (February-March), 61.
        Comments briefly on the influence of French poetry on
    Cummings. In French.

24 RICH, DANIEL CATTON. On Cummings, in The Dial and The Dial
    Collection. Edited by the Worcester Art Museum. Worcester,
    Massachusetts: Worcester Art Museum, pp. 16, 18.
        Comments briefly on Cummings as a modernist contributor
    to The Dial.

25 RIZZARDI, ALFREDO. "L'Ultimo Cummings," in his La Condizione
    Americana: Studi su Poeti Nord-Americani. Bologna:
    Cappelli, pp. [165]-72.
        Comments on 95 poems and discusses generally Cummings'
    style and themes. In Italian.

26 RIZZARDI, ALFREDO. "Un Clown del Nostro Tempo: E. E. Cum-
    mings," in La Condizione Americana: Studi su Poeti Nord-
    Americani. Bologna: Cappelli, pp. [131]-63.
        Reprint of 1957.19.

27 ROSENTHAL, M. L. "Three Windows on Cummings." The Nation,
    188, no. 2 (10 January), 34-35.
        Reviews 95 poems, E. E. Cummings: A Miscellany, and
    Norman's The Magic-Maker: E. E. Cummings. Rosenthal finds
    that Cummings' work "has not changed essentially...except
    that quieter, more somber tones can occasionally be detected
    and that his weaknesses (sentimentality and an insistent
    presumption of his own superior sensitivity) loom larger
    than before." The prose pieces in A Miscellany he considers
    "journalistic" and "amateurish" with a few brilliant ex-
    ceptions.

28 SCHONBERG, HAROLD C. "At 65, Our Rebel Poet Still Rebels."
    New York Times Magazine (11 October), pp. 37, 66-68.
        Biographical-critical essay emphasizes Cummings' indi-
    viduality as man and poet. Reprinted in abridged form:
    1960.20.

1959

29 SCOTT, WINFIELD TOWNLEY. Review of 95 poems. Saturday Review,
    42, no. 1 (3 January), 13.
        Examines 95 poems; argues that "Cummings has restored
    joy to poetry" and calls his work "the latest important ex-
    pression of the New England Transcendental tradition."

30 SNODGRASS, W. D. Review of 95 poems. The Hudson Review, 12,
    no. 1 (Spring), 119-20.
        Notices 95 poems as a falling off, alleging that in it
    even the major efforts fail and that its virtues slip in
    almost by accident. "His poetry has undergone a general
    weakening; he has known his answers too long for his voice
    to keep its impulsion."

31 UNTERMEYER, LOUIS. "E. E. Cummings," in his Lives of the
    Poets: The Story of One Thousand Years of English and
    American Poetry. New York: Simon and Schuster, pp. 709-11.
        Gives basic biographical information and makes brief
    critical remarks on the "double" quality of Cummings' work.

32 VOISIN, LAURENCE. On Cummings. Europe, 37, nos. 358-359
    (February-March), 35-37.
        In a discussion of modern American poetry, describes
    Cummings as an inveterate romantic who is impassioned by
    life, by being, by form and color, and who produces uneven
    but pleasant verse. In French.

33 WEGNER, ROBERT E. "The Poetry and Prose of E. E. Cummings:
    A Study in Appreciation." Ph.D. dissertation, Western
    Reserve University.
        Examines self-discovery as a motive for Cummings' art,
    Cummings' attitude toward life as demonstrated in his dis-
    tinction between individuals and "mostpeople," his emphasis
    on freedom and his elevation of feeling over thinking, the
    development of his themes, his satires, and his forms and
    techniques. The dissertation was reprinted in book form
    and a longer annotation will be found under that entry:
    1965.30.

34 WILLIAMS, WILLIAM CARLOS. "E. E. Cummings." Evergreen Review,
    2, no. 7 (Winter), 214-15.
        Reviews 95 poems. "[T]he feeling of a primitive lan-
    guage pervades the book, a country atmosphere of New Eng-
    land...," but the world of the poems is, in fact, one of
    Cummings' own creation.

<u>1960</u>

1   ANON. "A Love of Lower Case." <u>The Times Literary Supplement</u>
(25 March), p. 192.
Comments on Cummings in a review of Norman's biography,
taking up such matters as Cummings' affinity with nineteenth-century American writers, the distance between his
ambitions and achievements, his didacticism, his anti-
scientific stance, his sentimentality, his excessive evocation, and his rhetorical (ràther than poetic) skill. For a
response and counter-response, <u>see</u> 1960.15 and 1960.2.

2   ANON. Reply. <u>The Times Literary Supplement</u> (1 April), p. 209.
Replies to Newby's defense (<u>see</u> 1960.15) against an
earlier review (<u>see</u> 1960.1), agreeing that Cummings is a
"considerable writer" and commenting further on the use of
idiom in "Buffalo Bill's."

3   BEACH, JOSEPH WARREN. On Cummings, in his <u>Obsessive Images:
Symbolism in Poetry of the 1930's and 1940's</u>. Edited by
William Van O'Connor. Minneapolis: University of Minnesota Press, pp. 241-42, 273-75, 289-93, 306, 374-75.
Discusses Cummings' criticism of civilization's triumph
over the "'soul,'" describes him as a "primarily personal
and philosophical" poet concerned not with society but with
the individual, and comments on his "denunciation of progress" and his "revulsion against science."

4   BENSTOCK, BERNARD. "All the World a Stage: The Elements of
Drama in the Poetry of E. E. Cummings," in <u>Studies in
American Literature</u>. Louisiana State University Studies,
Humanities Series, no. 8, edited by Waldo McNeir and Leo B.
Levy. Baton Rouge: Louisiana State University Press,
pp. 104-131.
Argues that Cummings has demonstrated, in his works from
the twenties through the fifties, "a keen sense of the
dramatic,...particularly in the characterizations he has
created. These 'people' seem to provide a strong basis of
reality in what is usually considered a rather difficult
poetry.... If a decline in poetic power is observed in
Cummings' later poetry, perhaps it is due not merely to
surface obscurities..., but also to the underlying loss in
the poems of the forties and fifties of the poet's inherent
sense of characterization." Cummings' use of places, abstract values, ideas, types, and individuals as dramatic
characters is discussed and exemplified.

1960

5   COMBECHER, HANS. On Cummings. <u>Die Neueren Sprachen</u>, 9, no. 1
     (January), 28-32.
         In an essay on war poetry, analyzes Cummings' "my sweet
     old etcetera" as a comic-ironic juxtaposition of the atti-
     tudes of those on the home front with the attitudes of the
     men in the field, with special attention to the poem's
     shifting use of the word "etcetera." In German.

6   FIEDLER, LESLIE A. On Cummings, in his <u>Love and Death in the</u>
     <u>American Novel</u>. New York: Criterion Books, p. 454.
         Describes <u>The Enormous Room</u> as one of the few modern war
     novels which approaches the gothic form without betraying
     it to sentimentality. Revised editions--1966.14; 1966.15;
     and 1969.13--leave the Cummings comments unchanged.

7   FIRMAGE, GEORGE J. <u>E. E. Cummings: A Bibliography</u>. Middle-
     town, Connecticut: Wesleyan University Press, 138 pp.
         A descriptive bibliography cataloguing books and pamph-
     lets by Cummings; his contributions to periodicals, books,
     pamphlets, programs, catalogues, and to a musical score;
     translations of his books, poems, and essays into foreign
     languages; musical settings of his poems; recorded readings;
     and reproductions of his drawings, watercolors, and oils.
     With an index of titles and first lines of Cummings' works
     and a general index. Reprinted: 1974.7.

8   FRIEDMAN, NORMAN. <u>E. E. Cummings: The Art of His Poetry</u>.
     Baltimore, Maryland: The Johns Hopkins Press, 204 pp.
         Analyzes in detail Cummings' vision and technique. After
     asserting in his introduction that Cummings' work, although
     not of a piece with that of the other poets of his genera-
     tion, is nevertheless informed by a serious artistic vision
     and executed with high craft, Friedman, in chapter one, de-
     fines Cummings' major themes. He argues that Cummings'
     poetic persona is a detached observer who dwells apart in
     the service of true response and accurate expression. The
     chief aid to the true response is love; the chief obstacle,
     submission to mass life. Cummings' speaker radically
     separates the two, sees the world as "cleanly divided be-
     tween good and evil, right and wrong, and, in so doing,
     simply rises above the whole struggle into a transcendental
     world which is one, and full of love." From this position
     of transcendence and from a position which sees man as un-
     fallen and therefore the creator of whatever good or evil
     there is in the world, the persona observes and judges. He
     has ideas about four areas of human life and thought: "love,
     death, and time; the natural and the artificial; society and
     the individual; and dream and reality." In each of these

1960

areas, opposition can be transcended by disciplined acceptance and surrender so that love transcends death and time,
the natural transcends the artificial, the individual
transcends society, and dream transcends reality. The
persona celebrates such transcendence and deplores its absence. These informing ideas explained, the remainder of
the first chapter discusses Cummings' development and use
of a "conceptual language" for their expression and comments on his most frequent subjects and image clusters:
love and lovers, the external worlds of nature and the
city, ideas, the demimonde, and individual persons or types
he admires or despises.

The second chapter examines the kinds of responses
typically acted out by Cummings' speaker; they are remark-
ably varied and involve all of the usual lyric stances except the meditative. Each of the other responses—
description, praise and eulogy, satire, reflection, and
persuasion—is discussed in terms of its characteristics,
its relative frequency of appearance, and its growth or
decline over Cummings' career. Chapter three explores the
area of style. Rejecting the idea that Cummings' language
is often unintelligible, Friedman finds at its center a
"neutral mode," a "modified romantic style" which juxta-
poses "romantic" words with antipathetic ones, thus per-
mitting Cummings to intensify or modify traditional
associations. This flexible neutral mode "allows him to
meet the demands of intelligibility by suiting the history
of language, on the one hand, to the needs of the individual
poem, on the other." The clash of vocabularies which this
suggests is the crucial fact of Cummings' style, and these
clashes and their varied significances are discussed at
length. Variations from the neutral norm are also examined.
Those to the extreme right produce a purely archaic, serious, formal, and reverential style; those to the extreme
left, a purely violent, vulgar, burlesque, and mock style.
These variations are, respectively, efficient modes for
poems of praise and satire, two of Cummings' dominant forms.
Many poems "mix" the three styles.

Chapter four explores Cummings' technical devices with
detailed attention to the growth and development of his
figurative language, to his metrical and stanzaic practices,
word-coinage, syntactical distortion, and typography. The
fifth chapter demonstrates Cummings' careful craftsmanship
by a close examination of "rosetree,rosetree," comparing
its finished form with earlier manuscript versions. The
conclusion notes Cummings' growth, making explicit an argument implicit throughout the book: that, although Cummings
has not demonstrated development by crisis or reversal, his

1960

poetry does reveal significant developments in thought,
expression, form, and technique. This growth is evidenced
by a comparison of the early "consider O" with the late
"now all the fingers of this tree (darling) have." A post-
script reviews 95 poems, characterizing it as treating
familiar themes freshly, reaffirming "anew an even more
transcendental faith in his characteristic acceptance of
life and love," being less venomous and more compassionate,
and exploiting a new vein of paradox. Revised edition:
1967.11.

9   GROSSMAN, D. JON. "Introduction," in his E. E. Cummings: En
    Traduction, Vingt-trois Poèmes. Paris: Pierre Seghers,
    pp. 9-[13].
        Provides general bibliographical and critical informa-
    tion as background to a translation of Cummings' poems.
    In French.

10 HIGHET, GILBERT. On Cummings, in his The Powers of Poetry.
    New York: Oxford University Press, pp. 105, 143-50, 218.
        Notes that Cummings is an heir to Emerson, comments on
    the ways in which "skillfully distorted syntax, punctua-
    tion, and spelling" function in "un," and finds Cummings'
    work "curiously ineffective" and limited in range.

11 HILLYER, ROBERT. On Cummings, in his In Pursuit of Poetry.
    New York: McGraw-Hill Book Co., pp. 195-97.
        A brief general comment on Cummings' poems. Hillyer
    prefers Cummings' more traditional work and notes the pos-
    sible influence of Emily Dickinson in some of the love
    poems.

12 HOWARD, LEON. On Cummings, in his Literature and the American
    Tradition. New York: Doubleday & Co., p. 290.
        Mentions Cummings as a minor poet of Eliot's generation
    and comments briefly on The Enormous Room and the poetry
    in a discussion of tradition in the twenties.

13 LAUTER, PAUL. "E. E. Cummings in Scholarland." The New
    Leader, 43, no. 38 (3 October), 23-24.
        Argues, in a review of studies of Cummings by Norman
    Friedman and Charles Norman, that Cummings' world view is
    oversimplified and that he has failed to grow.

14 LECHNER, SISTER JOAN MARIE, O.S.U. "E. E. Cummings and Mother
    Nature." Renascence, 12, no. 4 (Summer), 182-91.
        Discusses Cummings as a "nature poet" who practices a
    romantic identification with the natural world. He

frequently makes use of the metamorphic tradition "when he
turns to nature and through its symbols attempts to create
the ideal life and love he is seeking." His romantic
primitiveness is more typical of twentieth-century poetry
than is sometimes recognized. Several of Cummings' nature
poems are examined.

15 NEWBY, P. H. Letter to the Editor. The Times Literary Sup-
    plement (1 April), p. 209.
        Responds to the anonymous reviewer's strictures against
    Cummings in a review of Norman's biography (see 1960.1),
    defending Cummings as a "considerable writer" and charging
    the reader with missing the American idiom of "Buffalo
    Bill's." (For a reply, see 1960.2.)

16 NORMAN, CHARLES. On Cummings, in his Ezra Pound. New York:
    The Macmillan Co., pp. 78, 225, 247, 265, 266, 267, 284,
    289, 290, 303, 343, 358, 361, 371, 377, 381, 402, 409, 415,
    428, 435, 436, 440, 446, 447, 448, 449, 465, 466.
        Passing references to Cummings in relation to Pound.
    Norman notes such matters as the influence of Pound's "The
    Return" on Cummings, their correspondence, Cummings' con-
    tribution to Pound's defense through Julien Cornell, and
    his visits to Pound at St. Elizabeth's.

17 NYREN, DOROTHY. "Cummings, Edward Estlin," in her A Library
    of Literary Criticism. New York: Frederick Ungar Publish-
    ing Co., pp. 127-32.
        Reprints brief excerpts from twenty-one commentaries on
    Cummings.

18 OLSON, CHARLES. On Cummings, in The New American Poetry.
    Edited by Donald M. Allen. New York: Grove Press, p. 393.
        Reprint of 1950.16.

19 ROSENTHAL, M. L. On Cummings, in his The Modern Poets: A
    Critical Introduction. New York: Oxford University Press,
    pp. 145-52.
        Describes Cummings as "absorbed in the problem of defi-
    nition through the trapping of a state of awareness" and
    asserts that most details of his technical unorthodoxy are
    functional. The "chief effect of his technique is to re-
    discover and release the energies buried in the convention-
    al." What is lacking in Cummings is the negative side of
    romantic experience, and his range is narrow. With comment
    on several individual poems.

1960

20 SCHONBERG, HAROLD C. "At 65, Our Rebel Poet Still Rebels," in America's Taste, 1851-1959, The Cultural Events of a Century Reported by Contemporary Observers in the Pages of the New York "Times." Edited by Marjorie Longley, Louis Silverstein, and Samuel A. Tower. New York: Simon and Schuster, p. 309.
Abridged reprint of 1959.28.

21 SHAPIRO, KARL. On Cummings, in his In Defense of Ignorance. New York: Random House, p. 161.
Notes that "Cummings has advanced the sonnet to a new fame." This remark, with another, is reprinted in Start With the Sun, a book Shapiro authored with James E. Miller, Jr. and Bernice Slote (1960.22).

22 SHAPIRO, KARL. On Cummings, in his Start With the Sun: Studies in Cosmic Poetry. Co-authored by James E. Miller, Jr. and Bernice Slote. Lincoln: University of Nebraska Press, pp. 202, 212.
Adds to the reprinted remark on Cummings' use of the sonnet (see 1960.21) a comment on his "peevishness at the vulgarity of modern city life."

23 THORP, WILLARD. On Cummings, in his American Writing in the Twentieth Century. The Library of Congress Series in American Civilization, edited by Ralph Henry Gabriel. Cambridge: Harvard University Press, pp. 26, 214-15.
Describes The Enormous Room as one of the best books about World War I and surveys the poems, noting their visual emphasis. Cummings is our best sonneteer and the finest writer of erotic verse since the Earl of Rochester.

24 WALTERS, RAYMOND, JR. Review of 50 Poems. New York Times Book Review (1 May), p. 36.
Notices a paperback reprint of 50 Poems in an omnibus review, commenting on its "romanticist's concern with love and death."

25 WEST, PAUL. On Cummings. English, 13, no. 73 (Spring), 8-9.
Examines Cummings' abandonment "of sequence and linear consistency" for effect in an essay on modern poetic form.

1961

1 AARON, DANIEL. On Cummings, in his Writers on the Left: Episodes in American Literary Communism. New York: Harcourt, Brace & World, pp. 76, 79, 92, 107, 112, 175, 176-77, 411, 419.

Passing comments on Cummings' largely tangential relationship to American literary communism. He snipes at both
capitalism and communism, at the latter especially after
the events chronicled in <u>Eimi</u>. Reprinted: 1974.1.

2 BODE, CARL. "E. E. Cummings and Exploded Verse," in his <u>The
Great Experiment in American Literature</u>. New York:
Frederick A. Praeger, pp. 81-100.
Expands Bode's earlier criticisms of Cummings, emphasizing the role in his failures of such typically American
traits as the constant search for the new, the drive for
the better, and an eternal restlessness. At the end of the
essay, Bode softens earlier judgments, noting the energy of
Cummings' indignation and irreverence and the successful
experimentation of some of his love poems. Revision of
1955.1. Reprinted: 1965.4.

3 BRADLEY, SCULLEY, RICHARD CROOM BEATTY, and E. HUDSON LONG.
"E. E. Cummings," in their <u>The American Tradition in Litera-
ture</u>. Second edition. Vol. 2. New York: W. W. Norton &
Co., pp. 1476-77.
Slightly updated entry. Revised edition of 1956.2.

4 BURTIS, MARY ELIZABETH and PAUL SPENCER WOOD. "E(dward)
E(stlin) Cummings, 1894--," in their <u>Recent American Litera-
ture</u>. The New Littlefield College Outline Series, No. 72.
Paterson, New Jersey: Littlefield, Adams & Co., pp. 87-90.
Encyclopedia entry provides biographical and publication
information and presents, in near digest form, general
critical opinion on Cummings' themes and techniques.

5 CUNLIFFE, MARCUS. On Cummings, in his <u>The Literature of the
United States</u>. Second edition. London: Penguin Books,
pp. 224, 264, 282, 304, 313, 317-19, 320, 364.
Although the book is revised, the Cummings entry is unchanged. Reprint of 1954.11.

6 ESSLIN, MARTIN. On Cummings, in his <u>The Theatre of the Absurd</u>.
Garden City, New York: Anchor Books, Doubleday & Co.,
pp. xxii, 288-89.
Comments on Cummings' <u>Him</u> as it relates to the absurdist
drama, describing it as "a perfect statement of the philosophy of the Theatre of the Absurd in which the world is seen
as a hall of reflecting mirrors, and reality merges imper-
ceptibly into fantasy." Revised edition: 1969.12.

7 GARGANO, JAMES W. "Cummings' 'Pity This Busy Monster, Manunkind.'" <u>The Explicator</u>, 20, no. 3 (November), Item 21.

1961

Finds Britton's reading (see 1959.8) correct but somewhat narrow because of its emphasis on the "unwish" passage.
Gargano emphasizes instead the image of modern man as a
"monster" who "has lost his specifically human relation
with the natural world." See 1969.21. Reprinted: 1966.16.

8   LASSER, MICHAEL L. "The Agony of E. E. Cummings." The
    Literary Review, 5, no. 1 (Autumn), 133-41.
        Argues that Cummings is a successful paradigm of his own
    concept of the artist as a scorner of security and a seeker
    of intensity, and describes his agony as coming from his
    constant, unending "personal struggle to discover, to ap-
    preciate, and to express himself."

9   LOGAN, JOHN. "The Organ-Grinder and the Cockatoo: An Intro-
    duction to E. E. Cummings." The Critic, 20, no. 2 (October-
    November), 39-40, 42-43.
        Asserts that reading Cummings requires the "paradigms of
    love as well as those of language," comments on Cummings'
    feeling "that machines have destroyed man's sense of him-
    self," presents some anecdotes, and argues that his work
    contains the purities of art and of the heart. The purity
    of the heart in Cummings dissolves the dichotomy between
    artist and art. The purity of his art accounts for his
    uses of typography for controlling evocation and for explod-
    ing the clichéd response. All of these matters Logan exem-
    plifies in an analysis of "that melancholy," in which he
    also finds Cummings' central theme: "'the immortality of
    the creative imagination and the indomitability of the hu-
    man spirit.'" Revised edition: 1970.10.

10 PEARCE, ROY HARVEY. "Cummings," in his The Continuity of
    American Poetry. Princeton, New Jersey: Princeton Univer-
    sity Press, pp. 359-66.
        Says Cummings' "subject has always explicitly been him-
    self." In his poems, "self-transcendence turns out to be
    only self-realization." Technically, they are set up "to
    force us to attend to the quality of an individual experi-
    ence as it is occuring" and to "inhibit the 'normal' tenden-
    cy to generalize." His technique is concerned "to rescue
    language from the...abstractness that threatens to deaden
    it." At times, this is successful; at times, "excessively
    'verbal.'" On occasion, poems which would free their read-
    ers from manipulation can themselves become manipulative.
    This results in sentimentalism. The often exclusionary
    negations of his satire are the obverse of that sentimental-
    ism. Revision of 1952.14.

1962

*11   TAKUWA, SHINJI. "Some Impressions of Henry Adams, Hart Crane,
         E. E. Cummings, and Others." Studies in English Literature
         and Language, no. 11, pp. 19-53.
              Cited in 1962 MLA Bibliography, p. 184, item 5446.

12   TURNER, W. PRICE. "E. E. Cummings: Selected Poems 1923-1958."
         Stand, 5, no. 1, 59-62.
              Reviews Selected Poems 1923-1958. Cummings is a major
         poet who is the "champion of the individual and the scourge
         of the conformist mob."

13   WHICHER, STEPHEN and LARS AHNEBRINK. "E. E. Cummings," in
         their Twelve American Poets. New York: Oxford University
         Press, pp. 154-57, 190-91.
              After a short biographical sketch, headnote to ten Cum-
         mings poems describes him as a renewer of clichés of subject
         and form and as the "Last of the Romantic Egoists," although
         his positive stance is qualified by the exclusiveness of
         his negations. With a brief bibliography and notes on the
         anthologized poems.

1962

1   AARON, DANIEL. "American Writers in Russia: The Three Faces
        of Lenin." Survey: A Journal of Soviet and East European
        Studies, no. 41 (April), pp. [43]-57.
             Discusses the anti-Soviet Eimi in the context of the
        generally pro-Soviet writing of the twenties and thirties.
        Aaron places Cummings in the traditions of Emersonian and
        Thoreauvian individualism and of Twain's Innocents Abroad,
        and compares and contrasts Eimi with two roughly contempor-
        ary reports on the Soviet Union, Waldo Frank's Dawn in
        Russia and Edmund Wilson's Travels in Two Democracies.

2   ANON. "E. E. Cummings." New York Times (9 September), 4,
        p. 12.
             Editorial describing Cummings as an "old-fashioned poet"
        who "wrote about love and death, the graces of nature and
        the disgraces of civilization." His technique too was an-
        cient, the "realization of a lost art."

3   ANON. "E. E. Cummings Dies of Stroke; Poet Stood for Stylistic
        Liberty." New York Times (4 September), pp. 1, 33.
             Obituary notice recalls the facts of Cummings' life and
        comments generally on his characteristic subjects, styles,
        and themes.

1962

4   ANON. "E. E. Cummings: Poet of the Heart." Time, 80, no. 11
     (14 September), 102.
          An obituary notice, reviewing Cummings' "unique satiri-
     cal and lyrical achievement," noting his mixed critical re-
     ception, and arguing that, although his tools were secular,
     he practiced the "romantic individualist's religion of the
     heart."

5   ANON. "E. E. Cummings, RIP." National Review, 13, no. 12
     (25 September), 221.
          Obituary notice comments on Cummings' achievement of
     verbal analogues of "the multidimensional simultaneity" of
     certain twentieth-century paintings and his struggle "to
     define himself as a free individual in a society that makes
     this so difficult and continuous a task."

6   ANON. "The Enormous Poet." Newsweek, 60, no. 12 (17 Septem-
     ber), 99.
          Obituary notice calls Cummings--with Frost--America's
     finest lyric poet of this century, briefly reviews his life,
     and rewrites "Buffalo Bill's" in tribute.

7   ANON. "A Talented American Poet: The Late Mr. E. E. Cum-
     mings." The Illustrated London News, 241, no. 6424 (15
     September), 415.
          Brief obituary notice.

8   ANON. "Waitress Mourns Poet: 'Beautiful Person' Died."
     New York Times (4 September), p. 33.
          Anecdote of waitress who owned two of Cummings' books
     and mourned his passing.

9   BAUM, S. V., ed. ΕΣΤΙ: eec E. E. Cummings and the Critics.
     East Lansing: Michigan State University Press, 235 pp.
          Introduced by Baum, reprints twenty-six reviews of and
     essays on Cummings and his work. In the introduction,
     "Cummings and the Critics" (pp. vii-xv), Baum traces the
     development of Cummings criticism, with special emphasis on
     the major statements, both positive and negative, and on
     changes in attitude toward Cummings' experimental techniques
     and the question of growth or lack of it in his poetry.
     The reprinted pieces are: "[Strainings and Obscurities,]"
     Anonymous (pp. 3-4), "Off the Shoals" by John Dos Passos
     (pp. 4-9), "Syrinx" by Gorham B. Munson (pp. 9-18), "Flare
     and Blare" by Harriet Monroe (pp. 21-24), "Wallace Stevens
     and E. E. Cummings" by Edmund Wilson (pp. 24-27), "People
     Stare Carefully" by Marianne Moore (pp. 31-33), "Modernist
     Poetry and the Plain Reader's Rights" by Laura Riding and

1962

Robert Graves (pp. 34-43), "<u>Him</u>" by Stark Young (pp. 47-49),
"Notes on E. E. Cummings' Language" by R. P. Blackmur
(pp. 50-67), "Cummings's Non-Land of Un-" by William Troy
(pp. 71-72), "The Enormous Cummings" by Paul Rosenfeld
(pp. 72-80), "When We Were Very Young" by Francis Fergusson
(pp. 80-83), "Two Views of Cummings" by Philip Horton and
Sherry Mangan (pp. 87-92), "Is Indeed 5" by S. I. Hayakawa
(pp. 92-98), "[Merely a Penumbra]" by Yvor Winters (pp. 98-
99), "The Poems and Prose of E. E. Cummings" by John Peale
Bishop (pp. 99-109), "ee cummingesq" by Babette Deutsch
(pp. 112-13), "[An American Poet]" by F. O. Matthiessen
(pp. 117-18), "Technique as Joy" by Theodore Spencer (pp.
119-23), "The Poet of Brattle Street" by Horace Gregory and
Marya Zaturenska (pp. 123-132), "Prosody as the Meaning" by
Karl Shapiro (pp. 132-44), "Cummings Times One" by Lloyd
Frankenberg (pp. 144-69), "Anti-Semitism and E. E. Cummings:
[A Critical Round Robin]" by Alex Jackinson, Ludwig Lewisohn,
Stanton A. Coblentz, Charles I. Glicksberg, Leslie A. Fiedler, Harry Roskolenko. and William Carlos Williams (pp. 173-
82), "E. E. Cummings and His Fathers" by Alfred Kazin
(pp. 185-88), "A Poet's Own Way" by Randall Jarrell (pp.
191-92), and "[The Imaginative Direction of Our Time]" by
Louise Bogan (pp. 193-94). The book also contains "By eec:
A Primary Bibliography" (p. 195), "About eec: A Secondary
Bibliography" (pp. 196-213), and an "Index of Poems Quoted"
(pp. 215-18). Annotations of the reprinted pieces appear
with the entries for their original appearances.

10   BLACKMUR, R. P. "Notes on E. E. Cummings' Language," in
     <u>Literary Opinion in America</u>. Third edition. Edited by
     Morton Dauwen Zabel. New York: Harper & Row, Publishers,
     pp. 296-314.
        Reprint of 1931.1.

11   CIARDI, JOHN. "To Speak an Age." <u>Saturday Review</u>, 45, no. 39
     (29 September), 10.
        An obituary notice stressing Cummings' excessive simpli-
     fications, his subtle perceptions, his clear sense of his
     times, and his intense integrity.

12   DOUGHERTY, JAMES PATRICK, JR. "E. E. Cummings' <u>The Enormous
     Room</u> and its Relation to His Poetry." Ph.D. dissertation,
     University of Pennsylvania.
        Emphasizing theme and symbol, argues that the central
     idea of <u>The Enormous Room</u> and of many of Cummings' poems
     concerns the recognition "that the true individual will be-
     come disillusioned with any situation, and to survive must
     proceed or grow." Thus <u>The Enormous Room</u> and many other

1962

Cummings works can be viewed as segments "of a cyclic, unending pilgrimage, an ethical quest for self-knowledge and
self-perfection." These matters are discussed in terms of
Cummings' concern with art as self-expression, "the dialec-
tical and parenthetical framework of his mind, his desire
to stop the flow of time, and his opposition of an ideal
and real world," as well as in terms of his several conceptions of individualism and nonindividualism.

13 FERGUSSON, FRANCIS. On Cummings, in Literary Opinion in Ameri-
    ca. Third edition. Edited by Morton Dauwen Zabel. New
    York: Harper & Row, Publishers, pp. 519-21.
       Reprint of 1930.3.

14 FRIEDMAN, NORMAN. "E. E. Cummings and the Modernist Movement."
    Forum, 3, no. 10 (Spring-Summer), 39-46.
       Discusses the interrelation of romantic and modernist
    elements in Cummings' poetry. For the modernist, two-dimen-
    sional reality is complex and, therefore, poems must be
    complex. "Tension, conflict, reconciliation of opposites,
    ambivalence, metaphor, drama, paradox—these are the basic
    terms of modernist criticism.... But Cummings' picture of
    the world is somewhat different, and so his techniques vary
    accordingly in their nature and function." For Cummings,
    "to lose the two-dimensional everyday world is to gain the
    three-dimensional world of understanding. This is a world
    without conflict..., a world without contingency, without
    compromise, without limits, without fixity. It is the
    world of what's possible, and hence is the source of all
    our values." His "view of poetry is correspondingly
    simple." Thus, lyrics and satires. But, as the three-
    dimensional world of value indicates, Cummings, like the
    modernists, conceives of "'another kind of truth.'" And
    his concept of poetic form is as organic as the modernists'
    However, his problem is, in a sense, the reverse of theirs:
    "rather than framing a complex mirror to reflect a complex
    reality, he is treating simple subjects and attitudes in a
    complicated way." The complication freshens what might seem
    ordinary.

15 FRIEDMAN, NORMAN. "Pan and Buffalo Bill." College English,
    23, no. 8 (May), 672.
       Disagrees, in a letter, with Ray's suggestion (in a foot-
    note to his article on irony in Cummings, see 1962.24) that
    the "goat-footed balloon Man" is "a symbol of the tainted
    adult world waiting to betray the childhood world of inno-
    cence." Friedman also rejects Ray's larger claim that Cum-
    mings treats Buffalo Bill ironically. (For Ray's response,
    see 1962.25.)

1962

16 HENRY, NAT. "Cummings' '305.'" The Explicator, 20, no. 6
    (February), Item 49.
        Explains the devices of the poem ("The Mind's("), espe-
    cially its use of phonetic spelling of the spoken forms of
    words, in exploring its satire of the false, one-dimensional
    world of cinema and particularly cinema sex. See 1962.29.
    Reprinted: 1966.23.

17 HENRY, NAT. "Cummings' '275.'" The Explicator, 20, no. 8
    (April), Item 63.
        Analyzes Cummings' special use of tmesis in this poem
    ("go(perpe)go") to explain its satirizing of society's ten-
    dency to hold up the ant's empty, mechanical, and "compul-
    sive diligence as an end in itself." Reprinted: 1966.24.

18 HERZBERG, MAX J. "Cummings, E[dward] E[stlin]," in his The
    Reader's Encyclopedia of American Literature. New York:
    Thomas Y. Crowell Co., pp. 228-29.
        Comments generally on Cummings' work, asserting that
    "most of his technical innovations possess a genuine poetic
    content" and that The Enormous Room "is one of the half-
    dozen best American novels of the 20th century."

19 KUNTZ, JOSEPH M. Explications of Poems by Cummings, in his
    Poetry Explication: A Checklist of Interpretation since
    1925 of British and American Poems Past and Present.
    Second edition. Denver, Colorado: Alan Swallow, pp. [66-
    70].
        A checklist of explications. Revised edition of 1950.3.

20 MEI, FRACESCO. "Cummings e L'Avanguardia." La Fiera
    Letteraria, 17, no. 39 (30 September), 3.
        Compares and contrasts Cummings with several other mem-
    bers of the American literary avant-garde. In Italian.

21 PHILLIPS, PAUL. "A Note on E. E. Cummings." Mainstream, 15,
    no. 11 (November), 22-25.
        Argues that Cummings' "life-long romance with individual-
    ism eventually deteriorated into a desperate cynicism" and
    surveys his typography, lyricism, Chaplinesque wit, and in-
    creasing estrangement.

22 POORE, CHARLES. "Too Good to be Obvious." New York Times
    (4 September), p. 33.
        Writing on the day after Cummings' death, Poore describes
    him as "a magnificent poet" and comments on his syntax, his
    "essential clarity," his creation of "elliptical tensions,"
    and his reputation.

1962

23   PRATT, JOHN CLARK. On Cummings, in his <u>The Meaning of Modern</u>
     <u>Poetry</u>. New York: The Welch Scientific Co., pp. 158, 161,
     163, 166, 167, 168, 169, 173, 176-77, 179, 180, 185.
         Presents a question-and-answer study of "Buffalo Bill's"
     for readers wishing to teach themselves to read modern
     poetry.

24   RAY, DAVID. "The Irony of E. E. Cummings." <u>College English</u>,
     23, no. 4 (January), 282-90.
         Complains of failures, especially of the British, to
     attend to Cummings' idioms, and examines the irony of Cum-
     mings' "Buffalo Bill's." The poem is "an assault on every-
     thing held dear by a sentimentalist or a hero-worshipper,"
     attacking all but "a sense of fundamental decency outraged
     with everything that corrupts life or makes it fraudulent."
     A footnote comments on "the goat-footed balloon Man." (For
     responses, <u>see</u> 1962.15 and 1962.25.)

25   RAY, DAVID. "Reply." <u>College English</u>, 23, no. 8 (May), 672.
         Reasserts his original opinions on Cummings' uses of the
     balloon man and on "Buffalo Bill's" (<u>see</u> 1962.24) in re-
     sponse to Friedman's disagreements (<u>see</u> 1962.15).

26   ROCHE, DENIS. "E. E. Cummings." <u>Tel Quel</u>, no. 11 (Autumn),
     pp. [66]-67.
         Obituary notice presenting general information on Cum-
     mings' career and techniques. In French.

27   STRAUMANN, HEINRICH. On Cummings, in his <u>American Literature</u>
     <u>in the Twentieth Century</u>. London: Hutchinson & Co.,
     p. 159.
         Reprint of 1951.15.

28   UNTERMEYER, LOUIS. "E. E. Cummings," in his <u>Modern American</u>
     <u>Poetry</u>. New and Enlarged edition. New York: Harcourt,
     Brace & World, pp. 469-70.
         Updated introduction to a selection of sixteen Cummings
     poems. Revised edition of 1925.6.

29   WAGENER, W. YEATON. "Cummings' '305.'" <u>The Explicator</u>, 21,
     no. 2 (October), Item 18.
         Expands Henry's reading of the poem ("The Mind's(") (<u>see</u>
     1962.16) to point out that the first and last lines further
     emphasize the speaker's disgust with Hollywood and can be
     juxtaposed to form a title, thus allowing the parenthetical
     element to be seen as a poem contained by a split title.
     Wagener also notes that the scatological language of line
     twelve is the punch line of a well known bawdy joke.

30 WHITE, JAMES E. "Cummings' 'I.'" The Explicator, 21, no. 1
(September), Item 4.
Notes that Cummings' use of tmesis in "l(a" causes all
of the poem's details to emphasize the fact of loneliness
and to further fuse idea with image. "The effect is one of
simultaneity."

<u>1963</u>

1 ABEL, LIONEL. "Cummings' Daisy." The Nation, 197, no. 20
(14 December), 420-21.
Reviews 73 poems, describing Cummings as a poet of ecstasy and of arguments for ecstasy and praising 73 poems
for having more ecstasy and less argument.

2 BABCOCK, SISTER MARY DAVID, O.S.B. "Cummings' Typography:
An Ideogrammic Style." Renascence: A Critical Journal of
Letters, 15, no. 3 (Spring), 115-23.
Argues that the capture of "aliveness" is the goal of
much of Cummings' typography and also the basic quality of
the Chinese ideogram and that—perhaps unconsciously—Cummings imitates the spirit of the Chinese written character
in an attempt to get beyond the limits of grammar to a mode
of simultaneous patterns. Several poems are examined as
examples.

3 BARTON, CYNTHIA. "Cummings' 'Memorabilia.'" The Explicator,
22, no. 4 (December), Item 26.
Feels that Kilby (see 1953.7), although correct in his
other comments, fails to understand the poem's basic structure, which is derived from the phrase 'Stop look & / lis-
ten.'" Barton also combines the different readings of the
word "Cincingondolanati" given by Kilby and Griffiths (see
1954.14), suggests that the allusion to Browning may ameli-
orate some of the poem's harshness, posits a pictorial reading of the words "metope" and "triglyph," and notes that
the phrase "nel mezzo del cammin'" is from the first stanza
of Dante's Inferno.

4 CIARDI, JOHN. Review of 73 poems. Book Week (27 October),
p. 6.
Notices 73 poems, discussing the need to distinguish between Cummings' "word-game poems" and his "'developed'"
poems. The latter sort are "achievements not only in a
style but in the essential human perception that only style
can make possible."

1963

5   CLENDENNING, JOHN. "Cummings, Comedy, and Criticism." The
     Colorado Quarterly, 12, no. 1 (Summer), 44-53.
         Asserts that Cummings is not a modernist since he is un-
     affected by modernist principles and themes. Nevertheless,
     his "uniqueness of mind and technique has enriched American
     verse." His technique stems from "the tradition of American
     humor, not that of English poetry. The basis of his craft...
     is the surprise ending, the shocking detail, the double-
     take." This aspect of Cummings Clendenning discusses at
     length. He also comments on the inability of modernist
     criticism to comprehend Cummings at his best.

6   CONNOLLY, CYRIL. "E. E. Cummings," in his Previous Convictions.
     New York: Harper & Row, Publishers, pp. 313-16.
         Pays memorial tribute to Cummings, calling him a "natural
     anarchist" and comparing him to Fitzgerald and his poems to
     those of Catullus.

7   DE RACHEWILTZ, MARY. "Nonintroduzione" and "Notizia biografi-
     ca," in Poesie, di E. E. Cummings. Translated by Mary de
     Rachewiltz. Milan: Lerici-Scheiwiller, pp. 9-16 and 19-20.
         An introduction to a translation of Cummings' poems into
     Italian commenting generally on his lyrics and satires and
     quoting from several American critics. With a brief bio-
     graphical note. In Italian.

8   DEUTSCH, BABETTE. On Cummings, in her Poetry in Our Time.
     Second edition. Garden City, New York: Doubleday & Co.,
     Anchor Books, pp. 92, 121-27, 393-95, 412.
         Although the book is revised, the remarks on Cummings
     are unchanged. Revised edition of 1952.6.

9   DOS PASSOS, JOHN. "Off the Shoals," in A Dial Miscellany.
     Edited by William Wasserstrom. Syracuse, New York: Syra-
     cuse University Press, pp. 106-11.
         Reprint of 1922.6.

10 DUFFEY, BERNARD. On Cummings. The Centennial Review, 7, no.
     2 (Spring), 228.
         Notes that Cummings' turn to the "subjective lyric" is
     one of several points which mark the loss of the hold of
     "the romantic coherence" on the American imagination.

11 HENRY, NAT. "Cummings' '303' ('Nor Woman')." The Explicator,
     22, no. 1 (September), Item 2.
         Rearranges the poem to demonstrate that it suggests "the
     body of a young girl violated and left dead in a park. The
     poet skilfully minimizes the horror of the deed to highlight
     the pathos of the picture."

12   HENRY, NAT. "Cummings' '262.'" The Explicator, 21, no. 9
       (May), Item 72.
          Paraphrases the unconventional language of the poem
       ("sh estiffl"), pointing out that Cummings' punctuation is
       sometimes diversionary and sometimes pictorial.

13   JACOBSEN, JOSEPHINE. "Legacy of Three Poets." The Commonweal,
       78, no. 7 (10 May), 189-92.
          Obituary comments on Cummings, Frost, and Williams. Al-
       though the three are "profoundly different," they share a
       vision of life which, while never minimizing reality and
       without easy optimism, is grounded in faith. Cummings'
       hatred of death-in-life and his "spontaneous and indestruc-
       tible confidence in the value of being alive" are discussed.

14   JARRELL, RANDALL. On Cummings. Prairie Schooner, 37, no. 1
       (Spring), 17-19.
          Comments on Cummings in a survey of fifty years of Ameri-
       can poetry, describing him as an expert in "illegal syntac-
       tic devices..., a magical bootlegger...of language."

15   MATTHIESSEN, F. O. On Cummings, in Literary History of the
       United States: History. Third edition. Edited by Robert
       E. Spiller, Willard Thorp, Thomas H. Johnson, Henry Seidel
       Canby, and Richard M. Ludwig. New York: The Macmillan Co.,
       pp. 1351-52.
          Reprint of 1947.9.

16   MEZINIS, GEORGE K. "Cummings: An Introduction." Kobe Gaidai
       Ronso, 13, no. 5 (February), 101-109.
          Discusses Cummings' traditional subjects and modern
       techniques and analyzes "hist whist."

17   MOTTRAM, E. N. W. "Cummings, E[dward] E[stlin]," in The Con-
       cise Encyclopedia of English and American Poets and Poetry.
       Edited by Stephen Spender and Donald Hall. New York:
       Hawthorne Books, p. 112.
          Brief encyclopedia entry presents general information
       and considers Cummings' poetry without development and
       "tarnished" by "a vulgar lack of self-criticism."

18   NORMAN, CHARLES. "Bristling With Surprises." New York Times
       Book Review (3 November), p. 22.
          Reviews 73 poems, noting its intensity, the skill of its
       sonnets and versification, and its continuing revelation of
       Cummings as a lover of the country as well as the city.

1963

19   PRATT, WILLIAM. "Introduction," in his The Imagist Poem:
     Modern Poetry in Miniature. New York: E. P. Dutton & Co.,
     pp. 12, 23.
          Brief references to Cummings' relation to the Imagists.

20   TUCKER, ROBERT G. and DAVID R. CLARK. "Freedom, Joy & Indig-
     nation: Letters from E. E. Cummings." The Massachusetts
     Review, 4, no. 3 (Spring), 497-528.
          Reprints, with explanatory and transitional comments,
     letters from Cummings concerning the attempted censorship
     of a taped reading (of poems on freedom) he had made for
     the New England Anthology series produced by the Literary
     Society of the University of Massachusetts for the National
     Association of Educational Broadcasters. Reprinted:
     1972.27.

21   WASSERSTROM, WILLIAM. On Cummings, in his The Time of the
     "Dial." Syracuse, New York: Syracuse University Press,
     pp. 58-59, 60, 61, 90, 95, 100-101, 117, 131, 168n., 173n.,
     182n.
          Brief comments on Cummings' relationship with The Dial,
     including a letter on Cummings' punctuation by Kenneth
     Burke.

1964

1   ALLEN, WALTER. On Cummings, in his The Modern Novel in Britain
    and the United States. New York: E. P. Dutton & Co.,
    pp. 41, 140, 180.
         Notes similarities between Cummings' poetry and the
    writing of Ronald Firbank, calls The Enormous Room--"only
    dubiously a novel"--"a notable and highly individual piece
    of experimental prose," and remarks the similarity in kind
    of that work to Djuna Barnes' Nightwood. Allen's book was
    published in England by Phoenix House of London in the same
    year under the title Tradition and Dream: The English and
    American Novel from the Twenties to Our Time. Pagination
    is identical.

2   ANON. "An Individual Voice." The Times Literary Supplement
    (16 April), p. 312.
         Reviews 73 poems, stressing Cummings' individual voice
    and commenting on his delicate rhythmic skills and "senti-
    mental use of language."

3   ANON. Review of 73 poems. The Virginia Quarterly Review, 40,
    no. 2 (Spring), lxi.

Notices Cummings' last volume, finding that it continues to demonstrate his old powers without any new development. His power of control, however, rendered him "a major poetic voice of the American twentieth century."

4   CIARDI, JOHN. "'what if a much of a which of a wind.'" Saturday Review, 47, no. 43 (24 October), 18, 72.
    Discusses "what if a much of a which of a wind," finding it "a poem that contains elements beyond the reach of any exegesis, and yet one that declares itself to the reader as an instant and compelling experience." See 1967.4 for a response.

5   CLARK, DAVID R. "Cummings' 'Poem' ('it's / so damn sweet when Anybody--')." The Explicator, 22, no. 6 (February), Item 48.
    Compares an earlier version of the poem with the one actually published in The Massachusetts Review to demonstrate Cummings' art in revising the poem to increase its effectiveness. Reprinted: 1972.6.

6   DICKEY, JAMES. "E. E. Cummings," in his The Suspect in Poetry. Madison, Minnesota: Sixties Press, pp. 85-91.
    Reprint of 1959.12.

7   FITTS, DUDLEY. Review of 73 poems. Saturday Review, 47, no. 18 (2 May), 34.
    Examines Cummings' 73 poems in an omnibus review. The volume "repeats his usual form: four or five poems of a beauty and a power that annihilate objection, accompanied by a number of minor pieces." Fitts comments briefly on "now does our world descend."

8   FRIEDMAN, NORMAN. "E. E. Cummings and His Critics." Criticism, 6, no. 2 (Spring), 114-33.
    Analyzes the critics of Cummings "in order to see what their views of the poet reveal about themselves, and what this in turn reveals about the present state of twentieth-century criticism and scholarship, its powers and limitations." Friedman argues "that many critics have been unable to grasp the meaning of Cummings' art because Cummings is a modern Romantic and they have been unable to understand the significance of Romanticism and the import of its relationship to the Modernist tradition." At the center of Cummings' art "there is a transcendental and paradoxical vision of timelessness" which most critics have missed and which provides the raison d'etre for nearly everything in his work. Friedman explores this vision in some detail, explaining its

1964

connections with both Romanticism and Modernism, and examines the collective failure of Cummings' critics to
understand these matters. He concludes that twentieth-
century criticism has been too monistic in its insistence
on "a peculiarly twentieth-century view of the tragic vision" and in ignoring the "oriental and Romantic tradition
of mystical and intuitive accord with natural process, a
tradition in which suffering is not wished away but is
rather accepted gladly as the condition of freedom," and a
tradition to which Cummings belongs. Includes a bibliography of Cummings criticism, arranged by decade and with the
individual pieces classed as "Favorable," "Unfavorable," or
"Mixed." (This bibliography is reprinted as an appendix to
the revised edition of Friedman's E. E. Cummings: The Art
of His Poetry, 1967.11, where it has been updated to include works appearing between April 1962 and July 1965.)

9   FRIEDMAN, NORMAN. E. E. Cummings: The Growth of a Writer.
     Carbondale and Edwardsville: Southern Illinois University
     Press, 203 pp.
        Traces the development of Cummings' vision of life and
     of his techniques for expressing that vision. Because such
     development implies purposeful growth toward a goal, Fried-
     man's introductory chapter begins by trying to explain the
     meaning of Cummings' mature work. Like other modern writers,
     he is concerned with the "more" beyond the surfaces of re-
     ality. His attitude toward this "more" is that of a free-
     dom-Paradoxer (as opposed to a discipline-Paradoxer). That
     is, Cummings believes "that order is achieved through free-
     dom" and that "there is a natural order which can only be
     achieved by discarding the artificial orders which man is
     always trying to impose upon it." But the matter is rather
     more complex than this, for if Cummings is a freedom-Para-
     doxer, his vision nonetheless requires discipline. He
     demands renunciation, not of freedom but of the ordinary
     world. It is this which allows transcendent insight.
     Friedman proceeds to summarize Cummings' mature vision
     "under four related headings: the nature of the true world,
     knowing it, acting in it, and depicting it. Technically,
     these refer to his metaphysic, his epistemology, his poli-
     tics, and his aesthetic." Cummings' true world is that of
     natural process, "a timeless world of the eternal present."
     It is known by wisdom rather than knowledge, since ultimate
     values lie beyond logic. Cummings' politics are love and
     the individual. His aesthetic is Romantic.
        Friedman then turns to the craft by which Cummings ex-
     presses these ideas and attitudes. Generally, his technique
     is both experimental and traditional, but for all its use of

the past his technique is marked by spectacular innovations. "Not artistic flauntings of sense, they are best understood as various ways of stripping the film of familiarity from language in order to strip the film of familiarity from the world." Cummings' problem--the problem of most modern writers--is, then, "how to reverse the drag of language toward deadness without losing intelligibility altogether." Where others found their answer in metaphor, "Cummings found his chiefly in the magic of the word itself. Concerned less with the interplay of ambiguities than with the vitalizing of movement, he has coined a [conceptual] vocabulary in which nouns are made out of verbs, thus preserving sense while at the same time creating motion." Other aspects of Cummings' technique, including his typography, are discussed under this aegis.

Having laid this groundwork, Friedman examines--in order chronologically by decade and by genre--Cummings' published works preceding the posthumous 73 poems. Where appropriate, each of these is supplied with biographical and publishing background; the contents of each are catalogued, categorized, summarized, and compared with those of earlier and later volumes; the relationship of each to the development of Cummings' mature vision and art is examined. With a bibliographic note. The introductory chapter is reprinted with minor changes in 1972.10.

10   GREGORY, HORACE. "E. E. Cummings." The Commonweal, 79, no. 24 (13 March), 725-26.
     Reviews 73 poems, describing many of Cummings' poems as "among the classics of modern poetry" and praising the uniqueness of his achieved "lyrical integration of satire, religious feeling and art." Cummings is also discussed in terms of the sixteenth and seventeenth century Courtly Makers and is compared with Emily Dickinson.

11   GROSS, HARVEY. "E. E. Cummings," in his Sound and Form in Modern Poetry: A Study of Prosody from Thomas Hardy to Robert Lowell. Ann Arbor: The University of Michigan Press, pp. 122-26.
     Describes Cummings as an employer of a "typographical prosody" which is a by-product of the push by Imagist techniques of the image and then words themselves toward "prosodic isolation." But Cummings goes further; not "only does he break down the line into visual shapes and give the separate word rhythmic autonomy, but he fragments words themselves. Each letter of the alphabet assumes importance in the rhythmic scheme." Poems 1 and 13 from no thanks are discussed in demonstration. Cummings' pictorial poems

1964

(especially the famous grasshopper poem) are also discussed.
They display a special form of synaethesia which, unfortun-
ately, often fails to span the "metaphorical gap between eye
and ear." Finally, Cummings' "shape poetry" operates on the
level of intellect, not perception or emotion. His visual
poems are compared and contrasted with those of the Meta-
physicals. Gross notes that "Cummings also writes the kind
of shape poem where meter as well as visual pattern make a
prosody" and concludes his discussion by remarking the importance of the typewriter to Cummings' work and to modern
writing in general.

12   JOOST, NICHOLAS. On Cummings, in his Scofield Thayer and "The
      Dial": An Illustrated History. Carbondale and Edwards-
      ville: Southern Illinois University Press, pp. 16, 22-23,
      37, 38, 51, 57, 58, 72, 78, 97, 112, 125-26, 127, 130-31,
      132, 154, 181, 188, 201, 224, 257, 262.
         Presents information on Cummings as a contributor to The
      Dial and a friend of its editors.

13   LEVIN, SAMUEL R. "Poetry and Grammaticalness," in Proceedings
      of the Ninth International Congress of Linguists. Edited
      by H. Lunt. The Hague, Netherlands: Mouton & Co.,
      pp. 203-10.
         Discusses a line from Cummings' "anyone lived in a pretty
      how town" in a commentary on generative grammar and deviant
      phrases and sentences in poems. The development of a gram-
      mar that would generate the phrase "he danced his did," al-
      though possible, would generate thousands of unwanted
      sentences. For a reply, see 1967.15. For comment, see
      1969.14. Reprinted: 1967.22.

14   McLUHAN, MARSHALL. On Cummings, in his Understanding Media:
      The Extensions of Man. New York: McGraw-Hill, pp. 260-61.
         Comments on the importance of the typewriter to Cummings'
      verse. "In Just-" is discussed as an example. Reprinted:
      1964.15.

15   McLUHAN, MARSHALL. On Cummings, in his Understanding Media:
      The Extensions of Man. New York: The New American Library,
      pp. 229-30.
         Reprint of 1964.14.

16   MARKS, BARRY A. E. E. Cummings. Twayne's United States Au-
      thors Series, No. 46. New York: Twayne Publishers, 156 pp.
         Because previous studies gained comprehensiveness at the
      cost of attention to individual works, Marks intends to il-
      luminate Cummings' attitudes and themes as they appear in

116

1964

specific poems. Chapter one presents detailed explications of four representative poems: "1(a," "nonsun blob a," "Among these red pieces of day," and "anyone lived in a pretty how town." The second chapter examines Cummings' interest in and use of two characteristics of the special sort of consciousness most typical of children (and of some artists): their open, uncultivated, and therefore unobstructed response to the world and to others, and their corollary ability to detach themselves from the world and others in the spirit of imaginative play. Also stressed is Cummings' mature awareness that children cannot be made final arbiters of value, as expressed in his qualifying sense of their often excessive egoism. Chapter three discusses the use of sex in Cummings. He employs sex as a sign of "natural vitality in contrast to sterile human conventionality." Discussion of Cummings' combining of traditional and experimental strategies for dealing with this subject is included, as is an examination of his attempts to expand its thematic implications into such areas as the humanizing of modern life. Several poems which include both sex and death are analyzed to demonstrate Cummings' belief that even these apparent opposites must be contained in any full vision of life.

Chapter four concentrates on Cummings' relation to some of the characteristic aesthetic ideas of his age: the overlapping of genres, especially of painting and poetry; the new realism of the cubists and others; the tendency to include the ugly as a necessary concomitant of beauty; and the emphasis on fragmentation and motion demanded by the discoveries of modern science. Chapter five concentrates on another aspect of the aesthetics of Cummings and his generation--the concept of formalism, with its view of the artist as craftsman-like maker and as creator of order. Chapters two through five support their generalizations with many close readings of individual poems. The sixth chapter describes Cummings as a typically American poet, typical because he expresses America's optimism, intensity of spirit, and millenial drive for perfection. At the same time, he sees the dark side of these virtues, especially in their frequent expression in materialistic and pragmatic rather than spiritual ways. Running throughout the book is a suggestion that Cummings is a religious writer whose religious sense is typified by the virtue of humility. Marks' emphasis is almost exclusively on the poetry; he includes a chronology and a brief bibliography. Passages reprinting analyses of "1(a" and "anyone lived in a pretty how town" appear in 1972.15 and 16 respectively. Reprinted: 1964.17.

1964

17 MARKS, BARRY A. E. E. Cummings. Twayne's United States Au-
thors Series, No. 46. New Haven, Connecticut: College and
University Press, 156 pp.
Reprint of 1964.16.

18 MARTZ, LOUIS L. Review of 73 poems. The Yale Review, 54, no.
2 (December), 285, 297-98.
Notices 73 poems in an omnibus review, finding Cummings
a still powerful master. "Something of this sort has maintained the acuteness of Cummings' poetry, an archaic but
nevertheless viable belief in the existence of a platonic
ideal."

19 MORSE, SAMUEL FRENCH. "Speaking of Books." New York Times
Book Review (20 September), p. 2.
Discusses Cummings' popularity with young readers, commenting on his transcendentalism, his romanticism, his use
of syntax to renew values, and his irreverence ("a kind of
civil disobedience").

20 MOTTRAM, ERIC. On Cummings. The Review, nos. 11-12, p. 39.
Complains that Cummings' poems of the thirties were
"simplifications" and therefore a form of "conservation of
the status quo" in a period of political and economic
pressures.

21 NORMAN, CHARLES. E. E. Cummings: The Magic-Maker. Second
edition. New York: Duell, Sloan and Pearce, 255 pp.
Revised edition of 1958.19, marked by the removal of
some documentation and by the addition of a brief chapter
updating the biography to the time of Cummings' death in
1962.

22 QUASIMODO, SALVATORE. "The Poetry of e. e. cummings," in his
The Poet and the Politician and Other Essays. Translated
by Thomas G. Bergin and Sergio Pacifici. Carbondale:
Southern Illinois University Press, pp. 118-20.
Reprint in English of 1953.12.

23 SHAPIRO, KARL. On Cummings. The Carleton Miscellany, 5, no.
3 (Summer), 21-23.
Describes Cummings, in a personal survey of authors, as
"a domesticated Baudelaire." Because Cummings didn't believe in original sin, he is a "minor poet." His poetry is
what "is left of the poetry of pleasure, poetry for the joy
of improvisation." Reprinted: 1968.24.

1965

24   WALSH, ROBERT C. "Cummings' 'Anyone Lived in a Pretty How
      Town.'" The Explicator, 22, no. 9 (May), Item 72.
           Beginning with Carr's thesis (see 1952.4) that the poem
      is both a love and an unlove story, paraphrases the entire
      poem to demonstrate that the pattern of the unlove story--
      the loss of love that accompanies growing up--fits each of
      the stanzas.

25   WELLS, HENRY W. On Cummings, in his New Poets From Old: A
      Study in Literary Genetics. New York: Russell & Russell,
      Inc., pp. 85, 141, 149, 152-53, 232-38.
           Reprint of 1940.5.

26   WILLIAMS, PAUL O. "Cummings' 'kind).'" The Explicator, 23,
      no. 1 (September), Item 4.
           Disentangles the poem's "merged and superimposed syntax"
      --a syntax which supports the poem's anticonventional theme
      --to demonstrate that it is "a satiric comment on the at-
      tempts of the scientific mind to explain the universe in
      terms of mathematics and trivial, explainable shapes."

                              1965

1   ANON. Review of E. E. Cummings: A Miscellany Revised. Ameri-
      can Literature, 37, no. 3 (November), 360.
           Briefly notices the appearance of the revised edition of
      Cummings' "fugitive" prose pieces edited by George J.
      Firmage.

2   BAUTISTA, CIRILO F. "The Bright Monolith: A Note on the
      Poetry of E. E. Cummings." Saint Louis Quarterly, 3, no. 4
      (December), 517-54.
           A general study of Cummings, examining his poetic quali-
      ties and his "renovations" of poetic tradition, with analy-
      ses of several poems. Bautista also examines the question
      of Cummings' intelligibility and attempts to define his
      position in American and world literature.

3   BIANCHI, RUGGERO. On Cummings, in his La Poetica Dell'
      Imagismo. Milan: U. Mursia & Co., pp. 7, 201.
           Briefly notes Cummings' debt to Imagism in his use of
      fragmentation for distilling the quintessence of a moment.
      In Italian.

4   BODE, CARL. "E. E. Cummings and Exploded Verse," in his The
      Half-World of American Culture: A Miscellany. Carbondale:
      Southern Illinois University Press, pp. 226-42.
           Reprint of 1961.2.

1965

5   CASTY, ALAN. "Tennessee Williams and the Small Hands of the
    Rain." The Mad River Review, 1, no. 3 (Fall-Winter), 27-43.
        Discusses Williams' use of the last line of Cummings'
    "somewhere i have travelled, gladly beyond" as the motto to
    The Glass Menagerie and argues that the "constellation of
    images and qualities" the line evokes has been the center
    of Williams' vision of life.

6   COWLEY, MALCOLM and ROBERT COWLEY. On Cummings. American
    Heritage, 16, no. 5 (August), 37.
        Includes, in a collection of documents from and about
    the twenties, Cummings' "workingman with hand so hairy-
    sturdy," which, in a brief headnote, is described as an
    expression of expatriate disaffection with Paris.

7   DAVIS, CHARLES T. "E. E. Cummings," in American Literary
    Scholarship: An Annual, 1963. Edited by James Woodress.
    Durham, North Carolina: Duke University Press, p. 172.
        Bibliographical essay describing works on Cummings pub-
    lished in 1963.

8   EATON, ANNE T. Review of Fairy Tales. Commonweal, 83, no. 5
    (5 November), 156.
        Notes the appearance of Fairy Tales. "Beautifully
    imagined, gently humorous, they will delight five- and six-
    year-olds."

9   FERRY, DAVID. On Cummings, in American Poetry. Stratford-
    Upon-Avon Studies, No. 7, edited by John Russell Brown,
    Bernard Harris, and Irvin Ehrenpreis. London: Edward
    Arnold (Publishers) Ltd., pp. 135-37, 147-50.
        In an essay on the diction of American poetry, compares
    Williams and Cummings in terms of the freedom with which
    they "use colloquial, slangy and generally non-literary
    language as an ordinary part of their style." Ferry finds
    that, although Cummings participates in the renovation of
    poetry by the reintroduction into it of "'unpoetic' terms,"
    his dissatisfaction with the accepted mode is only super-
    ficial, especially because he (unlike Williams) does not
    take the consequences of his style seriously.

10 FIRMAGE, GEORGE J. "Introduction," in E. E. Cummings: A
    Miscellany Revised. Edited by George J. Firmage. New York:
    October House, pp. vii-viii.
        Brief comments on the fugitive Cummings pieces collected
    in this volume, especially those added for this revision.
    Revised edition of 1958.8.

11 FORSYTH, JAMES. "Notes on E. E. Cummings." <u>Rebel Magazine</u>, 8
    (Winter), 29-40.
        Catalogues and gives examples of several of the "basic
    devices" of Cummings' poetry.

12 GREGORY, HORACE. "Introduction," in <u>E. E. Cummings: A Selec-
    tion of Poems</u>. New York: Harcourt, Brace & World, pp. 3-
    10.
        Calls Cummings "one of the greatest lyric poets of all
    time," comments on some of the "beliefs, places, and tradi-
    tions" that inform his poems, discusses his relationship to
    such French writers as Apollinaire, Michaux, and Cocteau,
    and examines his "comic spirit." In exploring Cummings'
    connection with his New England heritage, Gregory notes
    briefly but in detail similarities between Cummings and
    Emily Dickinson.

13 HART, JAMES D. "Cummings, E[dward] E[stlin]," in his <u>The Ox-
    ford Companion to American Literature</u>. Fourth edition.
    New York: Oxford University Press, p. 199.
        Slightly updated entry. Revised edition of 1941.7.

14 HOFFMAN, FREDERICK J. On Cummings, in his <u>The Twenties:
    American Writing in the Postwar Decade</u>. Second edition.
    New York: The Free Press, pp. 82-87, 254-55.
        Reprint of 1955.12.

15 JACKSON, CHARLOTTE. Review of <u>Fairy Tales</u>. <u>The Atlantic</u>, 216,
    no. 6 (December), 156.
        Brief notice of <u>Fairy Tales</u>.

16 JONES, A. R. On Cummings, in <u>American Poetry</u>. Stratford-Upon-
    Avon Studies, No. 7, edited by John Russell Brown, Bernard
    Harris, and Irvin Ehrenpreis. London: Edward Arnold (Pub-
    lishers) Ltd., pp. 125, 131.
        Notes that Cummings is indebted to the Imagists and that
    he "releases the romanticism latent in Imagism and allows
    it free lyrical play," often saving his poems from senti-
    mentality by use of "idiosyncratic phrasing and typography."

17 LURIE, ALISON. Review of <u>Fairy Tales</u>. <u>The New York Review of
    Books</u>, 5, no. 9 (9 December), 39.
        Notices <u>Fairy Tales</u> in an omnibus review and supposes
    that children "aren't going to like it much."

18 MILES, JOSEPHINE. On Cummings, in her <u>The Continuity of Poetic
    Language: The Primary Language of Poetry, 1540's-1940's</u>.
    New York: Octagon Books, pp. 385, 389, 391, 392, 393, 439,
    440-42, 444-45, 457, 476, 516, 517, 521.

1965

>   Reprint of 1951.13, with the addition of a note in the
>   forward on the importance of the word "mountain" in Cum-
>   mings' vocabulary.

19   MOORE, MARIANNE. "Humility, Concentration and Gusto," in her
>   A Marianne Moore Reader. New York: The Viking Press,
>   pp. 123-30, passim.
>   Reprint of 1955.24.

20   OLSON, CHARLES. On Cummings, in his Human Universe and Other
>   Essays. Edited by Donald Allen. San Francisco: The
>   Auerhahn Society, p. 58.
>   Reprint of 1950.16.

21   OSBORNE, WILLIAM R. "Cummings' 'The Bigness of Cannon' ('La
>   Guerre, I')." The Explicator, 24, no. 3 (November), Item
>   28.
>   Refutes Blackmur's use of the first line of this poem to
>   substantiate his thesis that Cummings' language is imprecise
>   (see 1931.1). Demonstrates that the word "skilful" is, in
>   fact, extremely precise. It ironically emphasizes the mis-
>   application of technology by the munitions makers and con-
>   tains the keen pun "is killful."

22   READ, DONALD R. "E. E. Cummings: The Lay of the Duckbilled
>   Platitude." Satire Newsletter, 3, no. 1 (Fall), 30-33.
>   Analyzes the "satire of political hypocrisy," "remarked
>   Robinson Jefferson," as resolving the formal paradox of
>   verse satire and as applying "the techniques of poetry to
>   satire in such a way as to realize potentialities of mean-
>   ing and integritas rarely realized in prose." Each of the
>   poem's satiric devices is explicated.

23   SCHROEDER, FRED E. H. "Obscenity and its Function in the
>   Poetry of E. E. Cummings." The Sewanee Review, 73, no. 3
>   (July-September), 469-78.
>   Argues that Cummings always uses obscene language or
>   allusion in connection with irony and satire to make moral
>   statements. "Cummings' satire is directed toward three
>   human foibles: pompous hypocrisy,...literary idealized
>   love,...and man's inhumanity to man." These attacks and
>   poems typifying them are discussed in some detail.

24   SCULLY, JAMES. "ee cummings," in Modern Poetics. Edited by
>   James Scully. New York: McGraw-Hill Book Co., pp. 119-20.
>   Headnote to a reprinting of Cummings' introduction to
>   Poems: 1923-1954 describes him as, for all his "eccentric
>   manners" and "satiric forays," "a lyric, affirmative

romancer" who battles "abstraction, intellectualization, or whatever seems 'artificial' and static."

25   SMITH, DAVID E.   "The Enormous Room and The Pilgrim's Progress." Twentieth Century Literature, 2 (July), 67-75.
     Argues that Cummings' work uses Bunyan's as its organizing principle and that the pilgrim-narrator's entry into a vision of human value and Christian community (the Delectable Mountains) requires his acceptance of human filth. This aspect of Cummings' work is related to Bunyan's allegorical use of the Slough of Despond and to portions of Swift's Gulliver's Travels. Reprinted: 1972.10. Revised edition: 1966.39.

26   STRAUMANN, HEINRICH.   On Cummings, in his American Literature in the Twentieth Century. New York: Harper & Row, p. 175.
     Reprint of 1951.15.

27   SUTTON, WALTER.   On Cummings, in American Poetry. Stratford-Upon-Avon Studies, No. 7, edited by John Russell Brown, Bernard Harris, and Irvin Ehrenpreis. London: Edward Arnold (Publishers) Ltd., pp. 175-76, 181, 191.
     Briefly comments, in an essay on criticism and poetry, on Cummings' denigration of criticism, his combining of traditional and experimental modes, and his development of a personal voice and manner.

28   THORNE, JAMES PETER.   "Stylistics and Generative Grammars." Journal of Linguistics, 1, no. 1 (April), 49-59.
     Argues at length that the total effect of "anyone lived in a pretty how town" is "controlled by the fact that the kind of irregularity it exhibits is regular in the context of the poem." The best linguistic method for approaching it is not to seek a generative grammar for Standard English that will produce its sentences, but to postulate an independent grammar and, so, an independent language. For comments, see 1969.14 and 1969.20.

29   TURNER, C. STEVEN.   "Cummings' 'In Just-.'" The Explicator, 24, no. 2 (October), Item 18.
     Argues that Felheim (see 1955.8) and Mayo (see 1947.10) fail to extend their readings of this poem sufficiently far. It points not only to a season of the year but also to a period of life, and while reveling in that time of youth it also implies its incipient loss.

30   WEGNER, ROBERT E.   The Poetry and Prose of E. E. Cummings. New York: Harcourt, Brace & World, Inc., 186 pp.

Described by its author as an <u>appreciation</u> of Cummings. Chapter one discusses the importance of self-discovery as a motive for Cummings' art and defines his paradoxical use of two key words: failure and nothing. The second chapter asserts that Cummings differs from his contemporaries in his "general attitude toward life, and in his method of employing subjects and images." His attitude is characterized by a distinction between individuals who are truly alive and "mostpeople" who fail or refuse to respond to life. Cummings himself presents not a system of thought, but a response to life. His central subjects are love, birth, growth, death, and their opposites. For him, love is all inclusive. His favored images (many of which are listed) are manifestations of the life force that infuses the universe.

The third chapter discusses Cummings' emphasis on freedom and individuality and his elevation of feeling over thinking as a guide to behavior; it also counters those critics who describe Cummings as an anarchist, solipsist, or nihilist and those who charge him with anticultural attitudes or with a failure to consider the tragic aspects of human nature. Countering another frequent critical complaint, that Cummings' poetry shows little growth, the fourth chapter discusses the poet's themes. These can be contained in an umbrella statement: "the purpose of life is the realization of love." This concept does not emerge full-blown but is developed through Cummings' career. This development is described in great detail.

Chapter five examines Cummings as satirist. Forces that stultify the natural, the spontaneous, the vital in life, Cummings sees as antagonists to be exposed, ridiculed, or "scorned to oblivion," and they are the objects of Cummings' satire. The final chapter examines Cummings' techniques and forms and finds that he is intensely aware of "the syntax of things." Whether experimentally or conventionally, Cummings uses forms and techniques skillfully to support, express, and embody his themes.

The book's arguments are supported with analyses of a large number of individual poems, and several of the prose works receive particular attention. Includes a chronological list of Cummings' books. Reprint of 1959.33.

31 W[ERSBA], B[ARBARA]. Review of <u>Fairy Tales</u>. <u>New York Times Book Review</u> (7 November), p. 40.
Examines <u>Fairy Tales</u>, describing its stories as "fragmentary and luminous, delicate, and blissfully unresolved; not so much 'about' things as the things themselves."

32   WESOLEK, GEORGE. "e. e. cummings: A Reconsideration."
      Renascence, 18, no. 1 (Autumn), 3-8.
           Argues that Cummings' poetic vision is more profound and
      intense than is usually recognized. "He confronts himself
      with cosmic dichotomies that take him to the core of man's
      reality." Wesolek explores Cummings' alienation from "most-
      people" and from the banal world and discovers that his
      isolation "forces him to turn in on himself and encounter
      whatever good or evil is there. The isolation also directs
      him to an Other, but an Other that is worthy of him--a Being
      that transcends even his visions." This being is both God
      and Love and something beyond. And finally, "neither God
      nor Love can fill the void in Cummings. The emptiness re-
      mains as a symbol of man's condition."

                              1966

1   ANON. "Dispraising Dogmata." The Times Literary Supplement
      (11 August), p. 726.
           Reviews E. E. Cummings: A Miscellany, finding that the
      collection reveals Cummings as self-contradictory and "over-
      simplifying," "a kind of pre-electronic sentimentalist."

2   ANON. Review of Fairy Tales. Saturday Review, 49, no. 4
      (22 January), 45.
           Brief notice of the publication of four children's
      stories written by Cummings for his daughter.

3   BARROWS, H. C., JR. and WILLIAM R. STEINHOFF. "'Anyone Lived
      in a Pretty How Town,'" in The Explicator Cyclopedia.
      Volume 1, Modern Poetry. Edited by Charles Child Walcutt
      and J. Edward Whitesell. Chicago: Quadrangle Books,
      pp. 35-36.
           Reprint of 1950.4.

4   BRAUER, GEORGE C., JR. On "(one!)," in The Explicator Cyclo-
      pedia. Volume 1, Modern Poetry. Edited by Charles Child
      Walcutt and J. Edward Whitesell. Chicago: Quadrangle
      Books, p. 41.
           Reprint of 1957.2.

5   BRITTON, JOHN. "'Pity This Busy Monster, Manunkind,'" in The
      Explicator Cyclopedia. Volume 1, Modern Poetry. Edited by
      Charles Child Walcutt and J. Edward Whitesell. Chicago:
      Quadrangle Books, pp. 41-42.
           Reprint of 1959.8.

1966

6   BUDD, LOUIS J. "'Buffalo Bill's Defunct,'" in The Explicator
      Cyclopedia. Volume 1, Modern Poetry. Edited by Charles
      Child Walcutt and J. Edward Whitesell. Chicago: Quadrangle
      Books, pp. 37-38.
         Reprint of 1953.2.

7   CARR, ARTHUR. On "anyone lived in a pretty how town," in The
      Explicator Cyclopedia. Volume 1, Modern Poetry. Edited by
      Charles Child Walcutt and J. Edward Whitesell. Chicago:
      Quadrangle Books, pp. 36-37.
         Reprint of 1952.4.

8   CLAGGETT, MARY FRANCES. "'Glory, Jest, and Riddle.'" English
      Journal, 55, no. 3 (March), 353-54.
         A discussion of "what if a much of a which of a wind,"
      emphasizing its pattern and images and the way in which its
      "riddle nature" might be used to effect in teaching the poem
      in the high school classroom.

9   CROWDER, RICHARD. "48," in The Explicator Cyclopedia. Volume
      1, Modern Poetry. Edited by Charles Child Walcutt and J.
      Edward Whitesell. Chicago: Quadrangle Books, pp. 47-48.
         Reprint of 1958.6.

10   DEMBO, L. S. "E. E. Cummings: The Now Man," in his Concep-
      tions of Reality in Modern American Poetry. Berkeley and
      Los Angeles: University of California Press, pp. 118-28.
         Discusses the relation of Cummings' ideas to Bergson's
      concept of "spontaneous existence," "physical and mental
      life as a perpetual birth and growth, as constant becoming."
      For Cummings, perception and response are crucial, and he
      makes the distinction between "the deluded rationalists
      (bourgeois society) and the enlightened irrationalists
      (poets)" typical of the objectivists. Cummings' ideas about
      the self and its relation to the world are also related to
      objectivist ideas. In Cummings, the self-transcending self
      treats objects not as abstractions but as "blossoming" in
      the mind. The "imitation of being and becoming" in the now
      of the poem is central to Cummings' poetic and determines
      much of his technique. It is the perceiving self which
      "resolves" the contradiction between growth as development
      in time and the idea of "'instantaneous growth.'" Cummings
      relates to objects both as an objectivist and a mystic.

11   DIAS, EARL J. "E. E. Cummings and Buffalo Bill." The CEA
      Critic, 29, no. 3 (December), 6-7.
         Argues that in "Buffalo Bill's" Cummings ironically de-
      nounces Buffalo Bill as a negator of life.

1966

12 DOS PASSOS, JOHN. On Cummings, in his <u>The Best of Times: An</u>
    <u>Informal Memoir</u>. New York: The New American Library,
    pp. 23-24, 61, 82-89, 132-35, 164-65.
        Reminiscences of Dos Passos' relations with Cummings at
    Harvard, in New York, and in Europe, with comments on Cum-
    mings' explosively extemporaneous conversation.

13 FELHEIM, MARVIN. "'In Just-,'" in <u>The Explicator Cyclopedia</u>.
    Volume 1, Modern Poetry. Edited by Charles Child Walcutt
    and J. Edward Whitesell. Chicago: Quadrangle Books,
    pp. 38-39.
        Reprint of 1955.8.

14 FIEDLER, LESLIE. On Cummings, in his <u>Love and Death in the</u>
    <u>American Novel</u>. Second edition. New York: Dell Publishing
    Co., A Delta Book, p. 479.
        The Cummings entry is unchanged in this revised edition
    of 1960.6.

15 FIEDLER, LESLIE. On Cummings, in his <u>Love and Death in the</u>
    <u>American Novel</u>. Second edition. New York: Stein and Day,
    Publishers, p. 479.
        The Cummings entry is unchanged in this revised edition
    of 1960.6.

16 GARGANO, JAMES W. On "Pity This Busy Monster, Manunkind," in
    <u>The Explicator Cyclopedia</u>. Volume 1, Modern Poetry. Edited
    by Charles Child Walcutt and J. Edward Whitesell. Chicago:
    Quadrangle Books, p. 42.
        Reprint of 1961.7.

17 GERBER, PHILIP L. On Cummings, in his <u>Robert Frost</u>. Twayne's
    United States Authors Series, No. 107. New York: Twayne
    Publishers, pp. 99-100.
        Contrasts Cummings' formal concerns with Frost's.

18 GOODWIN, K. L. On Cummings, in his <u>The Influence of Ezra</u>
    <u>Pound</u>. London: Oxford University Press, pp. 171-75.
        Explores Cummings' debt to Pound. His "major innovation,
    ...the careful placement of words on the printed page, owes
    something to Pound." Other areas in which Goodwin suggests
    influence are the use of dialects, a "penchant for indecen-
    cy," and "the technique of offering unpopular opinions in a
    demagogic way."

19 GRIFFITH, BEN W. On "Memorabilia," in <u>The Explicator Cyclo-</u>
    <u>pedia</u>. Volume 1, Modern Poetry. Edited by Charles Child

1966

Walcutt and J. Edward Whitesell. Chicago: Quadrangle
Books, p. 40.
Reprint of 1954.14.

20 GROSSMAN, D. JON. "Présentation," "Chronologie," "Les Poèmes,"
"La Prose--Le Théatre," "Les Peintures," "Témoignages," and
"Notes Pour Une Bibliographie Critique," in his E. E. Cummings. Poètes d'Aujourd'hui, No. 142. Paris: Pierre
Seghers, pp. [7]-12, [13]-19, [20]-57, [58]-78, [79]-85,
[86]-91, [185]-90.
    Presents a complex of materials as introduction and ap-
pendix to an extensive selection of Cummings' work. An
introductory note describes this edition of translations,
discusses Cummings in relation to French literature, and
remarks on his reputation in France. A chronology presents
detailed information on Cummings' life and publishing
career. A chapter on the poems examines each of Cummings'
volumes in sequence, describing them, placing them in context, suggesting influences on their poems, and commenting
on developments in their themes and techniques. A chapter
on the prose and plays does the same for the major prose
and dramatic works. A brief section discusses Cummings as
a painter, describing some of his creations, comparing them
with the works of other painters, and suggesting connections
between his paintings and writing. Grossman also collects
a number of short comments on Cummings by other critics.
With a selected bibliography. In French.

21 GURIAN, JAY. On "Buffalo Bill's." Colorado Quarterly, 15,
no. 1 (Summer), 75-77.
    Comments on "Buffalo Bill's" in an examination of Western
poetry and poetics, finding that "Cummings was satirizing
the hoax aspects" of the settlement of the West.

22 HENRY, NAT. On "These Children Singing in Stone A," in The
Explicator Cyclopedia. Volume 1, Modern Poetry. Edited by
Charles Child Walcutt and J. Edward Whitesell. Chicago:
Quadrangle Books, p. 45.
Reprint of 1955.11.

23 HENRY, NAT. "305," in The Explicator Cyclopedia. Volume 1,
Modern Poetry. Edited by Charles Child Walcutt and J. Ed-
ward Whitesell. Chicago: Quadrangle Books, p. 49.
Reprint of 1962.16.

24 HENRY, NAT. "275," in The Explicator Cyclopedia. Volume 1,
Modern Poetry. Edited by Charles Child Walcutt and J. Ed-
ward Whitesell. Chicago: Quadrangle Books, p. 48.
Reprint of 1962.17.

25   HYMAN, STANLEY EDGAR. "The Extremes of E. E. Cummings," in
      his <u>Standards: A Chronicle of Books for Our Time</u>. New
      York: Horizon Press, pp. 118-22.
          Discusses the extremes of Cummings' art: his failures
      of sentimentality and bitterness, his successes of beauty,
      love, and joy and of the "lifegiving and humane."

26   HYNES, SAM. "276," in <u>The Explicator Cyclopedia</u>. Volume 1,
      Modern Poetry. Edited by Charles Child Walcutt and J. Ed-
      ward Whitesell. Chicago: Quadrangle Books, p. 48.
          Reprint of 1951.11.

27   KENNEDY, RICHARD S. "Edward Cummings, the Father of the Poet."
      <u>Bulletin of the New York Public Library</u>, 70, no. 7 (Septem-
      ber), 437-49.
          Presents information on Cummings' father, describing him
      as "the dominant figure in the early life of his son."
      Among direct influences, Kennedy notes the "constant verbal-
      ization that was part of a minister's life," the father's
      love of word-play, his liberal use of metaphor and con-
      trolling image in his sermons (an extension of the New
      England emblematic habit of mind), and his humanistic,
      Unitarian world view.

28   KILBY, CLYDE S. "'Memorabilia,'" in <u>The Explicator Cyclopedia</u>.
      Volume 1, Modern Poetry. Edited by Charles Child Walcutt
      and J. Edward Whitesell. Chicago: Quadrangle Books,
      pp. 39-40.
          Reprint of 1953.7.

29   LASSER, MICHAEL L. "Cummings' 'Sonnet Entitled How to Run the
      World.'" <u>The Explicator</u>, 24, no. 5 (January), Item 44.
          Argues that, despite Freidman's suggestion (<u>see</u> 1964.9),
      the nine isolated capital letters in the sonnet may, al-
      though unpronounced, have a use close to the verbal, perhaps
      indicating that the words they precede are to be taken to-
      gether to form a comment on the poem as a whole. This would
      support the poem's themes of love, surrender, feeling, and
      transcendence.

30   LEVIN, GERALD. "'Poem (Love's function...),'" in <u>The Explica-
      tor Cyclopedia</u>. Volume 1, Modern Poetry. Edited by Charles
      Child Walcutt and J. Edward Whitesell. Chicago: Quadrangle
      Books, pp. 42-43.
          Reprint of 1958.17.

1966

31 LINDROTH, JAMES R. and COLETTE LINDROTH. <u>Monarch Literature</u>
    <u>Notes on the Poems of E. E. Cummings</u>. New York: Monarch
    (Simon & Schuster), 90 pp.
        An introductory study guide to Cummings' poems.

32 LORD, JOHN B. "Para-Grammatical Structures in a Poem of E. E.
    Cummings." <u>Pacific Coast Philology</u>, 1 (April), 66-73.
        Examines Cummings' use of certain recursive (e.g., "all
    by all and deep by deep") and nonrecursive (e.g., "wish by
    spirit and if by yes") structures as a kind of para-grammar
    which supports the meaning of "anyone lived in a pretty how
    town."

33 MORSE, SAMUEL FRENCH. Review of <u>Fairy Tales</u>. <u>The Horn Book</u>
    <u>Magazine</u>, 42, no. 1 (February), 52.
        Reviews the stories of <u>Fairy Tales</u> as "evocations of
    mood" combining "innocence, wonder, enthusiasm, and a
    special kind of gaiety."

34 MOSELEY, EDWIN M. "'These Children Singing in Stone A,'" in
    <u>The Explicator Cyclopedia</u>. Volume 1, Modern Poetry. Edited
    by Charles Child Walcutt and J. Edward Whitesell. Chicago:
    Quadrangle Books, pp. 43-44.
        Reprint of 1950.15.

35 RECK, MICHAEL. Review of <u>Fairy Tales</u>. <u>Commonweal</u>, 83, no. 18
    (11 February), 562.
        Notices <u>Fairy Tales</u>, describing its "immense parable of
    innocence" as being moving without being sentimental.

36 RUS, LOUIS "'(one!),'" in <u>The Explicator Cyclopedia</u>. Volume
    1, Modern Poetry. Edited by Charles Child Walcutt and J.
    Edward Whitesell. Chicago: Quadrangle Books, pp. 40-41.
        Reprint of 1957.20.

37 SANDERS, BARRY. "Cummings' 'All in Green Went My Love Riding.'"
    <u>The Explicator</u>, 25, no. 3 (November), Item 23.
        Suggests that the poem is specifically concerned with the
    goddess Diana and presents supportive evidence. The death
    in the last line is of a special sort, the death of the
    speaker's heart in the face of unrequited love, an ending
    appropriate to Diana's chasteness. <u>See</u> 1967.20 and 1968.23.

38 SHUCHTER, J. D. "E. E. Cummings and Joe Gould's 'Oral His-
    tory.'" <u>American Notes and Queries</u>, 4, no. 10 (June),
    148-49.
        Indicates that lines from a Cummings' poem (<u>see</u> <u>no</u>
    <u>thanks</u>, p. 27) express early doubt about the existence of
    the "Oral History."

39 SMITH, DAVID E. "The Enormous Room, The Pilgrim's Progress,
    and the 'Demonic Trinity,'" in his John Bunyan in America.
    Indiana University Humanities Series, No. 61, edited by
    Edward D. Seeber. Bloomington: Indiana University Press,
    pp. 105-19, 135-37.
       This revision of 1965.25 expands the original essay by
    expressing its arguments in greater detail and by increasing
    its evidentiary quotations.

40 SQUIER, CHARLES L. "Cummings' 'Anyone Lived in a Pretty How
    Town.'" The Explicator, 25, no. 4 (December), Item 37.
       Demonstrates that the poem's many themes "are carried by
    the bells which ring throughout it." They "mark the passage
    of time; they tell the seasons, signal birth, marriage, and
    death. Thus they underline the cyclical themes of the
    poem." But they also "mark or comment on the quality of
    the experiences suggested in the poem. The tone of the
    bells changes with the experience."

41 STANFORD, ANN. "E. E. Cummings," in American Literary Scholar-
    ship: An Annual, 1964. Edited by James Woodress. Durham,
    North Carolina: Duke University Press, pp. 186-89.
       Bibliographical essay describing works on Cummings pub-
    lished in 1964.

42 STANLEY, JULIA P. "An Analysis of E. E. Cummings' 'Actuali-
    ties: I.'" College Composition and Communication, 17,
    no. 3 (October), 130-34.
       Analyzes Cummings' use of "syntax, lexicon, and phonol-
    ogy" in "Actualities: I," discovering that "all work toward
    unification of the sonnet as an artistic totality." Stanley
    lists the sonnet's "kernel sentences" and comments on its
    use of "WH-transforms," of modification, especially spatial,
    of violation, and of formal structure.

43 STEINBERG, JACK. "'1 X 1,'" in The Explicator Cyclopedia.
    Volume 1, Modern Poetry. Edited by Charles Child Walcutt
    and J. Edward Whitesell. Chicago: Quadrangle Books,
    pp. 46-47.
       Reprint of 1949.12.

44 STETLER, CHARLES EDWARD. "A Study of the Transcendental Poetry
    of E. E. Cummings." Ph.D. dissertation, Tulane University.
       Concentrates on Cummings' poems of love and transcendence,
    demonstrating through many explications "the progressive
    deepening of Cummings' beliefs, the steady clarification of
    his transcendental vision, and the ever increasing control

1966

over materials used to communicate that vision." Concludes
that Cummings is not a "negativist" but a "positive romanticist."

45 STEVENS, WALLACE. On Cummings, in his Letters of Wallace
    Stevens. Edited by Holly Stevens. New York: Alfred A.
    Knopf, pp. 667, 785, 867, 868.
        Contains a letter to Cummings offering Stevens' sponsor-
    ship of his application for a Bollingen grant and letters
    to others commenting on a recording of song settings of
    Cummings' poems and on Stevens winning (over Cummings) the
    1954 National Book Award for Poetry.

46 SWADOS, HARVEY. "E. E. Cummings," in The American Writer and
    the Great Depression. Edited by Harvey Swados. The Ameri-
    can Heritage Series, edited by Leonard W. Levy and Alfred
    Young. Indianapolis, Indiana: The Bobbs-Merrill Co.,
    pp. 379-80.
        Headnote to "Speech from a Forthcoming Play" describes
    Cummings as a "congenital nonconformist" and a "romantic
    anarchist." In the "Speech" he shows himself as "a chron-
    icler of oppression and stoic resistance."

47 TUCKER, ROBERT G. "Cummings the Chivalrous," in The Twenties:
    Poetry and Prose, 20 Critical Essays. Edited by Richard E.
    Langford and William E. Taylor. Deland, Florida: Everett
    Edwards Press, pp. 25-27.
        Argues that Cummings is a chivalrous poet jousting with
    the modern monsters of "constrictive conventionalism" in
    order to "clear the air of lovelessness" and enable the
    celebration of love. The satires make redeeming love inde-
    pendent of time and the world.

48 VOWLES, RICHARD B. "'Space Being...Curved," in The Explicator
    Cyclopedia. Volume 1, Modern Poetry. Edited by Charles
    Child Walcutt and J. Edward Whitesell. Chicago: Quadrangle
    Books, p. 43.
        Reprint of 1950.23.

49 WEIMER, DAVID R. "Grassblades Assassinated: E. E. Cummings,"
    in his The City as Metaphor. Random House Studies in Lan-
    guage and Literature, No. 8, edited by Paul Fussell, Jr.
    New York: Random House, pp. [78]-87.
        Examines Cummings as a city poet, his technical use of
    the innovations of the "new art" introduced to America by
    the Armory Show of 1913, and his impulse to separate the
    born from the made, feeling from syntax, nature from city,
    and so on.

50   WHICHER, STEPHEN E.   "'What if a Much of a Which of a Wind,'"
      in The Explicator Cyclopedia. Volume 1, Modern Poetry.
      Edited by Charles Child Walcutt and J. Edward Whitesell.
      Chicago: Quadrangle Books, pp. 45-46.
          Reprint of 1953.17.

                              1967

1   BACKUS, JOSEPH M.   "Two 'No-Name' Poems." Names: Journal of
      the American Name Society, 15, no. 1 (March), 1-7.
          Analyzes Dickinson's "I'm Nobody! Who are you?" and
      Cummings' "anyone lived in a pretty how town" as examples
      of works which use "no-names" to indicate "'the denial of
      existence to any such-named person'" and "'a person...of no
      importance.'" In both poems, the "no-names" function
      literally and in ironic reversal of ordinary values.

2   BENEDIKT, MICHAEL.   "Santa Claus by E. E. Cummings," in his
      Theatre Experiment: An Anthology of American Plays. Garden
      City, New York: Doubleday & Co., p. [73].
          Describes Cummings' attitudes toward American culture
      and his sense of theatre as event as prophetic. Santa Claus
      is a "prenaturalistic play," a modern morality play with its
      pageant augmented by hints of circus, burlesque, and vaude-
      ville spectacle.

3   BRADLEY, SCULLEY, RICHARD CROOM BEATTY, and E. HUDSON LONG.
      "E. E. Cummings," in their The American Tradition in Litera-
      ture. Third edition. Vol. 2. New York: W. W. Norton &
      Co., pp. 1570-71.
          Slightly updated entry. Revised edition of 1956.2.

4   CHISHOLM, WILLIAM S.   "An Exercise in Syntactic Stylistics."
      Linguistics, 33 (July), 24-36.
          Responds to questions raised by Ciardi's remarks on "what
      if a much of a which of a wind" (see 1964.4), approaching
      the poem from the point of view of syntactic stylistics to
      isolate its points of grammatical innovation.

5   COAN, OTIS W. and RICHARD G. LILLARD.   "Cummings, E. E.," in
      America in Fiction: An Annotated List of Novels That In-
      terpret Aspects of Life in the United States, Canada, and
      Mexico. Palo Alto, California: Pacific Books, p. 123.
          Briefly annotates The Enormous Room as a realistic "and
      subtle analysis of a kind of Pilgrim's Progress through
      shock and horror."

1967

6   COOPERMAN, STANLEY. On Cummings, in his <u>World War I and the</u>
     <u>American Novel</u>. Baltimore, Maryland: The Johns Hopkins
     Press, pp. 69, 70, 80, 82, 95-96, 98, 106-107, 119, 143,
     169-75, 185, 189-90, 219, 242.
          Examines Cummings as a member of the literary generation
     shaped by the impact of World War I. Emphasis is on <u>The</u>
     <u>Enormous Room</u>, in which "the rhetoric of indignation becomes
     the drama of absurdity." Cooperman explores Cummings' em-
     phasis on the individual, his manipulation of language, the
     exasperating effect of his parody in so serious a context,
     and his use of La Ferté as controlling symbol.

7   COWLEY, MALCOLM. "Cummings: The Last of Lyric Poets," in his
     <u>Think Back on Us...A Contemporary Chronicle of the 1930's</u>.
     Edited by Henry Dan Piper. Carbondale and Edwardsville:
     Southern Illinois University Press, pp. 203-208.
          Reprint of 1932.3.

8   CUNLIFFE, MARCUS. On Cummings, in his <u>The Literature of the</u>
     <u>United States</u>. Third edition. London: Penguin Books,
     pp. 236, 276, 316, 325, 329-31, 332, 385.
          Although the book is revised, the Cummings entry is un-
     changed in this reprint of 1954.11.

9   FIRMAGE, GEORGE J. "Introduction," in <u>E. E. Cummings: Three</u>
     <u>Plays & A Ballet</u>. New York: October House, pp. vii-x.
          Presents brief, largely bibliographic background on <u>Him</u>,
     <u>Anthropos</u>, <u>Santa Claus</u>, and <u>Tom</u>, and quotes the "Imaginary
     Dialogue" by Cummings and the "thumbnail-analysis" by Isidor
     Schneider, both of which appear on the book jacket of the
     first edition of <u>Him</u>.

10   FRENCH, WARREN. On Cummings, in his <u>The Thirties: Fiction,</u>
     <u>Poetry, Drama</u>. Deland, Florida: Everett Edwards, p. 119.
          Notes that Cummings "continued to turn out...[his] fan-
     tastic mixture of typographical eccentricity and sentiment."
     His "poetry of the 30s looks--quite literally--like that of
     the 20s."

11   FRIEDMAN, NORMAN. <u>E. E. Cummings: The Art of His Poetry</u>.
     Second edition. Baltimore, Maryland: The Johns Hopkins
     Press, 218 pp.
          Augments the first edition with a lengthy bibliography
     of works on Cummings published from 1922 to 1965. Revised
     edition of 1960.8.

12   GAULL, MARILYN. "Language and Identity: A Study of E. E.
     Cummings' <u>The Enormous Room</u>." <u>American Quarterly</u>, 19, no.
     4 (Winter), [645]-62.

Argues that Cummings "assumed the multiple task of demonstrating not only the discrepancy between language and experience but also the corrosive effects of this discrepancy
on the human psyche, and, perhaps his most significant
achievement, offered a means for overcoming it in the creation of new relationships between language and experience."
His characteristic device for approaching these tasks is
"the manipulation of contexts, associating symbols with
their functional referents rather than traditional ones."
And, although this often causes confusion in the poetry, it
succeeds in The Enormous Room because it is "integral to the
form and theme of the novel." Gaull examines these matters
in terms of The Enormous Room, concluding that the book is
"a metaphor for the Edenic experience of the creating
imagination" as it reintegrates language and life. The
working out of this reintegration by the author is a para-
digm for the experience of the narrator.

13 GENTHE, CHARLES VINCENT. "Personal War Narratives in America,
    1914-1918." Ph.D. dissertation, Washington State Univer-
    sity.
        Comments briefly on the denunciation by Cummings and
    other "young apostates" of the romantic faith in war held
    by their "literary forebears."

14 HILL, ARCHIBALD A. On Cummings, in Essays on the Language of
    Literature. Edited by Seymour Chatman and Samuel R. Levin.
    Boston: Houghton Mifflin Co., p. 391.
        Notes that Cummings' adaptation of the linguistically
    unpredictable in "anyone lived in a pretty how town" is an
    example of that modernist technique which says "something
    nonsensical on the linguistic level, hoping that it will
    become meaningful on the stylistic level."

15 HILL, ARCHIBALD A. "Some Further Thoughts on Grammaticality
    and Poetic Language." Style, 1, no. 2 (Spring), 81-91.
        Disagrees with Samuel Levin's assertion (see 1964.13)
    "that all poetically deviant sentences are the result of
    processes like those of normal sentence formation" and
    argues instead that poetic "distortions" are special ef-
    fects, that the assumption that deviant sentences are inten-
    tional distortions of normal ones "solves all grammatical
    difficulties," and that the "underlying normal form" of
    such deviant sentences is recoverable. Cummings' "nonsun
    blob a" is one of several examples discussed in demonstra-
    tion. For a response, see 1971.12.

1967

16   HOFFMAN, FREDERICK J.   On Cummings.   Comparative Literature
      Studies, 4, nos. 1 and 2, 196.
           In an essay on "symbolisme" and modern American poetry,
      notes Cummings' use of symbol as motif in "my father moved
      through dooms of love."

17   IZZO, CARLO.   "Aldo, Tallone e Cummings," in his Civiltà Ameri-
      cana.   Volume 1, Saggi.   Biblioteca di Studi Americani, No.
      14.   Rome: Edizione di Storia e Letteratura, pp. 377-81.
           Brief general comments on Cummings.   In Italian.

18   IZZO, CARLO.   "In Morte di E. E. Cummings," in his Civiltà
      Americana.   Volume 1, Saggi.   Biblioteca di Studi Americani,
      No. 14.   Rome: Edizione di Storia e Letteratura, pp. 383-
      86.
           Obituary notice, commenting generally on Cummings' themes
      and techniques and praising him especially as a love poet of
      rare innocence.   In Italian.

19   JOOST, NICHOLAS.   On Cummings, in his Years of Transition:
      "The Dial," 1912-1920.   Barre, Massachusetts: Barre Pub-
      lishers, pp. 150, 169-70, 232, 261, 269, 273-74.
           Brief comments on Cummings in relation to the take-over
      of The Dial by Watson and Thayer.

20   JUMPER, WILL C.   "Cummings' 'All in Green Went My Love Riding.'"
      The Explicator, 26, no. 1 (September), Item 6.
           Rejects Sanders' reading of the poem (see 1966.37) be-
      cause it assumes the persona is male, whereas the poem's
      fifteenth-century sources indicate that the speaker is fe-
      male.   The poem is a literary ballad reconstructing an in-
      creasingly unlucky hunt during which the speaker's love is
      slain; it is not cyclic.   See 1968.23.

21   KALIN, BERKLEY.   "Social Criticism in Twentieth Century Ameri-
      can Poetry."   Ph.D. dissertation, St. Louis University.
           Contains a section examining Cummings as a poet who cre-
      ates an individual world in which his personality finds
      fulfillment.   He "urges the individual to rely upon sensual
      experience and to accept the essential mystery of life,
      namely love."

22   LEVIN, SAMUEL R.   "Poetry and Grammaticalness," in Essays on
      the Language of Literature.   Edited by Seymour Chatman and
      Samuel R. Levin.   Boston: Houghton Mifflin Co., pp. 224-30.
           Reprint of 1964.13.

23 LEWIS, R. W. B. On Cummings, in his <u>The Poetry of Hart Crane:</u>
   <u>A Critical Study</u>. Princeton, New Jersey: Princeton University Press, pp. 46, 74-77, 120.
   Notes that Crane's "Chaplinesque" helped establish the
   mood for "subsequent projections of the artist as comedian"
   by other artists, including Cummings. Cummings' projection
   in <u>Him</u> is discussed in particular.

24 MATTFIELD, MARY S. "Cummings' 'Let's From Some Loud Unworld's
   Most Rightful Wrong.'" <u>The Explicator</u>, 26, no. 4 (December), Item 32.
   Reads the poem as an example of Cummings' growth from
   his youthful negations to a more mature philosophy. This
   philosophy is an Emersonian transcendentalism, and the poem
   exhorts its speaker's beloved to turn from "nonexistence"
   and, through Nature, "to find identity with the noblest
   human values."

25 NORMAN, CHARLES. <u>E. E. Cummings: A Biography</u>. Second edition. New York: E. P. Dutton & Co., 354 pp.
   Revised edition, marked by the removal of some documentation and by the addition of a brief chapter updating the
   biography to the time of Cummings' death in 1962 and a new
   foreword. Revision of 1958.19.

26 OLSON, CHARLES. On Cummings, in his <u>Human Universe and Other</u>
   <u>Essays</u>. Edited by Donald Allen. New York: Grove Press,
   p. 58.
   Reprint of 1950.16.

27 PATTY, AUSTIN. "Cummings' Impressions of Communist Russia."
   <u>Rendevous</u>, 2, no. 1 (Spring), 15-22.
   Asserts that "ideas and attitudes about the individual
   and society formed before he even went to Russia" are manifested in Cummings' <u>Eimi</u>. Patty discusses <u>Eimi</u> and work
   preceding it from this angle.

28 SALZMAN, JACK. On Cummings, in <u>Years of Protest: A Collection</u>
   <u>of American Writings of the 1930's</u>. Edited by Jack Salzman.
   New York: Pegasus, pp. 377, 384.
   Describes Cummings as one of the outstanding literary
   individualists of the thirties and comments briefly on his
   attacks on both communism and capitalism in a syntax that
   itself attacks all that denies individualism.

29 SPRINGER, HASKELL S. "The Poetics of E. E. Cummings." <u>South</u>
   <u>Atlantic Bulletin</u>, 32, no. 4 (November), 8-10.

1967

Argues that Cummings' style is "directly related to traditional prosodic principles" and examines his uses of and
his attempts to disguise traditional poetics in several
poems. As "a general principle, he intentionally makes it
difficult for a reader to comprehend his verse" in order
"to force the reader to take part in the poetic process."
Springer also discusses several other aspects of Cummings'
language and technique. Reprinted: 1972.23.

30 STANFORD, ANN. "E. E. Cummings," in American Literary Scholarship: An Annual, 1965. Edited by James Woodress. Durham,
North Carolina: Duke University Press, pp. 215-17.
Bibliographical essay describing works on Cummings published in 1965.

31 WHITNEY, BLAIR. "American Poetic Drama: 1900-1966." Ph.D.
dissertation, University of Illinois.
Discusses Cummings' plays in an examination of American
poetic drama in this century. Like those of other part-
time dramatists, Cummings' plays suffer from insufficient
knowledge of stagecraft and dramatic structure, but they
"contain some excellent dramatic poetry."

32 WORTH, KATHERINE J. On Cummings' Him, in her "The Poets in
the American Theatre," in American Theatre. Stratford-Upon-
Avon Studies, No. 10, edited by John Russell Brown and
Bernard Harris. London: Edward Arnold (Publishers) Ltd.,
pp. 102-107.
Comments on Him as a "seminal play, which reflects or
anticipates many characteristic preoccupations of the poets
in the theatre" and discusses its theme, techniques, stag-
ing, and form (especially its discovery of a form for con-
veying "stream of consciousness"). At times, the play is
undisciplined and prolix, but its "achievement remains impressive." Similarities between Him and William Carlos
Williams' Many Loves and A Dream of Love are noted.

1968

1 ANON. "Lower Case Lover." The Times Literary Supplement
(28 November), pp. 1339-40.
Reviews Complete Poems, assessing Cummings as a relatively minor, if felicitous and surprising poet whose
revelations are often those of "a personal rhythm." He is
a characteristic American in his egocentrism and his dis-
owning of history. His morality is "loose," his faith
"easy."

1968

2   ANON. "Putting the Jerks into Joys." The Times Literary
     Supplement (22 August), p. 902.
          Reviews The Enormous Room and Three Plays and a Ballet.
     The former is described as a "Dadaist documentary." Its
     "language and syntax are amazingly fresh." As to the lat-
     ter, each of the four works it collects receives a brief
     comment.

3   BLACKMUR, R. P. "Notes on E. E. Cummings' Language," in
     Literary Opinion in America. Third edition. Edited by
     Morton Dauwen Zabel. Gloucester, Massachusetts: Peter
     Smith, pp. 296-314.
          Reprint of 1931.1.

4   CLINE, PATRICIA BUCHANAN TAL-MASON. "The Whole E. E. Cum-
     mings." Twentieth Century Literature, 14, no. 2 (July),
     90-97.
          Argues that Cummings demanded a "holistic experience of
     life." He posits two realms: the real world of "growth
     and decay in time" and the ideal world of "timeless and im-
     measurable absolutes." Nature and man exist in the real
     but participate in the ideal through love. But beyond this
     lies the possibility of growth, "the active striving toward
     contact with the absolute, 'to die in time and be reborn in
     timelessness,' through love." Growth and rebirth, the
     transcendence of the real and the incorporation of the ideal
     are his paradoxical means. The satires "are merely the
     other side of the same argument." The development of these
     ideas in Cummings' work is discussed. Reprinted: 1972.10.

5   DICKEY, JAMES. "E. E. Cummings," in his Babel to Byzantium:
     Poets and Poetry Now. New York: Farrar, Straus and Giroux,
     pp. 100-106.
          Reprint of 1959.12.

6   DOUGHERTY, JAMES P. "Language as a Reality in E. E. Cummings."
     Bucknell Review, 16, no. 2 (May), 112-22.
          While most modern poets have grounded themselves in "the
     phenomenological world of definite persons, things, and ac-
     tions" in order to escape the pitfalls of abstraction,
     Cummings--in his "idea-poems"--departs from that world. He
     vivifies his abstractions "not so much by tangible symbols
     as by an appeal to the tangibility of language itself."
     "Pity this busy monster, manunkind," "my father moved
     through dooms of love," and "anyone lived in a pretty how
     town" are discussed from this angle.

1968

7   EARNEST, ERNEST. On Cummings, in his <u>Expatriates and Patriots:</u>
    <u>American Artists, Scholars, and Writers in Europe</u>. Durham,
    North Carolina: Duke University Press, pp. 256, 264, 270,
    275, 280.
        Occasional comments on Cummings as a member of the ex-
    patriate generation of the twenties.

8   EVANS, OLIVER. Cummings Scholarship, in <u>American Literary</u>
    <u>Scholarship: An Annual, 1966</u>. Edited by James Woodress.
    Durham, North Carolina: Duke University Press, pp. 207,
    210, 211.
        Describes, in a bibliographical essay, works on Cummings
    published in 1966.

9   FAIRLEY, IRENE R. "Syntax as Style: An Analysis of Three
    Cummings Poems," in <u>Studies Presented to Professor Roman</u>
    <u>Jakobson By His Students</u>. Cambridge, Massachusetts:
    Slavica Publishers, Inc., pp. 105-111.
        Analyzes "Me up at does," "Chansons Innocentes, III,"
    and "a like a" from the point of view of stylistic linguis-
    tics. In the first of these, an inversion of syntactic
    units creates the poem's emotional content. In the second,
    the deletion of syntactic units provides spontaneity and
    drama. In the third, syntax "not only parallels, but car-
    ries the action of the poem."

10 FAUCHEREAU, SERGE. "E.-E. Cummings." <u>Les Lettres Françaises</u>
    (18 December), pp. 3-5, 7.
        General discussion of Cummings notes his relationships
    with imagism, dadaism, and surrealism and remarks his short-
    comings, his preoccupation with the problems of his genera-
    tion, his serene tone, and his connection with jazz. With
    a fairly detailed discussion of "(im) c-a-t (mo)" and a
    brief comparison of Cummings' poetry and the music of Edgar
    Varèse.

11 FERGUSSON, FRANCIS. On Cummings, in <u>Literary Opinion in</u>
    <u>America</u>. Third edition. Edited by Morton Dauwen Zabel.
    Gloucester, Massachusetts: Peter Smith, pp. 519-21.
        Reprint of 1930.3.

12 FRANCIS, ROBERT. "Non-Criticism," in his <u>The Satirical Rogue</u>
    <u>on Poetry</u>. Amherst: University of Massachusetts Press,
    p. 60.
        Satirical remark.

13 FRANKENBERG, LLOYD. On Cummings, in his <u>Invitation to Poetry:</u>
    <u>A Round of Poems from John Skelton to Dylan Thomas,</u>

Arranged with Comments. New York: Greenwood Press, Publishers, pp. 73-74, 257-60, 280-82.
Reprint of 1956.6.

14   GIDLEY, MICK. "Picture and Poem: E. E. Cummings in Perspec-
tive." The Poetry Review, 59, no. 3 (Autumn), 179, 181-95.
Examines Cummings' "poempictures," discovering that they
fall into three groups. In the first, Cummings "used typography as an extension of normal punctuation." In the
second, he used such devices as sudden capitalizations and
tmesis to record and recreate the spontaneous spontaneously.
In the third, he used typography to create a pictorial element adding to the poems' other elements. In all these
hieroglyphs, Cummings is creating "a vehicle for personal
conviction and insight" rather than, as earlier practitioners, "a vehicle for spiritual visions." Gidley also describes the satires as propagandistic, discusses poems using
the "child's-eye-view," examines the courtly love poems,
and comments on several rarely discussed poems and on Cummings' use of "syntactical transpositions."

15   GROSSMAN, D. JON. "Note du Traducteur," in his E. E. Cummings:
58 Poèmes. Paris: Christian Bourgois, pp. 153-54.
Comments briefly on the translation of Cummings into
French. In French.

16   GROSSMAN, MANUEL L. "Him and the Modern Theatre." The Quarterly Journal of Speech, 54, no. 3 (October), 212-19.
Examines Him in the context of the "Theatre of the Absurd" "to determine in what ways the play was a forerunner
of the modern theatre." Him and absurdist plays share
structures, the lack of clear plots and linear development,
and "the use of the conventions and techniques of the popular theatre." Despite these and other similarities, there
is one essential difference between Cummings and the ab-
surdists: he does not share their pessimism.

17   LUEDTKE, LUTHER S. "Cummings' 'The Noster Was a Ship of
Swank.'" The Explicator, 26, no. 7 (March), Item 59.
Examines the secondary and tertiary meanings of the Latin
and English words of this poem and finds that it argues
Cummings' "central conceptions of art and life and displays
the effect of artificiality in religion, philosophy, art,
and commerce on his highest human virtues, love and true
individuality."

18   MACKSEY, RICHARD A. On Cummings. The Johns Hopkins Magazine,
19, no. 1 (Spring), 42.

1968

> Comments briefly on Cummings in a discussion of the
> "originality, range, and extraordinary longevity" of
> several of the poets of the first generation of the twenti-
> eth century.

19   MACKSOUD, JOHN S. "Anyone's How Town: Interpretation as
     Rhetorical Discipline." <u>Speech Monographs</u>, 35, no. 1
     (March), 70-76.
         Asserts that, although literary critics read "anyone
     lived in a pretty how town" as a love story, it is, when
     viewed rhetorically (from the perspective of oral inter-
     pretation), a "philosophical commentary on the antagonism
     between knowledge and understanding." The "poem unfolds,
     by <u>means</u> of narrative, the consequences of the choice of
     'howness' rather than 'whyness.'" A lengthy discussion of
     the poem's two sets of nature-time images is produced in
     evidence of these considerations.

20   MAYO, ROBERT D. "Cummings' 'Chanson Innocente, I,'" in
     <u>Reading Modern Poetry: A Critical Anthology</u>. Second edi-
     tion. Edited by Paul Engle and Warren Carrier. Glenview,
     Illinois: Scott, Foresman and Co., pp. 114-17.
         Reprint of 1947.10.

21   MUNSON, GORHAM. Cummings Scholarship, in <u>American Literary</u>
     <u>Scholarship: An Annual, 1966</u>. Edited by James Woodress.
     Durham, North Carolina: Duke University Press, pp. 187,
     189, 200-201.
         Describes, in a bibliographical essay, works on Cummings
     published in 1966.

22   RECK, MICHAEL. On Cummings, in his <u>Ezra Pound: A Close-Up</u>.
     London: Rupert Hart-Davis, pp. 46, 58, 68, 82, 86-87, 91-
     92, 101, 114, 130, 142, 174, 193.
         Contains a number of brief biographical details on Cum-
     mings' relationship with Pound. Reck also notes that Pound
     is the unnamed subject of Cummings' "this mind made war"
     and suggests that Pound's care in the arrangement of words
     on the page in the later <u>Cantos</u> may have been learned from
     Cummings. Reprinted: 1973.23.

23   ROBEY, CORA. "Cummings' 'All in Green Went My Love Riding.'"
     <u>The Explicator</u>, 27, no. 1 (September), Item 2.
         Pursues Sanders' analysis of the classical elements in
     the poem (<u>see</u> 1966.37) but finds his explanation incomplete
     because it fails to account for the poem's medieval ele-
     ments. Robey considers the poem's subject the predatory
     female (this countering Jumper, <u>see</u> 1967.20) and finds that

142

this reading accounts for allusions both to the classical
goddess Diana and the "cruel mistress of the courtly love
complaint."

24 SHAPIRO, KARL. On Cummings, in his To Abolish Children and
    Other Essays. Chicago: Quadrangle Books, pp. 184-86.
    Reprint of 1964.23.

25 STETLER, CHARLES. "E. E. Cummings' 73 Poems: With Life's
    Eye." Xavier University Studies, 7, no. 1 (March), 5-16.
       Argues that Cummings' last volume continued to show his
    capacity for development and growth, especially "in the
    poems of love and transcendence." Stetler notes his con-
    tinuing ability to affirm in the face of death, an affirma-
    tion balanced by a continuing critical sense, and
    demonstrates that in 73 poems affirmation rises out of the
    negative instead of, as in earlier poems, transcending it.
    He also comments on the musical values of the poems.
    Several poems are discussed in support.

26 WAGER, WILLIAM. On Cummings, in his American Literature: A
    World View. New York: New York University Press, pp. 192,
    198.
       Notes the influence of Stein and Pound on Cummings with-
    out further comment.

27 WAGGONER, HYATT H. "The Transcendental and Extraordinary:
    E. E. Cummings," in his American Poets from the Puritans to
    the Present. Boston: Houghton Mifflin Co., pp. 511-25.
       Connects Cummings, through examination of his Transcend-
    entalist metaphysics, with Hart Crane and especially with
    Emerson. The connection with Emerson is also apparent in
    other aspects of Cummings' stance, for example in his in-
    tuitive epistemology, his Platonic and organic aesthetic,
    and his "mystical antinomianism." If these comments on the
    "what" of Cummings' poetry make him seem the twentieth-
    century embodiment of the "true poet" called for by Emerson,
    the "how" of the poems frequently denies him such stature.
    For although some percentage of the poems does successfully
    express his attitudes and ideas, too often his techniques
    are unimaginative and repetitive. On the other hand, Wag-
    goner defends Cummings against the frequent charge that he
    has failed to grow as a poet. Reprinted: 1970.19.

28 WOODRESS, JAMES. "Cummings, E. E.," in his Dissertations in
    American Literature: 1891-1966. Durham, North Carolina:
    Duke University Press, entries 515-19.
       Lists dissertations on Cummings written between 1954 and
    1962.

1969

1   ATTAWAY, KENNETH R. E. E. Cummings' Aloofness: An Underlying
    Theme in His Poetry. Research Paper Number 24, School of
    Arts and Sciences Research Papers. Atlanta: Georgia State
    College, 42 pp.
        Attempts to explain why "Cummings' attitude toward life
    and the poetic expression of that attitude do not fit to-
    gether." Cummings' philosophy of life is characterized by
    such concepts--instilled by his family and early environ-
    ment--as freedom from convention, individuality, radical
    equality, the primacy of love, and the ability of humanness
    to withstand false convention. But his youthful environment
    and war experiences violated these concepts and thus nar-
    rowed "his perception of life around him." Then, rather
    "than approach the people and events which make up life
    from an objective viewpoint, he retreated into a childlike
    emotional response to external occurences." This defensive-
    ness, in all its guises, can be characterized as "aloof-
    ness." The subjects, attitudes, and techniques of Cummings'
    poetry shut "his world off from mankind. What is wrong with
    his poetry is that the poet's simple and basic world is not
    communicated to the average reader. His continual verbal-
    izing of an emotional response to life does not give the
    reader any insight into existence; it is merely superficial
    and tedious." Includes a selected bibliography.

2   BROWN, ASHLEY. "Private Eye." Spectator, 222, no. 7340
    (28 February), 276.
        Reviews Complete Poems: 1913-1935 and 1936-1962, com-
    menting in general on Cummings' career and noting the
    strength (simultaneity) and weakness (fragmentation) of his
    dislocations of language and syntax.

3   CLARK, DAVID R. "Cummings' 'anyone' and 'noone.'" Arizona
    Quarterly, 25 (Spring), 36-43.
        Analyzes "anyone lived in a pretty how town," finding
    that in the poem and its paradoxes Cummings balances the
    virtues of uniqueness and integrity against the profound
    loneliness of the unloved individual in modern society.
    Reprinted: 1972.5.

4   DEKLE, BERNARD. "E. E. Cummings: Poet, Individualist," in
    his Profiles of Modern American Authors. Rutland, Vermont:
    Charles E. Tuttle Co., pp. 96-101.
        General comments on Cummings' individualism, his criti-
    cism of communism, his poetic expression of individuality,
    and his style.

5   DONOGHUE, DENIS. "Cummings and Goings." <u>The New York Review
    of Books</u>, 13, no. 6 (9 October), 48–50.
        Reviews <u>Selected Letters of E. E. Cummings</u>, finding the
    selection admirable and summarizing contents. Donoghue
    also suggests comparisons of Cummings with Plato and with
    the Cambridge Platonists.

6   DOUGHERTY, JAMES P. "E. E. Cummings: <u>The Enormous Room</u>," in
    <u>Landmarks of American Writing</u>. Edited by Hennig Cohen.
    New York: Basic Books, pp. 288–302.
        Discusses <u>The Enormous Room</u> as "an important imaginative
    record of that violent time when the 'modern' spirit was in
    birth"; "as a part of the literature of that well-known
    disillusion which followed the Great War; as a modern ex-
    tension of the American Radical tradition of Emerson,
    Thoreau, and Whitman; and as an anticipation of the post-
    modern world of the 1960's." The disillusionment of the
    book is not just an initiation into the realities of war,
    but a "loss of faith in the systems and categories" Cummings
    had been taught. It is the product of an unlearning pro-
    cess, and its experimental language is the unlearning of
    conventions which falsely manipulate reality.

7   DUPEE, F. W. "Foreword," in <u>Selected Letters of E. E. Cum-
    mings</u>. Edited by F. W. Dupee and George Stade. New York:
    Harcourt, Brace & World, pp. xv–xix.
        Contains an explanation of the editors' principles of
    selection and comments on the characteristics of the let-
    ters. The book also provides a chronology of events and
    characters referred to in the letters (pp. xxi–xxiv) and
    occasional explanatory footnotes.

8   DUPEE, F. W. and GEORGE STADE. "Foreword" to their "E. E.
    Cummings: Twenty-Three Letters." <u>Harper's Magazine</u>, 238,
    no. 1426 (March), 71–72.
        Quotes Dos Passos on Cummings (<u>see</u> 1966.12) and notes
    that his letters are sometimes marvelously extemporaneous
    and at other times have the effect "of an artist craftily
    catching the bright flow of his mind in intricate patterns
    of rhythm, language, image, and tone."

9   EASTMAN, MAX. "The Cult of Unintelligibility," in his <u>The
    Literary Mind: Its Place in an Age of Science</u>. New York:
    Octagon Books, pp. 57–78.
        Reprint of 1929.2.

1969

10 EASTMAN, MAX. "The Tendency Toward Pure Poetry," in his The
    Literary Mind: Its Place in an Age of Science. New York:
    Octagon Books, pp. 79-92.
        Reprint of 1929.3.

11 EPSTEIN, JACOB. "The Small-Eyed Poet." The New Republic, 160,
    no. 23 (7 June), 23-27.
        Reviews Selected Letters of E. E. Cummings, discovering
    that the letters reinforce a view of the life and the works
    as of a piece. His letters are "thin," but extremely read-
    able because of their "surpassing wit." Epstein also com-
    ments on the ways in which the letters illuminate Cummings'
    odd combination of lyric and satire.

12 ESSLIN, MARTIN. On Cummings, in his The Theatre of the Absurd.
    Second edition. Garden City, New York: Anchor Books,
    Doubleday & Co., pp. 8, 348-49.
        The Cummings material is unchanged in this revised edi-
    tion of 1961.6.

13 FIEDLER, LESLIE A. On Cummings, in his Love and Death in the
    American Novel. Second edition. New York: Dell Publishing
    Co., Laurel edition, p. 486.
        The Cummings entry is unchanged in this revision of
    1960.6.

14 FOWLER, ROGER. "On the Interpretation of 'Nonsense Strings.'"
    Journal of Linguistics, 5, no. 1 (April), 75-83.
        Comments on the grammatical analyses of "anyone lived in
    a pretty how town" by Levin and Thorne (see 1964.13 and
    1965.28), arguing that a principal skill involved in read-
    ers' ability to interpret Cummings' poem in spite of its
    several "nonsense strings" is the ability to retrieve "the
    syntax of an utterance" in both regular and secondary ways.

15 GENTHE, CHARLES V. On Cummings, in his American War Narra-
    tives: 1917-1918, A Study and Bibliography. New York:
    David Lewis, pp. 1, 32, 51.
        Brief references to Cummings in relation to American
    attitudes about World War I and as a member of the Norton
    Harjes ambulance corps.

16 GREGORY, HORACE and MARYA ZATURENSKA. On Cummings, in their
    A History of American Poetry, 1900-1940. New York: Gordian
    Press, pp. 336-47.
        Reprint of 1946.10.

17 HAMBURGER, MICHAEL. On Cummings, in his <u>The Truth of Poetry:</u>
    <u>Tensions in Modern Poetry from Baudelaire to the 1960's.</u>
    New York: Harcourt, Brace & World, pp. 108-109.
        Comments on Cummings' use of ambivalence "to disturb and
    make fun of...solemn humanitarian commonplaces" in such
    poems as "humanity i love you because you," "pity this busy
    monster, manunkind," and "what if a much of a which of a
    wind."

18 HART, JEFFREY. "Champion of Freedom and the Individual."
    <u>National Review</u>, 21, no. 33 (26 August), 864.
        Reviews Dupee's and Stade's selection of Cummings' let-
    ters, considering his radical individualism "refreshing."
    The letters' "powers of evocation" are impressive, all the
    more so "because casually exercised."

19 HEINRICHS, VINCENT L. "Cummings' '(IM) C-A-T (MO.'" <u>The</u>
    <u>Explicator</u>, 27, no. 8 (April), Item 59.
        Reconstructs this "image" poem's statement and analyzes
    its special use of the devices of punctuation, juxtaposition
    and dislocation of words, and capitalization.

20 HENDRICKS, WILLIAM O. On Cummings. <u>Journal of Linguistics</u>, 5,
    no. 1 (April), 1-9.
        Remarks, in an essay on models for a description of
    poetry, on Thorne's linguistic analysis of "anyone lived in
    a pretty how town" (<u>see</u> 1965.28).

21 HENRY, NAT. "Cummings' 'Pity This Busy Monster, Manunkind.'"
    <u>The Explicator</u>, 27, no. 9 (May), Item 68.
        Expands earlier interpretations by Britton (<u>see</u> 1959.8)
    and Gargano (<u>see</u> 1961.7) by offering two alternative read-
    ings of the sonnet's final imperatives.

22 JAMES, CLIVE. "An Instrument to Measure Spring With." <u>The</u>
    <u>Review</u>, no. 2 (March), pp. [38]-48.
        Discusses Cummings' poetry generally, noting that his
    "simple" ideas would bring an end to civilization and com-
    menting on the unity of his life and work. James describes
    the love poetry as based in and creating "a continuum be-
    tween the lady lusted after as pure gash and the lady con-
    templated as a divine revelation" and the satirical poetry
    as the necessary result for a poet who "asserts the divine
    as the sole level of reality and perpetual revelation as
    the only mode of vision." He also discusses Cummings' re-
    working of the sonnet as a "jazz solo" and his sonic and
    syntactical effects.

1969

23   LAWRENCE, FLOYD B. "Two Novelists of the Great War: Dos
      Passos and Cummings." The University Review, 36, no. 1
      (Autumn), 35-41.
           Argues that The Enormous Room, unlike Three Soldiers, is
      "a successful attempt to transcend the boundaries of uni-
      forms, prisons, regimentation, and all other local or his-
      torical threats to identity" and that, therefore, while
      lacking none of the verisimilitude of Three Soldiers, it
      "possesses that moral insight and artistic perfection which
      even the best war novel can never combine in an enduring
      fashion."

24   MATTHEWS, JACK. Review of Selected Letters of E. E. Cummings.
      New York Times Book Review (8 June), pp. 4, 66.
           Reviews Dupee's and Stade's selection of Cummings' let-
      ters as "rich with images, ideas, gripes, gossip and bril-
      liant spoofs." The letters become more controlled as the
      poet gets older.

25   PARKES, DAVID L. "Cummings, E. E.," in Twentieth Century
      Writing: A Reader's Guide to Contemporary Literature.
      Edited by Kenneth Richardson. London: Newnes Books,
      pp. 150-51.
           Encyclopedia entry describes Cummings as "a fairly ortho-
      dox and lyric romantic with a flair for unusual typography."

26   SCHLEINER, WINFRIED. "Drei Gedichte von E. E. Cummings."
      Literatur in Wissenschaft und Unterricht, 2, no. 1, 27-37.
           Explicates three Cummings poems, "maggie and milly and
      molly and may," "my sweet old etcetera," and "i sing of
      Olaf glad and big," concentrating on "translating" some of
      their technical and idiomatic difficulties for German read-
      ers and on Cummings' formal mastery. In German.

27   SOKOLOV, R. A. "Typewriter Art." Newsweek, 73, no. 23 (9
      June), 112-13.
           Reviews Dupee's and Stade's selection of Cummings' let-
      ters. "Epistolary prose has probably never come closer to
      poetry than with Cummings."

28   TRIEM, EVE. E. E. Cummings. University of Minnesota Pamphlets
      on American Writers, No. 87. Minneapolis: University of
      Minnesota Press, 48 pp.
           Presents an overview of Cummings' work and describes him
      as a transcendentalist, a troubadour, and an artist who uses
      the absurd to shock his readers into attention and, later,
      to "mean the truth of earthly living and a promise of etern-
      ity." After a biographical sketch, Cummings' techniques--

tmesis, typography, punctuation, stanza shape, distorted
syntax, word coinage, and so on—are discussed, and many of
their various functions outlined and evidenced. His use of
tradition, especially the sonnet, is also noted. Three of
Cummings' major themes—sensory awareness, the integrity of
the individual, and the true meaning of love—are examined
at length, and several of his better known poems are analyzed in demonstration of these themes and their development. Him, Eimi, and Santa Claus also receive attention.
With a bibliography. Reprinted: 1972.25; 1972.26.

29 UNTERECKER, JOHN. On Cummings, in his Voyager: A Life of
    Hart Crane. New York: Farrar, Straus and Giroux, pp. 234,
    294, 295, 327, 343-44, 358, 372, 393, 439, 518, 527, 569,
    597, 609, 616, 631-32, 634, 635.
        Brief comments on Cummings as an acquaintance of Crane
    and a member of his literary generation.

30 UNTERMEYER, LOUIS. "Quirky Communications from an Exuberant
    Unhero." Saturday Review, 52, no. 27 (5 July), 25-26.
        Reviews Selected Letters of E. E. Cummings, describing
    him as a prolific but far from great correspondent.

31 WEBER, BROM and JAMES WOODRESS. Cummings Scholarship, in
    American Literary Scholarship: An Annual, 1967. Edited by
    James Woodress. Durham, North Carolina: Duke University
    Press, pp. 210, 233.
        Describes, in a bibliographical essay, works on Cummings
    published in 1967.

32 WICKES, GEORGE. "E. E. Cummings and the Great War," in his
    Americans in Paris. Paris Review Editions. Garden City,
    New York: Doubleday & Co., pp. 69-118.
        Provides details of the events surrounding the incarcera-
    tion which gave rise to The Enormous Room. The book itself
    is described as one of the best prison books, rather than a
    war book, and is defined as an ironic political and moral
    allegory. Wickes notes that The Enormous Room records Cum-
    mings' stylistic evolution and comments on his uses of
    mock-heroic language, French, linguistic and grammatical
    play, typography, expressive spacing and punctuation, "tele-
    graphic technique," and precise timing. His friendship with
    Dos Passos is discussed. In an examination of Cummings'
    typographic verse, Wickes comments on his postwar trips to
    Paris and argues that he found his voice as a poet during
    the years when he was most exposed to French influences.
    The influences of cubism, Joyce, and especially Apollinaire
    are also explored. If Cummings' "calligrams are not

1969

strictly pictorial,...they are graphic." "r-p-o-p-h-e-s-s-
a-g-r" and "ondumonde" are discussed as examples. For an
adaptation of this essay, much condensed, see 1969.33.

33   WICKES, GEORGE. "E. E. Cummings at War." Columbia Forum, 12,
no. 3 (Fall), 31-[33].
Presents biographical data on Cummings' imprisonment and
comments briefly on The Enormous Room and its "light-hearted
tone" and "fierce irony." Adapted from 1969.32.

34   WILLIAMS, WILLIAM CARLOS. "Lower Case Cummings," in his Selec-
ted Essays of William Carlos Williams. New York: New
Directions Publishing Corp., pp. 263-67.
Reprint of 1946.23.

1970

1   BERUTTI, BETTY REVELEY. "A Grammatical Analysis of the Poetry
of E. E. Cummings." Ph.D. dissertation, The University of
Texas at Austin.
Applies several methods of language analysis to Cummings'
poems and compares the results to those arrived at by non-
linguistic methods. Berutti finds the former an effective
corrective to the latter, especially in adding precision
and clarity to the exercise of paraphrase, and she argues
that it does so because "formal grammar theories provide a
method of retrieving an underlying prose form for poetic
deviations." With many applications of the method to individual poems.

2   COWLEY, MALCOLM. "Introduction," in Viva. By E. E. Cummings.
New York: Liveright Publishers, unpaged.
Reprint of 1932.3.

3   DAVIS, WILLIAM V. "Cummings' 'All in Green Went My Love
Riding.'" Concerning Poetry, 3, no. 2 (Fall), 65-67.
Argues that the greenness--the innocence and naiveté--of
the mistress in "All in Green Went My Love Riding" tempers
her "'innate cruelty,'" but that her "naiveté with respect
to the love and courtship relationship" causes the death of
the narrator's interest in her.

4   DAVIS, WILLIAM V. "Cummings' 'next to of course god america
i.'" Concerning Poetry, 3, no. 1 (Spring), 14-15.
Discusses Cummings' combining of the Elizabethan and
Petrarchan sonnet forms, use of space on the page, one-line
couplet, and use of inverted syntax in "next to of course
god america i."

1970

5   DONAHUE, JANE. "Cummings' Last Poem: An Explication."
     Literatur in Wissenschaft und Unterricht, 3, no. 2, 106-108.
          Analyzes "all worlds have halfsight, seeing either with"
     as an amplification of Cummings' typical "concept of love
     as the key to a unifying and liberating view of life, his
     stress on the person rather than the 'world,' and his cele-
     bration of beauty and wonder." The poem's meter, unity,
     and offer of an alternative to the dilemma of dualism are
     examined.

6   ECKLEY, WILTON. The Merrill Checklist of e. e. cummings.
     Charles E. Merrill Checklists, edited by Matthew J. Bruccoli
     and Joseph Katz. Columbus, Ohio: Charles E. Merrill Pub-
     lishing Co., 36 pp.
          A bibliography listing selected primary materials, and
     selected secondary materials under the headings of bibliog-
     raphy, biography, and scholarship and criticism, this last
     including books, articles, and reviews.

7   ECKLEY, WILTON. The Merrill Guide to e. e. cummings. Charles
     E. Merrill Guides, edited by Matthew J. Bruccoli and Joseph
     Katz. Columbus, Ohio: Charles E. Merrill Publishing Co.,
     41 pp.
          After a biographical sketch, examines Cummings' technique
     and vision. His technical innovations create intensity and
     drama. They intend to rescue language from convention and
     cliché and to create that precision of expression which can
     "capture the essence of an experience or idea and present
     it with a sense of immediacy that...[can] pierce the lan-
     guage barrier between the reader and the poet." Cummings'
     vision is a traditional, essentially romantic vision which
     stresses an immediate awareness of life. He divides people
     into two categories, those who accept and celebrate life
     and those who reject and denigrate it. His poems fall into
     corollary categories, transcending lyric and pointed satire.
     The latter warn; the former offer hope. The center of Cum-
     mings' poetic vision is the transcendence of the negative
     self through love.

8   GRAVES, ROBERT. On Cummings, in his The Common Asphodel: Col-
     lected Essays on Poetry, 1922-1949. New York: Haskell
     House Publishers, Ltd., pp. 61-72, 75-76, 84-86, 92-93,
     96-98, 116-18, 125, 134, 160.
          Reprint of 1927.4.

9   LEARY, LEWIS. "Cummings, E. E.," in his Articles on American
     Literature: 1950-1967. Durham, North Carolina: Duke Uni-
     versity Press, pp. 99-102.

1970

A bibliography of Cummings scholarship published between 1950 and 1962.

10   LOGAN, JOHN. "The Organ-Grinder and the Cockatoo: An Intro-
     duction to E. E. Cummings," in Modern American Poetry:
     Essays in Criticism. Edited by Jerome Mazzaro. New York:
     David McKay Co., pp. 249-71.
        An enlarged version of 1961.9, making the same points,
     but more expansively and with more evidence. Revision of
     1961.9.

11   METCALF, ALLAN A. "Dante and E. E. Cummings." Comparative
     Literature Studies, 7, no. 3 (September), 374-86.
        Argues that Cummings' career indicates that Dante guided
     him first in hell and then in paradise. In the early work,
     the influence of Dante usually appears in "brief explicit
     references to passages from the Inferno, generally rein-
     forcing his satirical and negative vision of the modern
     world." In the later works, beginning with Eimi, he no
     longer quotes from the Inferno but turns to the Paradiso.
     His imagery (roses, bees) becomes increasingly reminiscent
     of Dante's. Metcalf also comments on "So shy shy shy," a
     Cummings poem with "a striking resemblance to a sonnet from
     the Vita nuova which Cummings knew and quoted."

12   MILLER, WAYNE CHARLES. On Cummings, in his An Armed America--
     Its Face in Fiction: A History of the American Military
     Novel. New York: New York University Press, p. 108.
        Notes that "Cummings' The Enormous Room is one of the
     most forceful antiwar novels ever written and an indictment
     of tyranny in any form" and that much of his poetry suggests
     a similar indictment.

13   MUNSON, GORHAM and ANN STANFORD. Cummings Scholarship, in
     American Literary Scholarship: An Annual, 1968. Edited by
     J. Albert Robbins. Durham, North Carolina: Duke University
     Press, pp. 239-40.
        Describes, in a bibliographical essay, works on Cummings
     published in 1968.

14   O'CONNOR, WILLIAM VAN. On Cummings, in his Sense and Sensibil-
     ity in Modern Poetry. New York: Gordian Press, pp. 60-61,
     76, 116, 124, 158-59, 183, 217-18, 230, 248.
        Reprint of 1948.11.

15   POWERS, RICHARD GID. "Cummings' 'I Will Be.'" The Explicator,
     28, no. 6 (February), Item 54.

Describes the poem as another use of Cummings' "machine-sex image" and explains how the poem's technique isolates the "linguistic and orthographic phallic symbols" concealed in its language. The poem involves the anticipation of an assignation and a fantasy of the expected lovemaking.

16   SHAW, ROBERT B. Review of <u>Selected Letters of E. E. Cummings</u>. <u>Poetry</u>, 115, no. 4 (January), 278-80.
      Examines Dupee's and Stade's collection of Cummings' letters in an omnibus review and finds in their revelation that his character was formed early and remained relatively unchanged an explanation for his frequently noted lack of poetic development. Shaw also comments on Cummings' humor.

17   SOLT, MARY ELLEN. On Cummings, in her <u>Concrete Poetry: A World View</u>. Bloomington: Indiana University Press, p. 47.
      Comments briefly on Cummings as a precursor of "projective" and "concrete" poetry.

18   SPEARS, MONROE K. On Cummings, in his <u>Dionysius and the City: Modernism in Twentieth-Century Poetry</u>. New York: Oxford University Press, pp. 82, 151-52, 167.
      Notes the need for a study of Cummings' use of the city and, after summarizing Cummings' Harvard graduation address, points out that for all his cogent defenses of modernism he always insists "that the only valid criterion for any form of art is the degree of its aliveness."

19   WAGGONER, HYATT H. "The Transcendental and Extraordinary: E. E. Cummings," in his <u>American Poets from the Puritans to the Present</u>. New York: Dell Publishing Co., pp. 511-25.
      Reprint of 1968.27.

20   WILSON, DAVID B. "'o to be in finland.'" <u>Neuphilologische Mitteilungen</u>, 71, no. 2 (June), 270-76.
      Analyzes "o to be in finland," arguing that its complexity goes beyond anything previously attempted in the poetry of political satire. Each of the poem's three units is based on a parody of a well-known phrase or quotation. The entire poem is both "a protest against American silence at the Russian invasion of Finland" and a more general critique of modern society.

<u>1971</u>

1   AARTS, JAN. "A Note on the Interpretation of 'he danced his did.'" <u>Journal of Linguistics</u>, 7, no. 1 (April), 71-73.

1971

> Discusses the ungrammaticality of the "did" lexeme in
> the line from "anyone lived in a pretty how town."

2   CHURCHILL, ALLEN. On Cummings, in his <u>The Literary Decade</u>.
>   Englewood Cliffs, New Jersey: Prentice-Hall, pp. 21-22,
>   58, 83, 86, 91, 92-93, 159, 197, 199, 212.
>   Occasional remarks on Cummings as a member of the liter-
>   ary generation of the twenties.

3   CROWDER, RICHARD. Cummings Scholarship, in <u>American Literary</u>
>   <u>Scholarship: An Annual, 1969</u>. Edited by J. Albert Rollins.
>   Durham, North Carolina: Duke University Press, pp. 252,
>   272.
>   Describes, in a bibliographical essay, works on Cummings
>   published in 1969.

4   DAVIS, WILLIAM V. "Cummings' 'Nobody Loses All the Time.'"
>   <u>American Notes and Queries</u>, 9, no. 8 (April), 119-20.
>   Examines the verbal and stanzaic games which explain the
>   presence of the apparently "unnecessary" seventh and eighth
>   stanzas of "nobody loses all the time."

5   DICKEY, JAMES. "E. E. Cummings," in his <u>Babel to Byzantium:</u>
>   <u>Poets & Poetry Now</u>. New York: Grosset & Dunlap, pp. 100-
>   106.
>   Reprint of 1959.12.

6   DUNDAS, DORIS. "Cummings' 'When God Lets My Body Be.'" <u>The</u>
>   <u>Explicator</u>, 29, no. 9 (May), Item 79.
>   Compares Cummings' poem with Kilmer's "Trees" to indicate
>   that Cummings is "subtly parodying Kilmer's popular poem."

7   FAIRLEY, IRENE ROSENSWEIG. "Syntactic Deviance in the Poetry
>   of E. E. Cummings: A Stylistic Investigation." Ph.D. dis-
>   sertation, Harvard University.
>   Discusses Cummings' poetry from a linguistic viewpoint,
>   concluding that an analysis of Cummings' dislocations of
>   syntax suggests that he is manipulating a limited set of
>   related rule constraints which, although innovative, depend
>   upon rules already existing within standard English or "deep
>   structure." The dissertation was, in slightly altered form,
>   published as a book, and a fuller annotation will be found
>   under the book entry: 1975.5.

8   FEENEY, JOSEPH JOHN, S.J. "American Anti-War Writers of World
>   War I: A Literary Study of Randolph Bourne, Harriet Monroe,
>   Carl Sandburg, John Dos Passos, E. E. Cummings, and Ernest
>   Hemingway." Ph.D. dissertation, University of Pennsylvania.

1971

Considers Cummings as one of a number of American anti-
war writers, examining his portrayal of the effects of war,
his ironic use of abstract words, and his occasional descriptions of war in "the imagery and diction of medieval
romance."

9   FINN, H. SETH. "Cummings' 'Memorabilia.'" The Explicator,
    29, no. 5 (January), Item 42.
    Suggests and explores the influence of Eliot's "The Love
    Song of J. Alfred Prufrock" on this Cummings poem.

10 FULLER, ROY. On Cummings, in his Owls and Artificers: Oxford
    Lectures on Poetry. New York: The Library Press, pp. 108-
    31, passim.
    Notes that the romanticism that was usually kept in check
    "by the arduous typographical preoccupations" of Cummings'
    free verse occasionally runs wild in "his later rollicking
    stanzas" and creates "Stuffed Owl stuff."

11 دكتور زاخر غبريال [GHUBRIYAL, ZAKHIR]. Introduction, in
    his شاعر أمريكا أ. أ. كمنجز
    [E. E. Cummings: American Poet]. General Society for Book
    and Periodical Publication, pp. 10-125.
    Introduces a translation of a selection of Cummings poems
    into Arabic, presenting a chronology, a primary bibliography,
    and a biographical study, and summarizing much earlier cri-
    ticism of Cummings' themes and techniques. In Arabic.

12 GUNTER, RICHARD. "Sentence and Poem." Style, 5, no. 1
    (Winter), 26-36.
    Responds to Hill (1967.15), arguing that his recovery of
    the "normal word order" of "nonsun blob a" does not produce
    "coherence" and offering another possible version, this one
    with less perfect sentences but greater thematic coherence.
    Gunter also suggests literal and metaphorical overlapping
    between Cummings' poem and Shakespeare's Sonnet 73.

13 LAUTER, PAUL. E. E. Cummings: Index to First Lines and Bibli-
    ography of Works By and About the Poet. Folcroft, Pennsyl-
    vania: Folcroft Library Editions, 46 pp.
    Reprint of 1955.17.

14 LOŽAR, TOMAŽ. "E. E. Cummings: The Poem as Improvisation."
    Acta Neophilologica, 4; 61-73.
    On Marshall McLuhan's suggestion (see 1964.14), considers
    Cummings in terms "of what we know about the creative moment
    from the jazzman's experience." Like jazz, Cummings' poems
    only function properly in performance. In both, "theater

1971

and music are united in a tendency towards the dance." For
such improvisational poetry, "traditional literary criticism will not do."

15   McBROOM, ROBERT L. "E. E. Cummings: Mirror and Arbiter of
His Age." Ph.D. dissertation, Texas Tech University.
Finds Cummings a mirror and arbiter of his age, a mirror
"in that through his poetry we see reflected the intensity
of tensions and complexity peculiar to the twentieth century," an arbiter "in that through satire, parody, irony,
and cynicism he judges and consequently condemns the century
of which he is a part." This dialectic is demonstrated by
analyses of the works. McBroom concludes, however, that
Cummings offers a synthesis of its oppositions by suggesting
"that through nature, love, and a renewed individuality
modern man may come to terms with his now fragmented
existence."

16   MACDONALD, BERNARD ANGUS. "E. E. Cummings: A Study of 'Epi-
thalamion' and 'Puella Mea.'" Ph.D. dissertation, The
University of Connecticut.
Analyzes two long poems from Tulips and Chimneys, discovering that their structural failure as long works and
the success of individual lines and stanzas in them is
characteristic of Cummings' genius. An examination of the
long prose works reaches a similar conclusion: "Cummings'
famed fragmentation of the physical world in his poems was
an inescapable tendency and not just an artistic device."

17   McILVAINE, ROBERT M. "Cummings' 'brIght.'" The Explicator,
30, no. 1 (September), Item 6.
Analyzes this short poem of religious affirmation, noting
its radical experimentation. It uses eleven words forty-
four times in a specific arithmetic pattern which expresses
a movement through doubt to increasing perception and finally to belief.

18   MOTTRAM, ERIC. "Cummings, E(dward) E(stlin)," in The Penguin
Companion to American Literature. Edited by Malcolm Brad-
bury, Eric Mottram, and Jean Franco. New York: McGraw-Hill
Book Co., pp. 67-68.
Brief encyclopedia entry presents general biographical
and critical information.

19   MOTTRAM, ERIC. "The Hostile Environment and the Survival
Artist: A Note on the Twenties," in The American Novel and
the Nineteen Twenties. Stratford-Upon-Avon Studies 13,
edited by Malcolm Bradbury and David Palmer. London: Edward Arnold (Publishers) Ltd., pp. 233-62, passim.

Describes The Enormous Room as "an early recognition of
the twentieth-century theft of dignity and freedom in America." Mottram connects Cummings' survival techniques--the
reinvention of language, the erasure of history, and the
reliance on "humane decency with an emphasis on privacy and
love which constitute an anarchist response to a disastrous
time"--to those of other "survival artists" in the "hostile
environment" of the postwar years.

20 MULLEN, PATRICK B. "E. E. Cummings and Popular Culture."
    Journal of Popular Culture, 5, no. 3 (Winter), 503-520.
        Discusses Cummings' concern, then unusual, with mass en-
    tertainment, his "avid interest in various forms of American
    popular culture." "To Cummings, burlesque and the other
    popular arts were alive with a spontaneous, unrehearsed
    quality. He wanted to capture the same quality of spontane-
    ity in his poetry, both in content and technique." Mullen
    discusses these matters in terms of Cummings' poems and his
    prose essays on entertainment.

21 PERRINE, LAWRENCE. "In Heavenly Realms of Hellas." Notes on
    Contemporary Literature, 1, no. 1 (January), 2-4.
        Examines Cummings' version, in "Heavenly Realms of Hel-
    las," of the myth of Hephaestus' snaring of his wife,
    Aphrodite, in adultery with Ares, and his summoning of the
    other gods to witness their shame (Odyssey, Book 8). In its
    complexly qualified contrast of Hephaestus and the lovers
    the poem draws a typically Cummingsesque "immoral moral."

22 POUND, EZRA. On Cummings, in his The Selected Letters of Ezra
    Pound: 1907-1941. Edited by D. D. Paige. New York: New
    Directions, pp. 201-202, 223, 227-28, 244-45, 265, 266,
    268-69, 277, 290-91, 292, 301, 325, 327, 328.
        Reprint of 1950.17.

23 REXROTH, KENNETH. On Cummings, in his American Poetry in the
    Twentieth Century. New York: Herder and Herder, pp. 85-88,
    96.
        Describes Cummings as a member of that group of writers
    shaped by the horrors of World War I and by the realization
    "that, under the surface of progress and high culture,
    Western Civilization had matured a militantly mindless and
    murderous bureaucracy which was now breaking through the
    ornamented façade and taking over." The poetry is charac-
    terized by an adolescence into which Cummings was frozen by
    the "moral catastrophe of the war." Reprinted: 1973.25.

1971

24 SCHNEIDER, EVELYN SEARS. "I. Glories and Glow-Worms: A
    Study of the Juxtaposition of Opposites in Three Plays by
    John Webster. II. The Changing Image of Charles Brockden
    Brown as Seen by American Critics from 1815 to the Present.
    III. Action, Motion and Being: The Technique of Kinesis
    in the Poems of E. E. Cummings." Ph.D. dissertation,
    Rutgers University.
        Examines, in part three of this omnibus dissertation,
    eight poems demonstrating three of Cummings' "modes of
    kinesis: the Verb; the destruction of conventional grammar,
    syntax, punctuation, and typography and the creation of new
    visual poetic experiences; the use of the child vision."
    Schneider also examines Cummings' frequent use of circular
    structure to steady his kinetic poems. Both the use of
    circular structure and the child vision contribute to Cum-
    mings' attempt to express the "timelessness and wholeness
    of the Self."

25 VANCE, THOMAS H. On Cummings, in Amerikanische Literatur im
    20. Jahrhundert / American Literature in the 20th Century.
    Edited by Alfred Weber and Dietmar Haack. Göttingen:
    Vandenhoeck & Ruprecht, pp. 252-55, 269.
        Discusses Cummings' "ygUDuh" as an antiwar poem in the
    Aristophanic spirit. The dramatic monologue reminds us that
    even a supposedly just war "produces a kind of blind auto-
    matic self-righteousness, a habit of thinking in destructive
    clichés." The poem's "oblique, marginal, minority protest"
    is contrasted with the "open, violent and emphatic" protests
    of such poems as Ginsberg's Howl. In English, with a sum-
    mary in German.

26 WEINBERGER, G. J. "E. E. Cummings' 'the people who.'" Re-
    search Studies, 39, no. 4 (December), 313-15.
        Argues that the difficulty of interpreting "the people
    who" "stems from Cummings' aiming at and trying to express
    the noumenal world" and analyzes the poem's theme of
    transcendent, transcending love.

1972

1 ANON. Review of Complete Poems, 1913-1962. Saturday Review,
   The Arts, 55, no. 49 (2 December), 84.
       Briefly notices the first complete edition of Cummings'
   poems published in America.

2 ANON. Review of Selected Letters of E. E. Cummings. Contemporary Review, 221, no. 1281 (October), 224.

1972

Briefly notices the appearance of Dupee's and Stade's
selection of Cummings' letters, remarking their "representative wit and wisdom."

3   ANON. "The Scourge of the Unpeople." The Times Literary
    Supplement (17 November), p. 1403.
        Reviews Dupee's and Stade's selection of Cummings' let-
    ters, discovering that, if nothing else, the letters do
    further demonstrate the innovativeness of his verbal
    imagination.

4   CHAO, PHEBE SHIH. "E. E. Cummings: Poet in the American
    Tradition." Ph.D. dissertation, Harvard University.
        Attempts to place Cummings within the context of American
    art, with special emphasis on his concern with the individu-
    al in society, a concern which places him in the intellectu-
    al line of Emerson, Whitman, and Thoreau. Like many modern
    writers indebted to the past for content, Cummings' origin-
    ality is in the areas of form and technique. Chao also
    examines Cummings' use of the artifacts of popular culture,
    especially the circus, which is a metaphor for his world
    and his world view.

5   CLARK, DAVID RIDGLEY. "E. E. Cummings: 'anyone' and 'noone,'"
    in his Lyric Resonance: Glosses on Some Poems of Yeats,
    Frost, Crane, Cummings & Others. Amherst: The University
    of Massachusetts Press, pp. [187]-94.
        Reprint of 1969.3.

6   CLARK, DAVID RIDGLEY. "E. E. Cummings: 'Poem,'" in his Lyric
    Resonance: Glosses on Some Poems of Yeats, Frost, Crane,
    Cummings, & Others. Amherst: The University of Massachu-
    setts Press, pp. [195]-99.
        Reprint of 1964.5.

7   CRIVELLI, RENZO S. "E. E. Cummings: La Poetica del Movimento."
    Studi Americani, 18; [313]-43.
        Discusses Cummings' "poetics of movement" by examining
    his comments on art and exploring his relation to the art
    movements of his time—especially cubism, with its interest
    in simultaneity. Crivelli suggests that Cummings, like
    John Marin, was influenced by Futurist techniques for
    achieving organic "poempictures" and examines his visual
    effects. He also considers Cummings' use of sound as a co-
    efficient of movement and connects his techniques to those
    of Stravinsky, Satie, and Schönberg. In Italian.

1972

8   CROWDER, RICHARD. Cummings Scholarship, in <u>American Literary</u>
    <u>Scholarship: An Annual, 1970</u>. Edited by J. Albert Robbins.
    Durham, North Carolina: Duke University Press, pp. 280,
    301-302.
        Describes, in a bibliographical essay, works on Cummings
    published in 1970.

9   CROWLEY, JOHN W. "Visual-Aural Poetry: The Typography of
    E. E. Cummings." <u>Concerning Poetry</u>, 5, no. 2 (Fall), 51-54.
        Argues that Cummings' typographical oddities are the re-
    sult of his exploitation of the "shift in poetry from an
    oral-aural to a visual-aural mode." "The typography is only
    incidentally emblematic and ideographic; its basic function
    is to shape and qualify the aural-oral impact of the poem."

10 FRIEDMAN, NORMAN, ed. <u>E. E. Cummings: A Collection of Criti-</u>
    <u>cal Essays</u>. Twentieth Century Views. Englewood Cliffs,
    New Jersey: Prentice-Hall, Inc., 191 pp.
        Introduced by Norman Friedman, reprints fourteen essays
    on Cummings. The introduction (pp. 1-14) asserts that Cum-
    mings' writing of the poetry of transcendence rather than
    ambivalence in a period dominated by the New Criticism ac-
    counts for the relative insufficiency of Cummings scholar-
    ship. Hoping that this collection will help remedy that
    situation, Friedman describes Cummings' major contributions
    as his expansion of the language, his continuance and de-
    velopment of the tradition of lyric style and structure,
    his social criticism, and his achievement of "moments of
    pure transcendence," and explains his choice of essays.
    The reprinted pieces are: "::2:1 The World and E. E. Cum-
    mings" by George Haines IV (pp. 15-30), "The Dangers of
    Security: E. E. Cummings' Revolt against the Future" by
    Barbara Watson (pp. 31-45), "The Meaning of Cummings" by
    Norman Friedman (a reprint of Chapter 1, "Introduction,"
    from <u>E. E. Cummings: The Growth of a Writer</u>, minus the
    first paragraph and the first sentence of the second para-
    graph) (pp. 46-59), "The Whole E. E. Cummings" by Patricia
    Buchanan Tal-Mason Cline (pp. 60-70), "E. E. Cummings" by
    Allen Tate (pp. 71-74), "Review of <u>50 Poems</u>" by R. P. Black-
    mur (pp. 75-78), "Latter-Day Notes on E. E. Cummings' Lan-
    guage" by Robert E. Maurer (pp. 79-99), "Lower Case
    Cummings" by William Carlos Williams (pp. 100-103), "E. E.
    Cummings: The Technique of Immediacy" by S. V. Baum (pp.
    104-120), "<u>The Enormous Room</u> and <u>The Pilgrim's Progress</u>" by
    David E. Smith (pp. 121-32), "E. E. Cummings' <u>Him</u>" by Robert
    E. Maurer (pp. 133-55), "The Voyages" by Paul Rosenfeld
    (pp. 156-67), "E. E. Cummings and His Fathers" by Alfred
    Kazin (pp. 168-71), and "Review of <u>i: Six Nonlectures</u>" by

Robert Graves (pp. 172-76). The book also contains a
"Chronology of Important Dates" (pp. 177-79) and a "Selected
Bibliography" (pp. 182-85). Annotations for the reprinted
essays appear with the entries for their original appearances.

11 GARELICK, JUDITH SPRITZER. "Marianne Moore, Modern Poet: A
Study of Miss Moore's Relationships with William Carlos
Williams, E. E. Cummings, T. S. Eliot, Wallace Stevens, and
Ezra Pound." Ph.D. dissertation, Harvard University.
Contains a chapter chronicling the biographical and
literary relationship of Moore and Cummings and includes
unpublished letters. Moore's critical response to Cummings'
poetry is discussed at some length, as is their sharing of
a desire to affirm life, of linguistic experiment, of "af-
fection for the child mind," and of such rhetorical devices
as unexpected uses of prefixes and suffixes, punning, adjective dislocation, "hidden" rhyme, innovative rhythmic and
visual patterns, and the employment of new vocabularies.

12 LANE, GARY. "Cummings' 'Sonnet Entitled How to Run the World.'"
The Explicator, 31, no. 1 (September), Item 7.
Describes the poem as "pitting the always possible Eden
of individual freedom against the world-negating limitation
of 'isms.'" Ironically, the poem's step-by-step "not-so-
easy-to-follow instructions" announce the futility of trying
to reduce the world to a system. Lane also indicates the
appropriateness of the poem's "violated sonnet" form to its
theme. Reprinted in somewhat different form in Lane's book
on Cummings: 1976.13.

13 LANE, GARY. "Cummings' 'Yes Is a Pleasant Country.'" The
Explicator, 31, no. 2 (October), Item 11.
Analyzes the poem and its twist on the carpe diem theme:
it is not the season which fosters love, but love which fosters the season. The poem and its lovers "move from the
relative uncertainty that cajoling proposition implies to
the delicious expectation of fulfillment." Reprinted in
somewhat different form in Lane's book on Cummings:
1976.13.

14 LITTELL, ROBERT. "The Enormous Room," in The Critic as Artist:
Essays on Books 1920-1970. Edited by Gilbert A. Harrison.
New York: Liveright, pp. 238-42.
Reprint of 1922.7.

15 MARKS, BARRY A. "'anyone lived in a pretty how town,' Interpretation," in Die Amerikanische Lyrik von Edgar Allen Poe

1972

bis Wallace Stevens. Edited by Martin Christalder. Darmstadt: Wissenschaftliche Buchgesellschaft, pp. 310–17.
Reprinted from 1964.16.

16   MARKS, BARRY A. "'1(a,' Interpretation," in Die Amerikanische
Lyrik von Edgar Allen Poe bis Wallace Stevens. Edited by
Martin Christalder. Darmstadt: Wissenschaftliche Buch-
gesellschaft, pp. 304–309.
Reprinted from 1964.16.

17   MARTY, MARTIN. Review of Complete Poems: 1913–1962. Commonweal, 97, no. 10 (8 December), 237.
Brief notice of the appearance of Complete Poems: 1913–
1962.

18   MOTT, PETER H. "E. E. Cummings: Two Texts on the God in Man."
Ph.D. dissertation, Columbia University.
Explicates Eimi and "my father moved through dooms of
love" as expressions of a central Cummings theme: "the
unity of man and god in the idea of the Self." The analysis
of the book concentrates on its "climactic passages of
prophecy and revelation," the analysis of the poem on its
use of seasonal structure as an "emblem of wholeness."

19   NORMAN, CHARLES. E. E. Cummings: The Magic-Maker. Boston:
Little, Brown and Co., 380 pp.
Reprint, with a new introduction, of 1958.19.

20   NORMAN, CHARLES. E. E. Cummings: The Magic-Maker. Indian-
apolis, Indiana: The Bobbs-Merrill Co., 380 pp.
Reprint, with a new introduction, of 1958.19.

21   NORMAN, CHARLES. On Cummings, in his Poets & People. Indian-
apolis, Indiana: The Bobbs-Merrill Co., pp. 61, 62–69, 70,
74, 84–87, 102, 115–16, 149, 166, 171, 191, 197, 199, 209,
212, 219, 231–33, 242, 244, 256, 264–65, 273, 274–78, 297,
[299]–308.
Presents anecdotal material on Cummings as an acquaint-
ance of the author and background on the source of poem 28
of 73 poems.

22   SCHMIDER, CARL LUDWIG. "Precision Which Creates Movement:
The Stylistics of E. E. Cummings." Ph.D. dissertation,
University of Denver.
A descriptive and critical investigation of the stylistics of Cummings' poetry in relation to his desire to create
"precise movement." Cummings' stylistics are enumerated,
categorized, and described, and the relationships among

stylistics, voice, form, and movement in individual poems is assessed.

23 SPRINGER, S. HASKELL. "The Poetics of E. E. Cummings," in Modern American Poetry: Essays in Criticism. Edited by Guy Owen. Deland, Florida: Everett / Edwards, pp. 165-72. Reprint of 1967.29.

24 TANNER, JAMES EDGAR, JR. "The Grammar of Poetry: An Introduction to the Analysis of Style in Literature." Ph.D. dissertation, University of North Carolina at Chapel Hill.
    Includes examination of Cummings' poetry from a linguistic point of view, discovering that its "'transformational' operations...delete information from the content on which they operate." Tanner concludes that Cummings' preference for this type of device results from his characteristically idealistic attitude toward language.

25 TRIEM, EVE. "E. E. Cummings," in American Writers: A Collection of Literary Biographies. Edited by Leonard Unger. Vol. 1. New York: Charles Scribner's Sons, 428-50. Reprint of 1969.28.

26 TRIEM, EVE. "E. E. Cummings," in Six American Poets from Emily Dickinson to the Present: An Introduction. Edited by Allen Tate. Minneapolis: University of Minnesota Press, pp. 159-94, 244-46. Reprint of 1969.28.

27 TUCKER, ROBERT G. and DAVID R. CLARK, eds. "Freedom, Joy & Indignation: Letters from E. E. Cummings," in Lyric Resonance: Glosses on Some Poems of Yeats, Frost, Crane, Cummings & Others. By David Ridgley Clark. Amherst: University of Massachusetts Press, pp. [221]-50. Reprint of 1963.20.

28 TURPIN, ELIZABETH RICE. "Rhetoric and Rhythm in Twentieth-Century Sonnets by Hopkins, Auden, Frost, Cummings, Thomas, and Merrill Moore." Ph.D. dissertation, Texas A&M University.
    Includes commentary on both "traditional" and experimental sonnets by Cummings, arguing that he continues and revitalizes the sonnet form, achieving the "effective rhetorical and rhythmical correlation of persona, theme, and structure characteristic of the early Italian sonnets" while adapting the form to the demands of modern poetics.

1972

29   WHITTEMORE, REED. Review of <u>Complete Poems: 1913-1962</u>. <u>The</u>
<u>New Republic</u>, 167, no. 15 (21 October), 32-33.
Reviews <u>Complete Poems: 1913-1962</u>, wishing for fewer
poems and some notes. Cummings is infatuated with "the
syntax of things," is "extraordinarily isolated," and has
social opinions which are, finally, antisocial.

30   WILSON, G. R., JR. "Cummings's '(Ponder, Darling, These
Busted Statues.'" <u>South Atlantic Bulletin</u>, 37, no. 4
(November), 66-69.
Analyzes "ponder, darling, these busted statues" as a
<u>carpe diem</u> poem in four movements, suggesting some parallels
with Marvell's "To His Coy Mistress."

31   WILSON, G. R., JR. "Cummings' 'TA.'" <u>The Explicator</u>, 31,
no. 3 (November), Item 17.
Describes Cummings' picture "in sight and sound of a
jazz piano player" as an example of his effort to capture
in poetry "a single momentary image that will transmit to
the reader the emotion...that the poet felt on perceiving
some particular event." The rhythm of the poem mimics the
pianist's rag-time beat.

<u>1973</u>

1   BROOKS, CLEANTH, R. W. B. LEWIS, and ROBERT PENN WARREN.
"E. E. Cummings," in their <u>American Literature: The Makers</u>
<u>and the Making</u>. Volume 2. New York: St. Martin's Press,
2179-85.
Headnote to a selection of Cummings' poems comments on
his connections with Imagism, his "odd typography and for-
mat," his themes, his use of American idioms, his rhythms,
his urban settings, and his lack of development. With a
biographical chart, a brief bibliography, and explanatory
headnotes to several of the poems anthologized.

2   COTE, DAVID DANIEL. "''Pray Always for Individuals': Technique
and Vision in the Poetry of E. E. Cummings." Ph.D. dissertation, Tufts University.
Considers Cummings' typographical innovations not only
as linguistic experiments but also as "emblems of his
transcendental vision." That vision is embodied in the
shape of his poems as well as their statements. The "im-
manence of the transcendental in the poetry's phenomenological and noumenological manifestations" explains Cummings'
central concerns "with the timelessness of time, with per-
sonhood and individuality," and his opposition to "egali-
tarianism, totalitarianism and the unlife of most people."

3   COWLEY, MALCOLM. "Cummings: One Man Alone," in his <u>A Second
     Flowering: Works and Days of the Lost Generation</u>. New
     York: The Viking Press, pp. 90-113.
          Reprint of 1973.4.

4   COWLEY, MALCOLM. "Cummings: One Man Alone." <u>The Yale Review</u>,
     62, no. 3 (March), 332-54.
          Combines criticism of Cummings' work with biographical
     information. Cowley examines Cummings' exaltation of feel-
     ing over knowledge and his aesthetic of the intensely alive
     and personal moment of feeling. He comments on the influ-
     ence of the style of <u>The Enormous Room</u>, on the critical re-
     actions to the early work, on Cummings' skill as a mono-
     loguist, and on his role as a spokesman for the generation
     of the twenties. He finds Cummings' technique typified by
     calligram, cryptogram, the use of negatives to imply special
     meanings, the transformation of parts of speech, and the
     conversion of words into positive or negative abstractions.
     In the thirties, Cummings lost his role as spokesman, and
     from then on continued his lyric work with less exuberance
     but with, at times, more depth and a more coherent attitude,
     Christian Emersonianism. Reprinted: 1973.3.

5   CROWDER, RICHARD. Cummings Scholarship, in <u>American Literary
     Scholarship: An Annual, 1971</u>. Edited by J. Albert Robbins.
     Durham, North Carolina: Duke University Press, pp. 277,
     290.
          Describes, in a bibliographical essay, work on Cummings
     published in 1971.

6   DAVIS, WILLIAM V. "Cummings' 'no time ago.'" <u>Research
     Studies</u>, 41, no. 3 (September), 205-207.
          Rejects Friedman's reading (in 1960.8) of "no time ago,"
     and argues that in it, as elsewhere, Cummings uses a paren-
     thesis to create a form that will suit his theme, here "his
     sense of mystery" in the religious experience the poem
     relates.

7   ELIAS, ROBERT H. On Cummings, in his "<u>Entangling Alliances
     with None</u>": An Essay on the Individual in the American
     <u>Twenties</u>. New York: W. W. Norton & Co., pp. 164, 178,
     184-88, 200.
          Notes that Cummings--with many other writers of the
     twenties--rejects the possibility of social participation
     as an acceptable mode of behavior. <u>The Enormous Room</u> is
     discussed as an example of the "philosophy of disengange-
     ment."

1973

8   FAIRLEY, IRENE R. "Meaning and Syntax in ee cummings' 'quick
     i the death of thing,'" in <u>Meaning: A Common Ground of</u>
     <u>Linguistics and Literature, In Honor of Norman C. Stageberg,</u>
     <u>Proceedings of a University of Northern Iowa Conference Held</u>
     <u>April 27-28, 1973</u>. Edited by Don L. F. Nilsen. Cedar
     Falls: University of Northern Iowa, pp. 42-49.
       Maintains that in "quick i the death of thing" Cummings
     uses carefully controlled gradations of ungrammaticality
     (from dislocation to inversion to intercalation) to support
     and extend the theme expressed in the poem's parallel nar-
     ratives, a devotional statement of man's smallness and God's
     omnipotence.

9   FAIRLEY, IRENE R. "Syntactic Deviation and Cohesion." <u>Lan-</u>
     <u>guage and Style</u>, 6, no. 3 (Summer), 216-29.
       Argues that Cummings' syntactic deviation often functions
     as a device of structural cohesion and therefore conjoins
     form and theme. "a like a," "Tumbling-hair," "Me up at
     does," "All in green went my love riding," and "when god
     lets my body be" are examined in support of this argument.
     Much of the material presented here appears in Fairley's
     <u>E. E. Cummings and Ungrammar</u>, 1975.5.

10   FANDEL, JOHN. "hee hee cummings' fonetty kinglish." <u>Common-</u>
     <u>weal</u>, 99, no. 10 (7 December), 264-66.
       Asserts that Cummings' typography and language are bar-
     riers to communication and defeat the immediacy he so
     desired.

11   GUIMOND, JAMES. On Cummings. <u>The Ohio Review</u>, 15, no. 1
     (Fall), 17.
       Notes in passing that Cummings was involved in "the dis-
     covery of the aesthetic value of mundane, surface reality,"
     as were William Carlos Williams, Charles Sheeler and the
     Precisionists, and Walker Evans and Dorothea Lange.

12   HEYEN, WILLIAM. "In Consideration of Cummings." <u>Southern</u>
     <u>Humanities Review</u>, 7, no. 2 (Spring), 131-42.
       Insists on the need for a closer reading of Cummings'
     poems. Heyen considers the question of Cummings' anti-
     intellectualism, disagrees with Blackmur's assertion that
     there is no separation between poet and speaker in Cummings
     (<u>see</u> 1931.1), gives close attention to "since feeling is
     first" and "raise the shade," suggests that "all of Cummings
     begins with the blunt fact of death and attempts to build
     from there," and argues that many of his poems have much
     duplicity and depth of irony inherent in them.

13 HOMBITZER, ELEANORE. "E. E. Cummings: 'a wind has blown the rain away...': Versuch einer Strukturalistischen Deutung." <u>Der Fremdsprachliche Unterricht</u>, 27, no. 3 (August), [25]-40.
      Analyzes "a wind has blown the rain away and blown" from a structuralist perspective, examining such matters as the poem's use of tense shifts, its sentence structure, rule deviations, and synchronic and diachronic aspects. In German.

14 HOWARD, PATSY C. "E. E. Cummings," in her <u>Theses in American Literature 1896-1971</u>. Ann Arbor, Michigan: The Pierian Press, pp. 35-36.
      Lists unpublished baccalaureate and masters theses on Cummings.

15 KIDDER, RUSHWORTH M. On Cummings' "1(a." <u>College English</u>, 34, no. 6 (March), 778-79.
      Uses Cummings' poem "1(a" to indicate ways in which poetic form might be discussed in the classroom.

16 LANE, GARY MARTIN. "Eimi: A Study of Cummings' Poems." Ph.D. dissertation, University of Michigan.
      Examines five of Cummings' major themes in terms of specific poems. The themes are seduction, individual and individualistic heroism, the transcendental unification of life and death, death in life, and love as means to and end of transcendence. The dissertation was later published in book form and a fuller annotation appears under the book entry: 1976.13.

17 MAHONEY, JOSEPH W. "E. E. Cummings Today: A Bibliographical Survey." <u>Literatur in Wissenschaft und Unterricht</u>, 6, no. 3 (15 November), 188-201.
      Surveys works by and about Cummings. The criticism is found to vibrate within a dialectic, one pole of which sees Cummings as an anticultural, anti-intellectual writer, the other as an artist interpreting his culture and making new demands on the intellect.

18 NIXON, NELL. "A Reading of 'one's not half two. It's two are halves of one:.'" <u>The Language of Poems</u>, 2, no. 2 (September), 26-33.
      A close analysis. Each line is examined in detail and a grammatical norm for each is given, as are a paraphrase and an "ordinary" phrase with a parallel grammatical structure (where possible and/or necessary), and a commentary. The poem is a love poem on one level and, on another, a

1973

discussion of "loving identification" as a means to perceiving the "ideal world and its basic truth." For a
response, see 1974.8.

19 O'BRIEN, MICHAEL WILLIAM. "Between Language and Voice: A
Study of Aesthetic Experimentation in Blake, Whitman, Cummings, and Concrete Poetry." Ph.D. dissertation, University
of Illinois at Urbana-Champaign.
    Includes discussion of Cummings from the point of view
of his experimentation "with the structural possibilities
of placing the poetic voice in the language of print." His
"unorthodox use of the typewriter controls the spatial arrangement of the constituent letters of words and allows
him to reflect the auditory pace of his persona's rhythm
and speed of expression. Thus, his control of space visual-
ly at the level of form is integrated with content, and
speaker with reader." O'Brien also examines Cummings in
connection with the concrete poets he to some extent in-
fluenced.

20 OLSON, CHARLES. On Cummings, in The Poetics of the New American Poetry. Edited by Donald Allen and Warren Tallman.
New York: Grove Press, p. 154.
    Reprint of 1950.16.

21 O'NEAL, LAUREL MAUREEN. "Cummings' 'What If a Much of a Which
of a Wind.'" The Explicator, 32, no. 1 (September), Item 6.
    Explains the poem as asserting "that life must necessar-
ily be rooted in transformation and growth." It explores
"two distinct approaches to the world, and to change and
growth. The first approach is seen as an inadequate and
static response based upon intellectual perceptions; the
second is seen as a more adequate approach based upon sense
awareness of the world."

22 ÖVERLAND, ORM. "E. E. Cummings' 'my father moved through dooms
of love': A Measure of Achievement." English Studies, 54,
no. 2 (April), 141-47.
    Examines the poem's rhythm, rhyme, typographically indi-
cated structure, and seasonal image pattern. This leads to
a detailed consideration of the poem's "non-conventional
linguistic structures," which are found to allow Cummings a
complex expression of his values and of his love and admiration for his father. "Paradoxically, in the communication
of the intensely private emotion of filial love E. E. Cummings's idiolect proves a universal language."

23　RECK, MICHAEL.　On Cummings, in his <u>Ezra Pound:　A Close-Up</u>.
　　　New York:　McGraw-Hill Book Co., pp. 46, 58, 68, 82, 86-87,
　　　91-92, 101, 114, 130, 142, 174, 193.
　　　　　Reprint of 1968.22.

24　R[EGIER], W. G.　Review of <u>Complete Poems:　1913-1962</u>.
　　　<u>Prairie Schooner</u>, 47, no. 3 (Fall), 280.
　　　　　Notices <u>Complete Poems:　1913-1962</u>, finding that the
　　　"vitality" of Cummings' poems has increased in the decade
　　　since his death.

25　REXROTH, KENNETH.　On Cummings, in his <u>American Poetry in the</u>
　　　<u>Twentieth Century</u>.　New York:　The Seabury Press, pp. 85-88,
　　　96.
　　　　　Reprint of 1971.23.

26　SLOTKIN, ALAN R.　"The Negative Aspect of Homo Faber:　A Read-
　　　ing of E. E. Cummings' 'pity this busy monster, manunkind.'"
　　　<u>The Language of Poems</u>, 2, no. 2 (September), 34-41.
　　　　　A close reading with special emphasis on the poem's
　　　"concept and use of negation" and its syntax and punctua-
　　　tion.　Each line is given detailed commentary as well as a
　　　grammatical norm.　Some lines are paraphrased and juxtaposed
　　　with "ordinary" phrases with parallel grammatical struc-
　　　tures.　For a response, <u>see</u> 1974.8.

27　SMITH, JAMES F., JR.　"A Stereotyped Archetype:　E. E. Cum-
　　　mings' Jean le Nègre."　<u>Studies in American Fiction</u>, 1,
　　　no. 1 (Spring), 24-34.
　　　　　Discusses the function of the character Jean le Nègre in
　　　<u>The Enormous Room</u>.　Cummings was one of the first "to por-
　　　tray the predicament of modern man in terms of a Negro
　　　character," and no matter how stereotyped the presentation
　　　of Jean le Nègre seems, he is in fact "an archetype of hu-
　　　manity confronting the inhumanity of a government suffering
　　　from acute war-hysteria."　Indeed, it is the very details
　　　of the stereotype which give Jean resilience in a desperate
　　　situation and which indicate his humanity.

28　STADE, GEORGE.　Review of <u>Complete Poems:　1913-1962</u>.　<u>New</u>
　　　<u>York Times Book Review</u> (22 July), pp. 17-18.
　　　　　Examines <u>Complete Poems</u>, commenting on Cummings' techni-
　　　cal oddities, his individuality, his pettiness and smugness,
　　　the absence of anxiety in his poetry, a poetry informed by
　　　a sense of play, his "bravura displays of dexterity," his
　　　concern with sex, and his popularity.

1973

29   STICKNEY, CHARLES JACOB. "The Distorted Word: Word Distortion
      in Modern British and American Literature." Ph.D. disserta-
      tion, The City University of New York.
          Contains chapters on word distortion in Cummings' prose
      and poetry in terms of its various uses: to catch the
      reader's attention, to enhance realistic presentation of
      sound or appearance, to telescope meanings, and so forth.

30   STRICKLAND, WILLIAM FRANKLIN. "E. E. Cummings' Dramatic
      Imagination: A Study of Three Plays and a Ballet." Ph.D.
      dissertation, The University of Florida.
          Examines the staging, action, and composition of <u>Him</u>,
      <u>Anthropos</u>, <u>Santa Claus</u>, and <u>Tom</u>. Strickland finds that the
      works' actions reflect Cummings' ironic and paradoxical idea
      "that the sensitive individual must make a descent into life
      before he can ascend toward artistic creation." He finds
      that their composition implies an ideal of organic unity.

31   SÜLZER, BERND. "Moglichkeiten linguistischer Interpretation
      im Unterricht: E. E. Cummings' 'Poem No. 151.'" <u>Neu-</u>
      <u>sprachliche Mitteilungen Aus Wissenschaft und Praxis</u>, 26,
      no. 3, 153-57.
          Analyzes Cummings' "lis," examining such matters as gram-
      matical, orthographic, and "usage" deviation to demonstrate
      Cummings' successful escape from convention. In German.

32   SUTTON, WALTER. On Cummings, in his <u>American Free Verse: The</u>
      <u>Modern Revolution in Poetry</u>. New York: New Directions Pub-
      lishing Corp., pp. 36, 38, 39, 46, 81, 87-102, 115, 156,
      172, 186, 203.
          Cummings differs from other moderns in his traditional-
      ism, in his embracing of romantic themes, in his refusal to
      accept the diminishment of self as a fact of modern life,
      and in his insistence on a direct, subjective, and discur-
      sive speech. His experiments with language, syntax, and
      meter create a technique "especially suited to his anti-
      intellectuality." If his technique is successful, his
      ideas are often weak. All of these matters are discussed
      in some detail.

33   THOMAS, BETHANY K. "Dialect in E. E. Cummings." <u>The Language</u>
      <u>of Poems</u>, 2, no. 2 (September), 49-51.
          Discusses the difficulties of isolating Cummings' dialect
      spellings from his other "misspellings" used for other pur-
      poses and suggests that dialect use is a significant clue
      in examining "how social attitudes find expression in
      literature."

34 THOMPSON, W. E. "Cummings and the Mystery of Stillness."
    Contemporary Poetry, 1, no. 1 (Spring), 35-43.
        Analyzes "n" as "creating the linguistic equivalent of
    stillness" and "insu nli gh t" as "an impressionistic word-
    painting." Technical considerations are stressed in both
    analyses.

35 TOWLES, J. L. "A Reading of 'if everything happens that can't
    be done.'" The Language of Poems, 2, no. 2 (September),
    42-48.
        Reads the poem as praising love, nature, and the unity
    of the world. Each line receives extensive comment, and
    some are paraphrased and juxtaposed with grammatical norms
    and "ordinary" phrases with parallel grammatical structures.
    For a response, see 1974.8.

36 UNTERMEYER, LOUIS. "E. E. Cummings," in his 50 Modern American
    and British Poets, 1920-1970. Edited by Louis Untermeyer.
    New York: David McKay Co., pp. 258-60.
        A brief biographical and critical note, describing Cum-
    mings' poetry as "lovely and limited."

37 VENDLER, HELEN. Review of Complete Poems, 1913-1962. The
    Yale Review, 62, no. 3 (March), 412-19.
        Reviews Cummings' Complete Poems in an omnibus review,
    discovering that it deepens rather than solves the mystery
    of his "great aborted talent." Vendler considers Cummings
    "abysmally short on ideas" and incapable of ambivalence.
    His "optimism excludes too much."

38 WEINBERGER, G. J. "Cummings' ')when what hugs stopping earth
    than silence is.'" Research Studies, 41, no. 2 (June),
    136-39.
        Analyzes the poem as treating "those timeless instants
    when lovers effect transcendence beyond the bounds of earth
    and its mortal concerns."

39 WEST, PHILIP J. "Medieval Style and the Concerns of Modern
    Criticism." College English, 34, no. 6 (March), 784-90.
        Discusses the way in which a formulaic analysis of "All
    in green went my love riding" might be used for classroom
    teaching, considering such matters as "the interplay of
    acoustic and visual space," transformational grammar, and
    the interplay of vernacular with "lettered" poetry.

1974

1974

1 AARON, DANIEL. On Cummings, in his <u>Writers on the Left: Epi-</u>
   <u>sodes in American Literary Communism</u>. New York: Octagon
   Books, pp. 76, 79, 92, 107, 112, 175, 176–77, 411, 419.
   Reprint of 1961.1.

2 BRADLEY, SCULLEY, RICHARD CROOM BEATTY, and E. HUDSON LONG.
   "E. E. Cummings," in their <u>The American Tradition in Litera-</u>
   <u>ture</u>. Fourth edition. Vol. 2. New York: Grosset &
   Dunlap, pp. 1027–29.
      The Cummings entry is slightly updated in this revised
   edition of 1956.2.

3 CLURMAN, HAROLD. Review of <u>Him</u>. <u>The Nation</u>, 218, no. 19
   (11 May), 604–605.
      Reviews the Circle Repertory Theatre's production of
   Cummings' play. Although "disjointed and flawed," it "still
   breathes with imagination and lyric life." Its anticipation
   of contemporary dramatic interests and effects is remarked.

4 DAVIS, WILLIAM V. "E. E. Cummings's 'except in your.'"
   <u>English Language Notes</u>, 11, no. 4 (June), 294–96.
      Analyzes "except in your" as a "statement of the artist's
   relationship to his muse dressed in the guise of a lady who
   orders the world, thereby allowing it to come to rest."

5 DUMAS, BETHANY K. <u>E. E. Cummings: A Remembrance of Miracles</u>.
   New York: Barnes & Noble Books, 157 pp.
      A general study. The opening chapter is biographical
   and traces Cummings' movement from Cambridge to Greenwich
   Village, the shifts of attitude which accompanied that movement, artistic influences on him, and his publishing history. The second chapter concentrates on the early poetry,
   commenting on the unpublished juvenilia, on early influences, and, in detail, on the poems included in the original
   1922 manuscript of <u>Tulips and Chimneys</u>.
      The third chapter examines the poems after <u>Tulips and</u>
   <u>Chimneys</u>, explores their use of the devices of disjunction,
   displacement, punctuation, and word coinage, and points to
   their use in creating accurate expression. Specific poems
   are examined in terms of four categories of style: romance,
   satire, appreciation, and epigram. Cummings' metrics, conceptual vocabulary, and handling of the sonnet form are
   also considered.
      The prose is discussed in chapter four. Unpublished
   juvenilia is examined; <u>The Enormous Room</u> is summarized, and
   its relation to <u>The Pilgrim's Progress</u> and use of inverted

values are noted; Eimi is also summarized, and its uses of
the pattern of The Divine Comedy and of the conceptual language of the poems are remarked. The essays collected in
A Miscellany Revised, i: Six Nonlectures, and the captions
for the photographs in Adventures in Value are discussed
briefly.

Chapter five summarizes the plays Him, Anthropos, and
Santa Claus, and the ballet Tom. Him is connected with ex-
pressionism and the theatre of the absurd, and its themes
are those of identity, love, and creation. Anthropos in-
dicts the primitiveness of modern society. Santa Claus
presents an allegorical contest between knowledge and understanding. Tom shows love triumphant over hate.

A concluding appraisal discusses Cummings as a linguistic
radical and maintains that his major accomplishments are
the multiplication of the poetic possibilities of the lyric
and the creation of a poetic language that forces his readers to look at reality from a new vantage. Includes a
bibliography and an index of first lines of poems discussed.

6   EVERSON, EDITH A. "Cummings' 'That Which We Who're Alive in
      Spite of Mirrors.'" The Explicator, 32, no. 7 (March),
      Item 55.
         Interprets this poem on the theme of renewal's accompani-
      ment of death by reference to its use and amendment of
      Elizabethan ideas and forms.

7   FIRMAGE, GEORGE JAMES. E. E. Cummings: A Bibliography.
      Westport, Connecticut: Greenwood Press, 139 pp.
         Reprint of 1960.7.

8   FRIEDMAN, NORMAN. "Notes and Comments: Reactions to the Cum-
      mings Issue: Vol. II, No. 2, September, 1973." The Lan-
      guage of Poems, 3, no. 2 (May), 31-33.
         Reactions to readings of Cummings poems in an earlier
      issue of the journal. Friedman asserts that Nixon's reading
      of "one's not half two" (see 1973.18) is marred by her use
      of the word "ideal" to characterize Cummings' transcenden-
      talism, since he finds transcendence not in an ideal world
      but in direct perception of nature. He rejects Slotkin's
      suggestion that "pity this busy monster, manunkind" is ad-
      dressed to God (see 1973.26) as inaccurate and comments on
      three details of Towles' analysis of "if everything happens
      that can't be done" (see 1973.35).

9   KROLL, JACK. "Full Circle." Newsweek, 83, no. 17 (29 April),
      108.

1974

Comments on Cummings' Him in a discussion of the Circle
Repertory Theatre's production of it and other plays. Although it is not realistic, it "epitomizes Cummings' positive, poetic humanism."

10   McCARTHY, HAROLD T. "E. E. Cummings: Eros and Cambridge,
     Mass.," in his The Expatriate Perspective: American Novel-
     ists and the Idea of America. Rutherford, New Jersey:
     Fairleigh Dickinson University Press, pp. 123-35.
     Examines The Enormous Room in terms of its hero's anomal-
ous joy in his imprisonment and his recognition of it as a
way of salvation and in terms of Cummings' American-patrician background. The book is in the tradition of those
American works which envision "the human spirit transcending
a cultural apocalypse." Although Cummings came from a
fortress of ruling-class culture, the experiences recorded
in the novel caused him to discover himself to be deeply
opposed to the values it guarded. This development is discussed at length. McCarthy also comments on Cummings' creation of an idiom for rendering his new attitudes, one that
would subvert conventional responses to the nonrational in
life and evoke new ones.

11   MATTHIESSEN, F. O. On Cummings, in Literary History of the
     United States: History. Fourth edition. Edited by Robert
     E. Spiller, Willard Thorp, Thomas H. Johnson, Henry Seidel
     Canby, Richard M. Ludwig, and William M. Gibson. New York:
     The Macmillan Co., pp. 1351-52.
     Reprint of 1947.9.

12   MELLER, HORST. "Edward Estlin Cummings: 'pity this busy
     monster, manunkind,'" in Die Amerikanische Lyrik, Von der
     Kolonialzeit bis zur Gegenwart. Edited by Klaus Lubbers.
     Düsseldorf: August Bagel, pp. 394-405.
     Analyzes "pity this busy monster, manunkind," explicating
some of its more innovative techniques and exploring its
theme in relation to works with similar themes by Henry
Adams, Emerson, Blake, and others. In German.

13   NADEL, ALAN M. "Cummings' 'When Faces Called Flowers Float
     Out of the Ground.'" The Explicator, 32, no. 6 (February),
     Item 47.
     Explicates the way in which, in "the tension between the
tone of the poem and the structure, Cummings has created a
world inside the poem that parallels the one about which he
is speaking" in this vibrant celebration of spring.

14   NASSAR, EUGENE PAUL. On Cummings. <u>Mosaic</u>, 7, no. 4 (Summer),
      123n.
          Notes that Cummings is among those modern poets who
      believe that each "man makes his own heaven...out of phe-
      nomenological reality."

15   NIXON, NELL. "A Reading of 'anyone lived in a pretty how
      town.'" <u>The Language of Poems</u>, 3, no. 2 (May), 18-31.
          A close analysis. Each line is examined in detail and
      a grammatical norm for each line is given, as are a para-
      phrase and an "ordinary" phrase with a parallel grammatical
      structure. Nixon concludes that the poem is an expression
      of Cummings' transcendental thought, with emphasis on in-
      tuited truth, the necessity of selfless love, the unreality
      of death, and the timelessness of the universe.

16   OLIVER, WILLIAM I. "<u>Him</u>--A Director's Note." <u>Educational</u>
      <u>Theatre Journal</u>, 26, no. 3 (October), 327-41.
          Asserts that, in <u>Him</u>, Cummings creates a profoundly
      complex mixture of surrealism, realism, and expressionism,
      "vindicates the mixture aesthetically, situationally, and
      thematically," and does so while still producing an in-
      tensely personal expression. The bulk of the essay is
      given over to Oliver's exploration of and attempts to solve
      the play's directorial problems in terms of his production
      of it at the University of California at Berkeley.

17   RANTA, JERRALD. "Palindromes, Poems, and Geometric Forms."
      <u>College English</u>, 36, no. 2 (October), 161-72.
          Examines the palindromic form of, among others, Cummings'
      "If you can't eat you got to," finding that the form, with
      its own repetition and monotony, "dramatizes" the exposure
      of emptiness that is the poem's content. Reprinted:
      1976.20.

18   ROSENFELD, ALVIN H. Cummings Scholarship, in <u>American Literary</u>
      <u>Scholarship: An Annual, 1972</u>. Edited by J. Albert Robbins.
      Durham, North Carolina: Duke University Press, pp. 312-13,
      328.
          Describes, in a bibliographical essay, works on Cummings
      published in 1972.

19   ROTHENBERG, JEROME. On Cummings, in his <u>Revolution of the</u>
      <u>Word: A New Gathering of Avant Garde Poetry 1914-1945</u>.
      New York: The Seabury Press, p. 15.
          Headnote suggests that Cummings' "use of typography,
      both as a notational device & as a basis for new visual
      forms, somewhere along the road to concrete poetry,"

1974

        signalled "that writing, far from being the normative
        state of a language, is itself derived from speech."

20   SMELSTOR, MARJORIE, S.C. "'Damn Everything but the Circus':
        Popular Art in the Twenties and him." Modern Drama, 17,
        no. 1 (March), 43-45.
            Explores Him in relation to the contemporary artistic
        scene. Its setting, dialogue, action, cast, theme, and
        thematic development all "reveal cummings' reliance upon
        the popular arts"; its significance is in its combination
        of "content and form so that the great and lively art dich-
        otomy is reconciled. For by handling a theme of 'high
        seriousness' through techniques which manifest 'high lev-
        ity,' cummings' presents him as his product of and response
        to the artistic dilemma of art in the twenties." The
        failure of contemporary critics to understand this accounts
        for their harsh response.

21   STAUFFER, DONALD BARLOW. "New Thresholds, New Anatomies," in
        A Short History of American Poetry. New York: E. P.
        Dutton & Co., pp. 292-97.
            Maintains that Cummings' experimental poetry represents
        the "defiant avant-gardism of the 'literary left.'" Like
        Stein, he believed "words are symbols that can embody con-
        cepts independently of their syntactical function," and,
        like Joyce, he "liked to play with words and with his read-
        er's expectations." But for all his relations with the
        avant-garde, Cummings cannot be lumped with any group. His
        combination of satires and lyrics "is not paradoxical, but
        stems from his central vision of life as a 'supremely wel-
        come mystery,' not to be violated by stupidity, greed,
        hypocrisy or cant." In addition to discussing these mat-
        ters, Stauffer examines Cummings' poetic "pose" and the
        variety of his poems.

22   WEINBERGER, G. J. "E. E. Cummings's Benevolent God: A Read-
        ing of 'when you are silent, shining host by guest.'"
        Papers on Language & Literature, 10, no. 1 (Winter), 70-75.
            Analyzes the poem as "a celebration of the love of an
        essentially unknowable God." This un-unknowableness "re-
        sults in the tentative nature of the poem." The poem also
        suggests that Cummings is capable of finding joy outside
        the self.

1975

1   AICHINGER, PETER. On Cummings, in his The American Soldier
        in Fiction, 1880-1963: A History of Attitudes Toward

<u>Warfare and the Military Establishment</u>. Ames: Iowa State University Press, pp. xvii, 3-99, passim.

Discusses Cummings' <u>The Enormous Room</u> in passing, comparing its "attitudes toward warfare and the military establishment" with those of American, English, and European war novels of the period from 1917 through 1963.

2   ANDREA, FLAVIA. "E. E. Cummings--Poetul Posibil." <u>Steaua</u>, 26, no. 8 (August), 46-47.

Surveys Cummings, commenting on his lyrics and satires, his simplification of all into evil or good, his transcendentalism, his setting of the methods of imagination against those of the machine, and his themes. He is a traditional poet, a modern romantic. In Romanian.

3   CROWDER, RICHARD. Cummings Scholarship, in <u>American Literary Scholarship: An Annual, 1973</u>. Edited by James Woodress. Durham, North Carolina: Duke University Press, pp. 319-21.

Describes, in a bibliographical essay, works on Cummings published in 1973.

4   DUMAS, BETHANY K. "E. E. Cummings in the Twenties," in <u>The Twenties: Fiction, Poetry, Drama</u>. Edited by Warren French. Deland, Florida: Everett / Edwards, Inc., pp. 365-75.

Argues that "Cummings the artist was largely formed during the twenties," with special emphasis on his development of a "spectatorial attitude" which provided him a toughness that helped him grow away from earlier romantic influences. Dumas comments specifically on Cummings' criticism of American capitalism and consumerism and on the portrait of the artist painted in <u>Him</u>.

5   FAIRLEY, IRENE R. <u>E. E. Cummings and Ungrammar: A Study of Syntactic Deviance in his Poems</u>. Searingtown, New York: Watermill Publishers, 202 pp.

Linguistic study explores Cummings' ungrammaticality, dealing with the question of how he can "include so much grammatical irregularity without losing the reader," and defines what irregularities are characteristic of his style. The discussions generally center on individual lines or passages rather than on entire poems. After an introductory chapter defining terms and explaining assumptions, the second chapter explores Cummings' assigning of new values to semantic indicators and of semantic content to "function words," and comments on his morphological innovations, his uses of compounding, affixation, and functional shift, and his orthographic and spatial innovations.

1975

Chapter three examines Cummings' syntactic innovations in
relation to the fact of syntactic and semantic overlap in
sentences, and treats such matters as deletion, repetition,
and selectional deviance. Chapter four analyzes Cummings'
use of adjective and adverb displacement. Here as else-
where the thematic functions of such grammatical deviation
are explored as the devices themselves are categorized.
Chapter five addresses Cummings' use of subject-verb-ob-
ject displacement and lists the permutations typical of
Cummings' style in this regard. Chapter six argues that
Cummings employs syntactic deviance not only in individual
lines but also for the creation of larger structural patterns, as "a major source of cohesiveness within a poem."
Several of Cummings' poems are discussed from this angle.
The final chapter provides a frame of reference for earlier
conclusions in a "matrix of rules" theory of literature and
explains that Cummings' deviations from grammar, in their
dependence on standard English, show that on this level
(as well as on other thematic and technical levels) he is
a "conservative revolutionary." With notes, a bibliography, and an index of first lines for entire poems discussed. Reprint, with minor changes, of 1971.7.

6 GELPI, ALBERT. On Cummings, in his The Tenth Muse: The Psyche
   of the American Poet. Cambridge: Harvard University Press,
   p. 91.
        Briefly connects Cummings' innovative techniques with
   those of other modern poets, considering them extensions of
   the experiments of Emerson.

7 HARMSEL, HENRIETTA TEN. "Christian Meanings in Cummings'
   'Jehovah buried, Satan dead.'" Christian Scholar's Review,
   5, no. 2, 119-22.
        Analyzes the poem as a "powerful statement of basically
   Christian concepts" combined with a critique of "the ma-
   terialism, conformity, and dehumanization of twentieth-
   century life."

8 HAULE, J. "E. E. Cummings as Comic Poet: The Economy of the
   Expenditure of Freud." Literature and Psychology, 25, no.
   4, 175-80.
        Analyzes Cummings' "listen my children and you" in terms
   of Freud's theory of the comic, finding that the former ful-
   fills the demands of the latter.

9 KENNER, HUGH. On Cummings, in his A Homemade World: The
   American Modernist Writers. New York: Alfred A. Knopf,
   p. xviii.

Explains Cummings' exclusion from the study by asserting that he "finally altered no verbal environment except his own." Reprinted: 1975.10.

10   KENNER, HUGH. On Cummings, in his <u>A Homemade World: The American Modernist Writers</u>. New York: William Morrow and Co., p. xviii.
Reprint of 1975.9.

11   KIDDER, RUSHWORTH M. "E. E. Cummings, Painter." <u>Harvard Library Bulletin</u>, 23, no. 2 (April), 117-38.
Maintains that Cummings was a serious painter and traces his "background in art" and his concern for the theoretical and aesthetic as well as the technical aspects of painting. Cummings' concern with the analytical intellect in both painting and writing (especially as evidenced in unpublished notes in Harvard's Houghton Library) belies his usual description as an anti-intellectual. Kidder also defines the development of Cummings' painting as a movement from the abstract to the representational. With comments on critical reviews of Cummings as a painter and photographs of several works.

12   KUNITZ, STANLEY. "E. E. Cummings: A Personal Note," in his <u>A Kind of Order, A Kind of Folly: Essays and Conversations</u>. Boston: Little, Brown and Co., pp. 244-46.
Presents reminiscences of Cummings and asserts that the joy of his "work is the product of his lifelong pursuit of folly, the folly of selfhood in a society of automatons, the folly of art in a time of the degradation of values."

13   MEAD, DAVID GODDARD. "E. E. Cummings: The Meaning of the Sonnets." Ph.D. dissertation, The University of Florida.
Examines Cummings' sonnets and his philosophy as developed in them. He began as a Platonic idealist; as he matured, he discovered that transcendental experience may be gained by the surrender of the self, through love, to others and the world; and, finally, he arrived at an "absolute acceptance of life in the temporal world." In terms of his aesthetics and innovative techniques, Cummings' experiments with the sonnet demonstrate his "belief that the artist must be true to his own creative impulse without regard to the aesthetic dictates of tradition or form."

14   MOORE, GEOFFREY. On Cummings, in <u>American Literature Since 1900</u>. Edited by Marcus Cunliffe. London: Barrie & Jenkins, pp. 124-26.
Discusses Cummings' ability to convey "a sense of delight in the present," remarks the importance of his

1975

> typographical experiments to the development of concrete
> poetry, and comments on Cummings' continuing "exploration
> of the boundaries of communication."

15   MORSE, DAVID.   On Cummings' <u>Him</u>, in <u>American Literature Since</u>
>   <u>1900</u>.   Edited by Marcus Cunliffe.   London: Barrie & Jen-
>   kins, pp. 84, 85-86.
>   Explores the experimentalism of <u>Him</u> and its "concern
>   with problems of identity and with the nature of mass
>   society."

16   REUTLINGER, DAGMAR.   "E. E. Cummings and <u>The Dial</u> Collection."
>   <u>The Massachusetts Review</u>, 26, no. 2 (Spring), [353-56].
>   Comments on eighteen Cummings drawings reproduced from
>   the Dial Collection at the Worcester Art Museum.   <u>See also</u>
>   1975.19.

17   STAFFORD, JEAN.   Review of <u>Fairy Tales</u>.   <u>The New Yorker</u>, 51,
>   no. 41 (December), 177-78.
>   Notices the paperback reissue of <u>Fairy Tales</u>.

18   TASHJIAN, DICKRAN.   "E. E. Cummings and Dada Formalism," in
>   his <u>Skyscraper Primitives: Dada and the American Avant-</u>
>   <u>Garde 1910-1925</u>.   Middletown, Connecticut: Wesleyan Uni-
>   versity Press, pp. [165]-87.
>   Explores Cummings' relations with the avant-garde move-
>   ments of the late teens and twenties, especially Dadaism.
>   In general, Cummings is more moderate than the Dadaists.
>   For example, he uses typographical experimentation for more
>   than shock value and does not "undergo the violently anar-
>   chic or destructive phase endemic to Dada."   He does employ
>   certain Dada methods "for the organic transformation of
>   form and content in his poetry" and shares their "apprecia-
>   tion of nonsense"; but as to the Dadaist writing of "ab-
>   stract poetry in an attempt to free the word from its
>   conventional syntactical pattern with assigned denotation,"
>   Cummings' poems never completely abandon the denotational
>   quality of words.   He uses certain Dadaist methods for
>   achieving simultaneity but extends them into more sophisti-
>   cated techniques.   Several of these are discussed and ex-
>   emplified.   Other aspects of the avant-garde which might
>   have influenced Cummings are touched on.   Tashjian also
>   notes that Cummings "borrowed Dada experiments for the
>   creation of spiritual values consonant with his New England
>   heritage of Transcendentalism" and examines his magazine
>   publishing during the first half of the twenties as another
>   way of exploring his connections to the avant-garde.   The
>   Dadaist and Surrealist aspects of <u>Him</u> are explored at some
>   length.

19   TUCKER, ROBERT. "E. E. Cummings As An Artist: The Dial Draw-
      ings." The Massachusetts Review, 26, no. 2 (Spring),
      [329]-53.
          Discusses Cummings' graphics (a number of which are re-
      produced) as they complement his poems. See also 1975.16.

20   WELLAND, DENNIS. On Cummings, in American Literature Since
      1900. Edited by Marcus Cunliffe. London: Barrie & Jen-
      kins, pp. 55-56.
          Briefly comments on the "exploration of the resources of
      language" in The Enormous Room.

21   WILSON, EDMUND. On Cummings, in his The Twenties. Edited by
      Leon Edel. New York: Farrar, Straus and Giroux, pp. xii,
      159, 205-207, 209-10, 281, 298, 350, 405-406, 429-30, 434,
      512, 514, 536.
          Presents largely anecdotal information on Cummings in
      the twenties.

                                1976

1   BROYARD, ANATOLE. "Puddle Wonderful." New York Times (21
      October), p. 37.
          Describes Cummings as typical of the adolescence of
      American literature and life, finds his "typographical
      antics" mere gimmickry, and considers his language impre-
      cise.

2   COXE, LOUIS. On Cummings, in his Enabling Acts: Selected
      Essays in Criticism. Columbia: University of Missouri
      Press, pp. 105-106.
          Notes that Cummings comes closest of modern New England
      poets to "a religion of humanity." He conveys "a sense of
      the sacred, the ineffable, in the small things that compose
      daily life.... Even his hatred seems holy."

3   CROWDER, RICHARD. Cummings Scholarship, in American Literary
      Scholarship: An Annual, 1974. Edited by James Woodress.
      Durham, North Carolina: Duke University Press, pp. 322,
      340-41.
          Describes, in a bibliographical essay, works on Cummings
      published in 1974.

4   DIEHL, PAUL BYRON. "The Renewal of Abstraction: E. E. Cum-
      mings' Sentiment, Sonnets, and Meters." Ph.D. dissertation,
      The University of Texas at Austin.

1976

Refutes the charge of sentimentality against Cummings
by describing the difference between an "open use of sentiment" and sentimentality, examines his sonnets to demonstrate a parallel growth of theme and technique in them,
and explores Cummings' "exploitation of the syllabic, Folk
Meter and foot-verse traditions."

5   FIRMAGE, GEORGE JAMES. "Afterword," in Tulips & Chimneys.
     By E. E. Cummings. Edited by George James Firmage. New
     York: Liveright, pp. 217-18.
         Discusses this volume's use of the four surviving copies
     of the original manuscript.

6   FORT, PAUL. "From '1 inga' to 'unders of dream': E. E. Cum-
     mings' Growth and Twentieth-Century American Poetry."
     Revue des Langues Vivantes / Tijdschrift voor Levende
     Talen, U. S. Bicentennial Issue, pp. 121-41.
         Maintains that Cummings is at the center of the dialec-
     tic of aestheticism and energy characteristic of twentieth-
     century American poetry, that his love poetry is his
     richest and most typical work, and that his love poems
     show dynamic growth and renewal. This growth (from "the
     new realism" to "transcendental vision" to an "increasing
     lucidity" which unifies the aesthetic and the energetic)
     is traced in detail. (The title given above is that
     printed over the article. In the volume's table of con-
     tents, the title appears as "From '1 inga' to 'overs of
     known': The Growth of E. E. Cummings' Love Poetry.")

7   GONZÁLEZ DE LEÓN, ULALUME. "e. e. cummings: el uno y el
     innumerable quién." Plural, 5, no. 4 (January), 31-42.
         Describes Cummings as having two voices: one, the voice
     of the prose, explores the "problems of the ordinary
     world"; the other, the voice of the poems, begins in "'an
     amputation of the world,'" is without "conflict and the
     drama of consciousness," and concerns itself with "love
     and indignation." Cummings' attitudes on ideology and his
     conception of salvation are discussed, as are his original-
     ity ("his success in rendering passion itself without di-
     minishing it") and his attempt to fabricate recognition
     rather than cognition. "nonsun blob a," "a-," and "r-p-o-
     p-h-e-s-s-a-g-r" are examined. In Spanish. Reprinted, in
     translation: 1976.8.

8   GONZÁLEZ DE LEÓN, ULALUME. "The One and the Not Numerable
     Whom." Translated by Paula Speck. Review, 17, no. 1
     (Spring), 82-92.
         Reprint, in English, of 1976.7.

9   KENNEDY, RICHARD S. "E. E. Cummings at Harvard: Studies."
     Harvard Library Bulletin, 24, no. 3 (July), 267-97.
          Examines Cummings' studies during the five years he
     spent at Harvard pursuing the A.B. and A.M. degrees. Ken-
     nedy pays special attention to those courses, relationships
     with professors, and other matters which played a part in
     the development of Cummings' mind and art, and points to
     the early influences of the Greek classics, medieval and
     other sorts of allegorical and emblem verse, and the poems
     of Keats and Rossetti on Cummings' work.

10   KENNEDY, RICHARD S. "Introduction," in Tulips & Chimneys.
     By E. E. Cummings. Edited by George James Firmage. New
     York: Liveright, pp. ix-xv.
          Introduces this printing of the original 1922 manuscript
     and the thirty-four additional poems from & by discussing
     the history of the manuscript and the history of Cummings'
     artistic development in the years up to its completion.
     Kennedy also argues that the three styles, Apollonian,
     Satyric, and Hephaestian, which account for nearly all of
     Cummings' poetic output, appear in these poems; he describes
     the characteristic subjects, attitudes, and techniques of
     each. If Tulips & Chimneys contains Cummings' major styles,
     it lacks the coherent outlook on life which is developed in
     and centers the later volumes.

11   KIDDER, RUSHWORTH M. "'Author of Pictures': A Study of Cum-
     mings' Line Drawings in The Dial." Contemporary Litera-
     ture, 17, no. 4 (Autumn), [470]-505.
          Examines the line drawings published by Cummings in The
     Dial. They "provide insights into the humor, economy, pre-
     cision, and movement of his poetry." Kidder connects the
     poetry and the drawings in terms of such matters as their
     interest in vitality, their "simultaneous presentation of
     opposites," their juxtaposition of disparate images, their
     "economy of expression" and "quick rendering," their "sup-
     pression of inessentials," their increasing stress on the
     "spontaneous and intuitive," and their replacement of an
     earlier "self-conscious lushness" by a "new firmness."
     With reproductions of sixteen line drawings.

12   KIDDER, RUSHWORTH M. "'Buffalo Bill's': An Early E. E. Cum-
     mings Manuscript." Harvard Library Bulletin, 24, no. 4
     (October), 373-80, Plates 1-3.
          Finds, in several manuscript pages from the Cummings
     Collection in Harvard's Houghton Library, evidence of the
     origin of this poem and of Cummings' process of composition
     in general. Kidder dates the poem as roughly equivalent

1976

with Cody's death on 10 January 1917 and demonstrates Cummings' drive for economy, accurate diction, and effective rhythmic and typographic arrangement. With photographs of the manuscript.

13   LANE, GARY. <u>I Am: A Study of E. E. Cummings' Poems.</u> Lawrence, Manhattan, and Wichita: The University Press of Kansas, 145 pp.

Presents Cummings as a poet who would by means of intensity teach his readers how to live. The introduction examines Cummings' vision, especially his essential egocentrism, his thematic dialectic of love, and his technical striving for immediacy of effect; and his major weaknesses, sentimentality, obscurity, and false ingenuity. Each of the five central chapters (two through six) "follows a motif as it expands into a major theme" and narrows its focus to specific poems. The first discusses the "seduction" theme with its sense of love as a "lively surrender, a death that can lead to growth." The theme is evidenced in analyses of "notice the convulsed orange inch of moon," "if i have made,my lady,intricate," "in Just-," "may i feel said he," and "yes is a pleasant country:." The second examines the theme of individual and individualistic heroism as manifested in those "who could integrate the diverse facets of personality into a unity of being." The poems explicated are "o by the by," "i sing of Olaf glad and big," "my father moved through dooms of love," "sonnet entitled how to run the world)," and "so many selves(so many fiends and gods." The third of the central chapters explores Cummings' transcendent unification of life and death and analyzes "when god lets my body be," "All in green went my love riding," "suppose," "dying is fine) but Death," and "wild(at our first)beasts uttered human words." The fourth examines the theme of death in life, the satirizing of the destroyers of individuality and love. Again, five exemplary poems are treated: "the Cambridge ladies who live in furnished souls," "proud of his scientific attitude," "MEMORABILIA," "here is little Effie's head," and "everybody happy?." The fifth discusses Cummings' mature vision of love as both the means to and end of transcendence. The explicated poems are: "one's not half two. It's two are halves of one:," "anyone lived in a pretty how town," "love's function is to fabricate unknownness," "SONG," and "all worlds have halfsight, seeing either with." The conclusion briefly reasserts the essentials of Cummings' vision and art and argues his importance. With a bibliographic note. Reprint, with minor changes, of 1973.16.

14   LAUTER, PAUL. E. E. Cummings: Index to First Lines and
     Bibliography of Works By and About the Poet. Norwood,
     Pennsylvania: Norwood Editions, 46 pp.
         Reprint of 1955.17.

15   LEVENSTON, EDWARD A. "Cummings' 'lucky means finding.'" The
     Explicator, 34, no. 5 (January), Item 36.
         Examines the poem as "an example of controlled serendip-
     ity: the faculty of making happy and unexpected discover-
     ies by design."

16   LIPSKI, JOHN M. "Connectedness in Poetry: Toward a Topologi-
     cal Analysis of E. E. Cummings." Language and Style, 9,
     no. 3 (Summer), 143-63.
         Suggests the possibility of applying topology, the
     branch of mathematics dealing with spatial properties, to
     the study of poetry; examines Cummings' use of "discon-
     nectedness" from a topological point of view in "a heuris-
     tic demonstration"; and, from this particular case,
     cautiously attempts to construct a formal model for topo-
     logical analysis of literary works.

17   MILLER, JORDAN Y. Cummings Scholarship, in American Literary
     Scholarship: An Annual, 1974. Edited by James Woodress.
     Durham, North Carolina: Duke University Press, pp. 383-84.
         Describes, in a bibliographical essay, works on Cummings
     published in 1974.

18   PAZ, OCTAVIO. "E. E. Cummings," in his The Siren and the Sea-
     shell and Other Essays on Poets and Poetry. Translated by
     Lysander Kemp and Margaret Sayers Peden. Austin: Univer-
     sity of Texas Press, pp. 131-36.
         Asserts that Cummings' work has "that rare alliance be-
     tween verbal invention and passionate fatality that dis-
     tinguishes the poem from the literary fabrication." If
     his work does not grow, neither does it descend. In addi-
     tion to this sort of general comment, Paz records his
     impressions and memories of visits with Cummings and re-
     marks briefly on his relationships with several American
     poets and other poets.

19   PEEK, GEORGE S. "The Narrator as Artist and the Artist as
     Narrator: A Study of E. E. Cummings' The Enormous Room."
     Ball State University Forum, 17, no. 4 (Autumn), 50-60.
         Examines Cummings' care, in The Enormous Room, to dis-
     tinguish the false from the true artist, especially as
     realized in the respective characters of Braggard and the
     narrator. The true artist goes beyond appearances and

1976

understands and affirms "significant truths about man"
through his immersion in the whole complex of reality.
The Enormous Room is "itself a representative piece of the
true artist's work."

20   RANTA, JERRALD. "Palindromes, Poems, and Geometric Forms."
        Visible Language, 10, no. 2 (Spring), 157-72.
            Reprint of 1974.17.

21   REINHART, TANYA. "Patterns, Intuitions, and the Sense of
        Nonsense: An Analysis of Cummings' 'anyone lived in a
        pretty how town.'" PTL, 1, no. 1 (January), 85-103.
            A linguistic analysis, concentrating on equivalence and
        succession patterns. Reinhart discovers three levels of
        meaning in the poem, each presenting a dichotomy. The
        first opposes singular and plural, the individual and the
        mass; the second moves from melodrama to irony; the third
        involves the way in which "giving sense to nonsense" be-
        comes content as well as device.

22   TANNER, JAMES E. "Experimental Styles Compared: E. E. Cum-
        mings and William Burroughs." Style, 10, no. 1 (Winter),
        1-27.
            Isolates the "dominant stylistic features" of Cummings'
        innovations in an attempt to quantify his experimentalism
        and maintains that what makes Cummings' style unique is
        not his violations of norms but the degree of those viola-
        tions. He next suggests that Cummings' style "is basically
        one that deletes from, rather than adds to, his cognitive
        content; and it consequently is one that demands a great
        deal of participation...from his readers." This may result
        from Cummings' view of language as "an organic force de-
        manding involvement in depth by all who come in contact
        with it." But it may also result from the opposite atti-
        tude, "from a retreat from the word, from a lack of faith
        in the adequacy of the residual statement." Throughout the
        essay, Cummings' experimentalism is compared and contrasted
        with Burroughs'.

23   VANDERBOK, JUDITH ANN JANKOVIAK. "E. E. Cummings and His
        Sonnets: A Quantitative Approach." Ph.D. dissertation,
        University of Colorado.
            Describes Cummings' 212 sonnets in terms of seventy-three
        artificially created variables measured by a computer. The
        results allowed certain substantive statements: there is
        a continuum through all established sonnet forms into Cum-
        mings' irregular form; there is clear formal, thematic, and
        technical development in the sonnets over time; "Cummings

personalized the sonnet form by his expansion of its formal
definition and his opening it to infinite variation"; Cummings belongs to the "American lyric tradition of innovation."

24   WALSH, JEFFREY. "The Painful Process of Unthinking: E. E.
Cummings' Social Vision in The Enormous Room," in The First
World War in Fiction: A Collection of Critical Essays.
Edited by Holger Klein. London: Macmillan, pp. [32]-42.
Maintains that Cummings' internment in La Ferté Macé
"acted as a catalyst in his artistic development" and explores "some of the ways in which The Enormous Room illus-
trates this change," especially in terms of Cummings'
developing social vision.

1977

1   CROWDER, RICHARD. Cummings Scholarship, in American Literary
Scholarship: An Annual, 1975. Edited by James Woodress.
Durham, North Carolina: Duke University Press, pp. 363,
372-73.
Describes, in a bibliographical essay, works on Cummings
published in 1975.

2   ENGEL, WILSON F., III. "Pilgrim as Prisoner: Cummings and
Vonnegut." Notes on Contemporary Literature, 7, no. 1
(January), 13-14.
Comments on the use of the pilgrim-prisoner motif in
Cummings' The Enormous Room and Vonnegut's Slaughterhouse-
Five.

3   KENNEDY, RICHARD S. "E. E. Cummings at Harvard: Verse,
Friends, Rebellion." Harvard Library Bulletin, 25, no. 3
(July), 253-91.
Biographical study of Cummings' Harvard years. Kennedy
examines the early poems, the discovery of Keats, the "increased awareness of imagery," the influence of Dory Miller,
Cummings' Greek teacher, the free translation from Aucassin
et Nicolette, and the conflict between the Harvard Monthly
and the Harvard Advocate. He explores Cummings' friendships
with S. Foster Damon, John Dos Passos, Scofield Thayer, J.
Sibley Watson, and Stewart Mitchell, and discusses his
graduation address on "The New Art." Kennedy also provides
information on Cummings' early love affairs, sexual esca-
pades, and drinking bouts, and his discovery of the popular
arts. The change that took place in his writing when he
was exposed to revolutionary art movements during the time

1977

he was a student in Dean Briggs' course in English versifi-
cation is explored. Many of the assignments turned in to
Briggs are reproduced and commented on, as are early versions of several poems which later appeared in Tulips &
Chimneys. Kennedy also discusses the difficulties these
changes in attitude caused in Cummings' relationship with
his father.

4 LAUTER, PAUL. E. E. Cummings: Index to First Lines and
   Bibliography of Works By and About the Poet. Philadelphia,
   Pennsylvania: R. West, 46 pp.
      Reprint of 1955.17.

5 SHADOIAN, CAROL FOSSETT. "E. E. Cummings: Cubist Poet. The
   Thought and Aesthetic of E. E. Cummings." Ph.D. dissertation, The University of Connecticut.
      Examines Cummings as a Cubist poet engaged in "the de-
   liberate destruction of a verbal and visual language system,
   along with their analogous philosophical assumptions, and
   the equally deliberate creation of another, which incorpor-
   ates a uniquely modern metaphysic / aesthetic."

A Note on the Index

The index interfiles author, title, and subject entries. All authors of works on Cummings are listed. All titles are listed, but in the case of reprints the index refers only to the original appearance of the item unless the title is altered in the reprint. Reprint information will be found in the annotation to the item's original appearance. Parts of books without special titles, untitled reviews, and the like are, of course, not listed. The subject entries index significant treatments of individual works by Cummings, including analyses of single poems (listed under titles and/or first lines as given in Complete Poems: 1913-1962). The user of the index is reminded that significant treatments in books on or general studies of Cummings (for a listing of these, consult the subject entry General studies) are not indexed separately. Further, reviews are rarely indexed as "significant treatments," although they may contain significant comments. In addition to important treatments of individual works, the following subjects are indexed: Bibliography, Biography, General studies, Linguistic studies, Painting (including line drawings, etc.), Reviews, and Techniques.

The major weakness of the indexing method described above is that it makes anonymous, untitled reviews of individual works which are not considered significant treatments (that is, most of them) difficult to find. Therefore, a listing of all reviews of works by Cummings, keyed to the titles of the works being reviewed, is included in the index under the subject entry Reviews.

All index references are to item rather than page numbers.

Index

and Merrill Moore,"
1972.28
Rice, Philip Blair, 1932.6
Rich, Daniel Catton, 1959.24
Riding, Laura, 1927.4; 1928.17
Rigor, Conrado B., 1949.10
Rizzardi, Alfredo, 1957.19;
1959.25, 26
Robey, Cora, 1968.23
Roche, Denis, 1962.26
Rodman, Selden, 1938.17; 1946.17
Rollins, Carl Purington, 1931.8
Rolo, Charles J., 1953.13
"The Romance of Actuality,"
1925.1
Rosenfeld, Alvin H., 1974.18
Rosenfeld, Paul, 1925.5;
1933.15; 1938.18; 1939-1940.1;
1946.18
Rosenthal, A. A., 1923.4
Rosenthal, M. L., 1950.18;
1954.24; 1959.27; 1960.19
Roskolenko, Harry, 1938.19;
1951.12
Rothenberg, Jerome, 1974.19
"Roughneck Verse," 1927.5
"r-p-o-p-h-e-s-s-a-g-r," 1951.11
Rus, Louis Calvin, 1955.27, 28;
1957.20; 1966.36
Russell, Peter, 1956.13
"Russia Revisited," 1949.4

S., K. G., 1931.9
Sage, Robert, 1927.5
Salzman, Jack, 1967.28
Sanders, Barry, 1966.37
Santa Claus, 1959.13; 1967.2;
1973.30
"Santa Claus by E. E. Cummings,"
1967.2
Saroyan, William, 1954.25
"Savagely A Maker," 1947.12
Schlauch, Margaret, 1942.3;
1955.29; 1956.14
Schleiner, Winfried, 1969.26
Schmider, Carl Ludwig, 1972.22
Schneider, Evelyn Sears,
1971.24
Schneider, Isidor, 1933.16;
1935.14
Schoeck, R. J., 1955.30

Schonberg, Harold C., 1959.28;
1960.20
Schroeder, Fred E. H., 1965.23
Scott, Winfield Townley,
1950.19; 1953.14; 1959.29
"The Scourge of the Unpeople,"
1972.3
Scully, James, 1965.24
"The Seductiveness of E. E.
Cummings," 1955.4
Seldes, Gilbert, 1928.18, 19
"Self Tail and All," 1950.2
Seltzer, Thomas, 1924.11
"Sentence and Poem," 1971.12
"Setting an Abstraction to Catch
an Abstraction," 1947.6
73 poems, 1968.25
Shadoian, Carol Fossett, 1977.5
Shapiro, Karl, 1945.1; 1946.19;
1949.11; 1960.21, 22;
1964.23; 1968.24
Shaw, Robert B., 1970.16
"sh estiffl," 1963.12
Shuchter, J. D., 1966.38
"Shy but Richly Comic," 1958.4
Sickels, Eleanor M., 1954.26
"since feeling is first,"
1973.12
Sitwell, Edith, 1934.7; 1958.24
"Six of One and Six Hundred of
the Other," 1955.20
Slotkin, Alan R., 1973.26
"The Small-Eyed Poet," 1969.11
Smelstor, Marjorie S. C.,
1974.20
Smith, David E., 1965.25;
1966.39
Smith, James F., Jr., 1973.27
Smith, L. E., 1923.4
Snodgrass, W. D., 1959.30
"Social Criticism in Twentieth
Century American Poetry,"
1967.21
Sokolov, R. A., 1969.27
Solt, Mary Ellen, 1970.17
"Some Further Thoughts on Gram-
maticality and Poetic
Language," 1967.15
"Some Impressions of Henry Adams,
Hart Crane, E. E. Cummings,
and Others," 1961.11

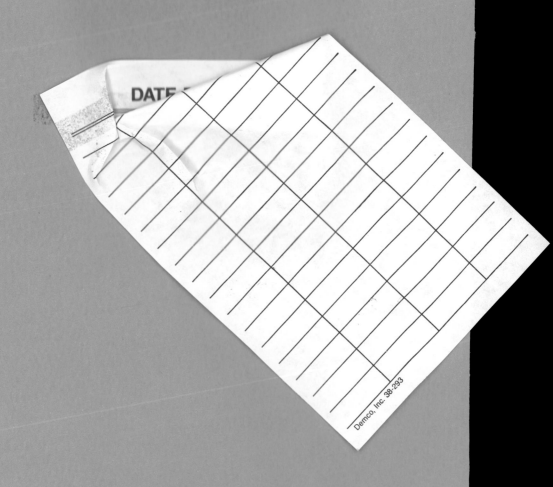

DATE

Demco, Inc. 38-293